Policy Studies Institute

CW01614873

Poverty and the Development of Anti-Poverty Policy in the United Kingdom

Policy Studies Institute

Poverty and the Development of Anti-Poverty Policy in the United Kingdom

Richard Berthoud and
Joan C. Brown
with Steven Cooper

A report to the Commission of the European Communities

H·E·B Heinemann Educational Books · London

Heinemann Educational Books Ltd
22 Bedford Square, London WC1B 3HH
LONDON EDINBURGH MELBOURNE AUCKLAND
HONG KONG SINGAPORE KUALA LUMPUR NEW DELHI
IBADAN NAIROBI JOHANNESBURG
EXETER (NH) KINGSTON PORT OF SPAIN

First published 1981

British Library Cataloguing in Publication Data

Berthoud, Richard
Poverty and the development of anti-poverty policy in the United Kingdom.—(Policy Studies Institute Series)
1. Poor—Great Britain—History
I. Title II. Brown, Joan C.
III. Series
305.5′6′0941 HC260.P6

ISBN 0-435-83102-X

Phototypesetting by Georgia Origination, Liverpool
Printed and bound in Great Britain by
Biddles Ltd, Guildford and King's Lynn

Contents

List of Tables, Maps and Figures

Maps

Figures

Preface

This study of United Kingdom poverty policy was sponsored by the Commission of the European Communities. It is one of a set of national reports on 'the nature, causes and extent of poverty, and policies being implemented to combat poverty' which have been prepared in each of the EEC member states. The project has been funded under the European Poverty Programme. This book is a slightly revised and edited version of the report on the United Kingdom presented to the Commission of the European Communities on December 1, 1980.

Many people have contributed directly to this book. The research team was led by Richard Berthoud, but Joan Brown was responsible for a large proportion of the research work. The primary responsibility for drafting each chapter has lain with one or the other of the two joint authors, as noted at the beginning of the chapter. They were assisted throughout the period of the study by Steven Cooper, and part-time by Susan Johnson. Gareth H. Williams prepared the bibliography. Tony Lynes wrote a background paper which provides the basis for the chapter on social security; Chris Paris and Stewart Lansley similarly provided the material for the chapter on housing. In a separate but allied project, W. D. Birrell and A. P. Williamson wrote a paper on voluntary organisations which has been consulted in the drafting of Chapter 9. The project secretary was Anne Auden. Several of the working documents prepared in the course of the study have been made available in PSI's Working Paper series.

The Policy Studies Institute is most grateful to Richard Layard (Centre for Labour Economics, London School of Economics) for access to his data file of the General Household Survey, which is used extensively in Chapter 2, and to the Office of Population Censuses and Surveys for permission to use this government copyright material.

The opinions expressed in this report are the responsibility of the authors, and should not be interpreted as the view of the Commission of the European Communities, the UK government or of the Policy Studies Institute.

1 Factors in the Development of United Kingdom Anti-Poverty Policies, 1950–1980

THE United Kingdom has a long history of social investigation and social reform, in certain policy areas going back several centuries. During the 19th century and the first half of the 20th century, many Royal Commissions and special committees of inquiry investigated and reported on major social problems. Influential individual social investigations have included Henry Mayhew's report on the *Life and Labour of the London Poor* in 1862, Charles Booth's study of poverty in London in 1887, and Seebohm Rowntree's detailed work on poverty in York in 1899, 1936 and 1950. A flow of social legislation was enacted throughout the 19th century and the first half of the 20th century.

In the 1940s there was a series of major landmarks in social legislation: the education system was reformed (1944); the National Health Service was established (1946); Family Allowances, National Insurance and National Assistance legislation based on the Beveridge Report was enacted (1945 to 1948); a new Childrens Act was passed (1948); and (although there was no 'landmark' legislation) governments accepted the prime responsibility for rebuilding the nation's housing. This complete revision of social programmes to create a 'welfare state' was intended as a comprehensive attack on the five 'giant evils' of Want, Idleness, Disease, Squalor and Ignorance.

The welfare state conferred substantial benefits throughout society, and general economic prosperity has improved people's standards of living. But from the mid-1960s onwards it became clear that poverty and inequality remained. Some of the shortcomings of the welfare state can now be seen to have been built in at the start; in other cases, inequality has failed to yield to what had seemed an appropriate line of attack. Over the years, demographic and economic changes have come to place strains on some aspects of social provision which they had not been designed to bear. These new problems have led to demands for alterations in the structure of the welfare state. On the one hand there have been demands for an extension of the welfare state to cover perceived failings and on the other hand, there have been demands for a retraction of the boundaries of state interference, to allow the private market to flourish.

Although it does not set out to be a history of the period, this study has had the objective of reviewing the development of anti-poverty policy since 1950, and of assessing the current position of the welfare state. This introductory chapter sets out some of the factual and analytical considerations on which the discussion of policies over the last 30 years has been based. The second chapter analyses the extent of inequality and the incidence of low incomes, in order to indicate the task facing policy makers today. The next chapters are devoted to the development of policies in the three fields most closely linked with income poverty: low pay, unemployment and social security. Chapters six, seven and eight then turn to the relationship between poverty and policies in three other central fields: housing, health and education. The analysis of policy in each of these six areas has attempted to describe the nature of the specific problem, and to assess the policies which have been implemented, or proposed, to deal with that problem. Since the 1940s, however, there has been little systematic attempt to propose an overall set of policies on poverty and inequality. Whatever the merits or failings of individual programmes, there has been a lack of coherence in the development of policies, so that the effect of one on another has not always been considered. The concluding chapter reviews the various approaches that have been adopted at different times and in different fields. Governments have worked over the past 30 years to reduce poverty, disadvantage and inequality. There is little emphasis on anti-poverty policy at present, but it is hoped that this analysis of past policies will indicate the direction for future programmes.

The social and economic context, 1950–1980

Some of the postwar changes in the structure of the United Kingdom population have tended to increase the calls upon the welfare state. During the 1950s and 1960s, the number of children increased by 18 per cent, so that by 1971 there were 40 children under the age of 15 for every 100 adults of working age.[1] But this trend has been reversed during the 1970s, so that the child dependency ratio is now no higher than it was in the immediate postwar years. On the other hand, the number of individuals over the official retirement age rose by 44 per cent between 1950 and 1980.[2] Although the steep increase in the total number of the elderly is expected to level off, the number of very old people will continue to rise in the decades to come.

The postwar period has also seen the growth of a new population group vulnerable to certain forms of poverty and disadvantage. Immigration, first from the West Indies and later from the Indian sub-continent and East Africa, has meant that there are now some 1.75 million members of ethnic minority groups in the UK, or 3 per cent of the total population.[3] Although the main phase of immigration appears to be over, the numbers in ethnic minority groups are expected to continue to increase through natural growth. The ethnic minorities are heavily concentrated in certain urban areas, where they may form as much as 20 per cent of the local population.

A third demographic change affecting poverty has been a great increase in the number of parents, mostly mothers, bringing up children on their own. Five per cent of all households, and 9 per cent of families with children are now headed by a lone parent.[4] This group suffers a strong risk of poverty, and there was little explicit provision for them in the early social security schemes.

A more widespread feature of the changes which have taken place has been an increase in the number of married women at work.[5] Their earnings make a major contribution to family incomes and there is a growing contrast between the incomes of families with two earners and those with none. Largely because of increased economic activity rates among women, the number of people available for work has risen by about three million since 1950,[6] but the economy has not provided an equivalent number of extra jobs. Throughout the 1950s and 1960s there was, taking one year with another, an underlying increase in unemployment.[7] During the late 1970s, unemployment increased even more dramatically and passed two million in August 1980. Changes in the industrial structure of the economy have made unemployment especially acute in certain parts of the country.

Nevertheless, the postwar period has seen improvements in our prosperity which, while modest in comparison with some other countries, have been exceptional by historical standards, and in marked contrast with the depression of the 1920s and 1930s. The 'index of (real) disposable income', for example, shows a 39 per cent improvement in standards of living during the 1950s, followed by a

31 per cent improvement during the decades of the 1960s and the 1970s.[8] Increasing prosperity has also been indicated by measures such as home ownership, the ownership of cars and the possession of consumer durables.[9] While social security and social assistance benefits were, when first introduced, set at a very low level in relation to earnings, the value of these payments has tended to be maintained broadly in line with increases in wages.[10] But if, as Chapter 2 suggests, inequality has not increased, neither has greater prosperity been a mechanism for a reduction in inequality. As items once considered luxuries have come to be seen as necessities, standards and expectations have been raised, and it is in this context of an altered perception of an adequate standard of living that poverty persists.

Much of the continued growth of the gross national product in the 1970s was attributable to the discovery of oil in the North Sea, and the natural growth of the non-oil economy of the 1950s and 1960s has not been sustained. The most serious problem, however, has been inflation. Between 1953 and 1967, the annual average rate of inflation reached 5 per cent only twice.[11] From 1967 to 1973, 5 per cent was exceeded every year as inflation climbed towards 10 per cent per annum. The 1973 oil crisis precipitated serious economic problems and inflation exceeded 25 per cent in 1975. This had been reduced to 10 per cent by 1978; it rose again to 20 per cent by mid-1980, but is now falling back again.

Many of the provisions of the welfare state require expenditure by central and local government through transfer payments or the provision of services. In 1975, the peak year for public expenditure, four of the five largest categories of state spending were in social fields: social security, education, health and housing.[12] Provision for social needs accounted for over half of all public expenditure and one quarter of the gross national product. Anti-poverty policy is therefore sensitive to public budgets. Since 1950 there have been three phases. In the first decade total public expenditure increased by 20 per cent (at constant prices), a rate somewhat below the expansion of the gross national product, so that as a proportion of gross national product, public expenditure declined somewhat. Between 1960 and 1975, public expenditure at constant prices more than doubled; it rose from 37 per cent of gross national product in 1960 to a peak of 55.5 per cent in 1975. There were two occasions in the early 1970s when restraints were placed on public expenditure; these were in fact reductions only in the projected rate of growth in expenditure, although they are often referred to as 'cuts'.

After 1975, reconsideration of public expenditure strategies was enforced by the decline in the performance of the national economy. The Labour Administration cut expenditure, at least partly as a condition for the provision of financial assistance from the International Monetary Fund. Public expenditure at constant prices declined by $2\frac{1}{4}$ per cent between 1975 and 1978, falling to 50 per cent of GNP. If the Labour Government had felt obliged to place restraints on expenditure, the Conservative Government elected in May 1979 adopted budgetary retrenchment as one of its main economic policies. By 1979/80, a $6\frac{3}{4}$ per cent overall reduction (at constant prices) had been implemented; further reductions totalling some 5 per cent of overall expenditure are planned to take effect by 1983/84.[13] This would reduce the overall level of expenditure to 39 per cent of GNP by the mid-1980s – little higher than the 1960 level. Projected increases in the number of claimants mean that social security expenditure is expected to continue to rise during this period but both health and education services will be reduced. Housing expenditure has received the severest cuts: it is expected to fall to only one-third of its 1974 peak level by 1983–84.

In summary, many of the postwar demographic trends have tended to increase the scale of demands on the welfare state. For much of the period, the economy was sufficiently buoyant to provide for those demands, although this in itself did not achieve a significant reduction in inequality. In recent years, the economy has been under strain and social policy has suffered in consequence.

The political context

The development of anti-poverty policies since the Second World War must also be viewed against the background of political and public opinion during the period. The major social reforms of the wartime and immediate postwar years emerged from a consensus between the three main political parties (Conservative, Labour and Liberal) and between governments and people as reflected in popular support for wartime plans for a better postwar society, and for successive items of social legislation. The consensus stemmed from a sense of social solidarity developed in the war years out of shared dangers and shared hardships and a determination that there should be no return to the unequal and divided society of the prewar depression years with mass unemployment, bitterness, despair and waste of human resources. The new postwar society, as envisaged in a series of reports and White Papers, would be a fairer and more equal society, a 'welfare state' in which the most vulnerable members would be helped and protected in a manner designed to preserve human dignity, in which common risks such as unemployment or illness would be shared (through social insurance and the tax system) and access to health services, good education and adequate housing would be determined not by income and class but by ability and need.

As a new generation began to grow up and memories of the depression years and the wartime experience faded a little, much of the passion for social reform also faded. Nevertheless, the consensus about the basic desirability of a welfare state and of increased equality held during the 1950s. The idea that prosperity should be shared with the less advantaged was politically and popularly acceptable and the Conservative Governments of 1951–64 maintained and expanded the country's social programmes.

A new impetus for social reform was given by the 'rediscovery of poverty' through a series of reports in the mid-1960s and by the concern generated by racial disharmony following the influx of West Indian and Asian immigrants. However, the mid-1960s also marked the beginning of persistent economic difficulties so that the need to take further measures to combat poverty and persistent inequality had to be considered not in the context of sharing prosperity, but against the need to find resources in a time of economic downturn. While the political welfare consensus survived until the early 1970s, it steadily became more fragile.

At the present time, consensus is not a word which springs readily to mind when considering the development of social policy. The Labour Party remains committed to the welfare state and to continued progress towards greater equality (and the Liberal Party supports this position in the main). The Conservative Party, on the other hand, is formally committed to pulling back the boundaries of the welfare state and to maximising self-help. Moreover, it is prepared to promote more inequality as a 'necessary' means of increasing economic incentives and preserving excellence. Although governments of both parties have adopted economic policies involving cuts in a wide range of social programmes, the Labour Party presented this as a regrettable economic necessity which would be set right at the earliest opportunity, while official Conservative policy is that, although some services might have a claim for greater resources after economic recovery, in the main the state is appropriately withdrawing from programmes in which it has become too heavily involved.

Official Labour and Conservative Party policies are not the whole story. Within the Conservative Party, a politically important minority still holds to elements of the welfare consensus, (in particular to the need to protect the most vulnerable) and to measures which preserve social cohesion. Within the Labour movement, some union members show considerably less commitment to equality than do the official union and Party spokesmen. Increasingly since the mid-1960s, there has been resistance, sometimes passive, sometimes active, to equalising programmes which would involve certain workers being held back in order that others (women, ethnic minorities, the low-paid) might advance. As economic conditions have worsened, there has been a tendency for each group to look out for its own interests and leave others to look after themselves. Public reaction to cuts in services has been a mixture of concern about any cuts affecting the elderly or the health services, protest about education cuts, passivity about public housing cuts and apathy tinged with hostility towards the unemployed.

As unemployment passes the two million mark and service cuts bite deeper, the situation may change again. There are signs that working class solidarity is re-emerging in Wales, Scotland and Northern England, where it has always been strongest, and government supporters who are uneasy about present policies are beginning to make their views known. In Northern Ireland, sectarian divisions and more than a decade of violence have cut across the more usual social divisions, but deep concern about increasing unemployment and poverty is one common factor. At this time, future directions in political and public attitudes on programmes needed to combat poverty cannot be predicted with any confidence.

Theories of poverty and their influence on policy

Individual and group deficiencies

The theorists of early industrial England had few doubts about the causes of poverty. On the one hand, the exercise of the virtues of diligence, prudence, sobriety, thrift and initiative was the pathway to affluence. On the other hand, poverty was caused by idleness, improvidence and intemperance, defects of character which the individual could, if he chose, overcome. While the existence of certain hazards of life (unemployment, sickness, old age, death of the breadwinner) was acknowledged, it was the mark of a provident man that he set aside savings to cover such risks.

It followed from this view of poverty that, although the completely destitute could not be abandoned, relief should be restricted to absolute necessities and provided in a form which both deterred the recipients from desiring to remain dependent upon it and deterred others from conduct which would lead to destitution. At the same time, a distinction between the standard of living offered to those in receipt of relief for their poverty and those who remained independent must be maintained. In the words of the 1832 Poor Law Commissioners, propounding what became known as the doctrine of less eligibility, 'The first and most essential of all conditions is that the situation of the individual relieved should not be made really or apparently so eligible as the situation of the independent labourer of the lowest class.'[14]

As the 19th century progressed, this theory was modified by the recognition that among those in poverty were decent, hardworking, good living, provident people who, in spite of personal effort, were defeated by successive or prolonged crises beyond their control. Rowntree, in his study of poverty in York in 1899,[15] theorised that there was a life cycle of poverty in which a family became poor as the number of children increased, moved into better times as the children grew up and became earners, and became poor again as the young people left home and the parents became too old to work. The death, incapacity (from illness or old age), unemployment or irregular employment of the chief wage earner (or unwillingness to take regular employment), and the combination of low or irregular wages and large families would produce primary poverty. Rowntree also identified secondary poverty due to mismanagement of income, for example, through drink, betting or poor housekeeping.

Based on this analysis, the poor could be divided (by the more affluent) into the 'deserving', that is, decent people poor through no fault of their own, and the 'undeserving', whose poverty was due to character defects, in particular laziness, drunkenness and immorality. The former might be given sympathetic aid and, if possible, helped back to independence. The latter should be subject to deterrent policies. In this assessment, the able-bodied unemployed were left uncomfortably on the fringe and, whether deserving or not, were seen to require the sting of poverty and relief with stigma to ensure they returned to work as quickly as possible.

This shift in emphasis damaged the theory that poverty stemmed from character defects because it acknowledged that a substantial proportion of poverty was the outcome of the functioning of the economic system and it might have been expected that, even in its modified form, such a theory could not survive the phenomena of mass unemployment and poverty of the depression years. In fact, the character deficiency approach has re-emerged in recent years in a new guise as a means of accounting for persistent poverty in otherwise affluent societies.

One such theory posits the existence of a sub-culture of poverty in which certain poor communities, in societies where the majority are prospering, develop a culture of their own which is at variance with the culture of the rest of society. Oscar Lewis, who put forward this theory in 1965 on the basis of studies in Mexico,[16] suggested that this sub-culture, once developed, perpetuated itself through the socialisation of the children within it, and both adults and children became immune to the influence of improved socio-economic conditions, and thus were not psychologically geared to take full advantage of changing conditions or increased opportunities which might occur.

A variant of this type of theory received prominence in 1972 in the UK, when Sir Keith Joseph, Conservative Secretary of State for Health and Social Security, propounded the theory of a cycle of deprivation in which deprivation/poverty is transmitted from one generation to another in certain families.[17] Parents who were themselves deprived provide inadequate socialisation for their children and thus the children do not acquire the motivation, skills and capacities necessary to avail themselves of educational and job opportunities. As a result, they remain poor in a society which otherwise could offer them prosperity.

Policies emerging from these two theories have been directed to intervening in the transmission of the 'culture' on an area or an individual base. Both theories have been subjected to fairly extensive research, much of which has questioned the validity of the basic premises or designated the theories as marginal to the process of identifying the causes of poverty.

Economic and class factors as causes of poverty

A different set of theories is based on the assumption that poverty is inherent in a capitalist economic system, an assumption which is shared by both supporters and opponents of the system.[18]

Advocates of a free market economy argue that, if left to function without interference, it is the most efficient way of producing prosperity for the majority. It is acknowledged that the functioning of the system can produce difficulties for some, for example, necessary technological change or changes in demand may involve displacement of workers. Moreover, the system requires inequality to function correctly. Jobs of markedly different levels of skills must be filled and must receive different rewards in order to attract personnel of the correct calibre. In any case, some persons are more able than others and the system will naturally pay them in accordance with their abilities and productivity. The 'fall-outs' from an otherwise beneficent system can be helped through the wealth produced by the system, provided the means of help chosen do not interfere with the system's functioning, either by being too costly in public or industry expenditure or by creating disincentives which interfere with the smooth operation of the system – for example, an unwillingness to accept low paid work. Failure to observe these rules will be counter-productive for both the poor and the more prosperous majority. It may be noted that this theory complements the view that the cause of poverty is to be found within the individual. It is the less able and the less hard-working who will be consigned to poverty through low pay or unemployment.

A less favourable description of the operation of wages and employment in the free market system is put forward by proponents of the dual labour market theory. This suggests that there is not a single labour market handing out rewards based on ability and productivity in an even-handed way, but a primary labour market consisting of 'essential' jobs in which employment is stable, pay is reasonable and conditions good, and a secondary market which operates as a pool of labour to be taken up or let go according to the fluctuations of the economy. In the secondary market, employment is unstable, pay is low, prospects of promotion are poor and working conditions often unsatisfactory. The poor are most likely to be found in this secondary market and, because of its nature, are less likely than those in the primary market to be unionised and thus acquire some countervailing power.

A further theory (termed the radical economic theory) forms a bridge between theories based wholly on the economic system and theories based on class structure. The radical economists suggest that while wages are determined by the operation of the market system and by ability, they are also determined by class divisions in society and by the relative distribution of social investment (for example, education) between social classes. Moreover, the labour market is not divided just into primary and secondary markets, but is stratified into manual and non-manual workers and, within these groups, into further strata involving qualifications and levels of skills. The employer negotiates separately with each stratum to set wages and conditions of service and, in so doing, maintains his own power, while some groups of workers receive concessions at the expense of other workers.

Class-based theories stemmed originally from the Marxist analysis, which explained class inequality as the result of the control of the means of production. On the one hand was the capitalist class – industrialists, bankers, landowners, shareholders and groups with associated interests, and on the other hand workers without capital and dependent upon wages, the former having substantial power over the latter, which was exercised for the benefit of the capitalist class and to the detriment of the workers. Certain groups which fell between these two major classes, but belonged to neither, tended to ally with the capitalist class, which they might hope to join, rather than with the workers, who were economically or socially below them.

Later class-based theories are concerned not only with power based on the ownership of capital, but with a wider command over resources of money, status and political power and influence. The class in possession of these resources exercises its power to maintain its favourable position and to resist a shift towards greater equality in the distribution of resources. Concessions will be made when other groups acquire sufficient power to challenge the possessing class, for example through the extension of the vote from restricted to universal franchise or the growth of unionism. Even so, whenever possible, any concessions granted will aim to preserve the basic status quo and minimise the loss of power of the class in possession.

A slightly different version of the economic and class-based theory asserts that poverty is a necessary component of the balance of these systems. Some must be poor in order that others may be wealthy, and some must be powerless in order that others may be powerful. As long as wealth and power are valued and will be strenuously defended, poverty and powerlessness will persist.

These economic and class theories of poverty have produced a variety of policies, depending on the extent to which a substantial change in the present economic system is regarded as desirable. They range from policies designed to shift economic power, for example, nationalisation of the 'commanding heights of the economy', state intervention in industry decision-making, or encouragement of unionisation; egalitarian policies designed to remove class-based disparities in health, education and housing; or, on the other hand, policies which accept the basic economic and class system and aim to create greater opportunities for access to its benefits. In addition, certain groups, in particular those outside the labour force, are seen as prone to poverty whatever ultimate balance of economic and class power emerges and must be provided for through some form of social security.

Poverty theory and policy

None of these theories of poverty can be regarded, on its own, as providing a full explanation of poverty or a wholly satisfactory basis for anti-poverty policy. Theories based on individual or group deficiencies obviously fail to take into account the operation of the economic and class system and the distribution of social investment. While anecdotal evidence can always be produced to support self-caused poverty theories, the theories based on economic and/or class factors offer broader-based, and thus more convicing, explanations. Nevertheless, these also have their weak elements. A pure market or capitalist system exists nowhere in western countries and, even when it did, it was substantially modified by class factors. Few of the wages and employment theories offer explanations for differentiation by sex, a significant element of low pay and, in the longer term, for female poverty in old age, nor can they handle questions of prejudice affecting capable disabled people or ethnic or religious minorities, or indeed, the poverty of those outside the labour force. Class/power-based theories offer rational explanations for the failure of many apparently well meant anti-poverty policies, but are much weaker on proposing effective means by which a 'have' and 'have not' division in society can be wholly avoided or a way in which a new 'have' group, even though changed in composition and perhaps greatly enlarged, can be prevented from defending itself against those still excluded from society's benefits.

Townsend, in his most recent study of poverty, has begun to develop a theory which recognises the highly complex sources of inequality and poverty.[19] He defines poverty as 'the lack of resources necessary to permit participation in the activities, customs and diets commonly approved by society' and sets out to examine a wide range of resources (not only capital and wages) and the scope, mechanisms and principles of distribution of each system controlling the distribution and redistribution of resources. He examines also the concept of 'minority group', for example, the aged, disabled, lone parent or immigrant, who may be assigned by society, temporarily or permanently, to some level or category of resources. This more comprehensive approach, which takes into account a wide range of factors which impinge upon the human condition, seems likely to be more effective than the single cause approach, which has distinguished many earlier theories. It remains to be seen how far it can influence policy-making.

In the meantime, policy makers have operated on the theories to hand. It should be noted that when analytical support for a theory weakens, its influence on public opinion and on policy does not necessarily die. In describing anti-poverty policies in this report, theories of self-caused poverty brought about by laziness, of poverty due to individual or family characteristics and of the need to maintain the less eligibility concept (whether economically relevant or not) will be seen to have a continuing and significant influence. At the same time, poverty problems created by the economic and social system have been recognised and acted upon to varying degrees and in different ways by parties of the left and right. Often a policy area will exhibit the operation of several types of theory at once and will experience changes of stress as governments change or as politicians respond to economic, social or political pressures.

Definitions of poverty

Although the term 'poverty' is applied generally to inequality and its various symptoms, the word is most commonly associated with the problem of low incomes. People are considered to be poor if their income is so low as to be intolerable; the problem of definition lies in determining what might be considered tolerable. Although, according to one view, poverty consists of an income so low as to lead to starvation, the majority of social analysts in the United Kingdom adopt a relative view of poverty. Inadequate incomes are to be defined as those which yield a level of living which is intolerable in the context of society's current standards. The difficulty lies in defining relative poverty in a way which is not simply a measure of inequality. An ideal definition of poverty ought to be applicable in a society in which, in spite of inequality, there was no poverty and, equally, in a society in which more than half of the population would be defined as poor, even on a relative basis. There have been various suggestions for defining a poverty line in the United Kingdom, but it must be admitted that none of them clearly and finally distinguishes between relative poverty and inequality.

A poverty line is essential, both for research and for policy, to provide some sort of estimate of the scale of the problem and to provide a sound basis for indicating changes from year to year. In fact, this latter criterion has proved as difficult to meet as the basic question of defining an adequate level of income. Two types of measure are appropriate for comparative purposes, but do not constitute a poverty line. A *distributional* poverty line simply focusses on, say, the lowest tenth or the lowest quarter of incomes. Such a measure can be used to compare the relative incidence of low incomes between economic or demographic groups within the country at a given time, but provides no measure of the extent of poverty.

A more useful measure is an *inequality* poverty line, defined in relation to some standard property of the income distribution – say, the mean, the median or the mode. Alternatively, the standard may be determined in relation to, for instance, the average earnings of male manual workers. This is theoretically less satisfactory, but is useful in practice because there are often clearer data available about earnings than about incomes. While this type of measure does not itself define an inadequate level of incomes, it is ideal for making comparisons from year to year, over at least a short period, or between neighbouring countries. Once a poverty line has been established, an inequality measure provides automatic recalibration (on a relative basis) to determine whether progress is being made towards the implied objective of reducing the extent of poverty.

There have been four approaches to defining a poverty line in the United Kingdom in the sense of a minimum level of living. Although the approaches are quite different, three of them can be seen to yield rather similar conclusions. The first is usually referred to as a subsistence poverty line, but this is misleading and it is better described as a *minimum consumption* poverty line.

The first attempt by Seebohm Rowntree to measure the extent of poverty in York in 1899[20] used a minimum consumption measure which can, indeed, be referred to as a subsistence definition. He designed a diet which, according to the medical opinion of his day, would provide a minimum quantity of nutrition for merely physical efficiency, but which took little or no account of what foods would actually be eaten by poor people. The cost of this diet, plus an allowance for housing costs and a very limited wardrobe, constituted Rowntree's poverty line. No allowance was made for anything (such as newspapers) not absolutely necessary for survival.

When he repeated his study in 1936, however, Rowntree changed his poverty line considerably;[21] while still a minimum consumption approach, it was based largely on current conventions, not on basic subsistence. The revised diet contained a variety of meats – meat is not the cheapest source of protein, and presumably not all of the meats included provided identical value for money. In historical terms, this provision was based on 20th century convention. So was the inclusion of tea in the diet, which provides no nutrition at all. The allowance for clothing was based on the observed purchases of poor people; this is a logically curious solution, but clearly includes a conventional element. This time, Rowntree included some small non-essentials, like newspapers, in his budget.

The 1936 poverty line was based on social convention and was, therefore, a measure of relative poverty. The principal weakness was that Rowntree had no objective measure of current conventions, nor of determining a point below which conventions could not be maintained. The poverty definition rested on his personal judgement. A second objection has been that a minimum consumption measure cannot be altered in response to changing conventions. However, if convention can determine the original definition, it can also determine its revisions. When Rowntree undertook his third study in 1950,[22] he did alter his poverty line slightly, still relying mainly on his own judgement; the real value of his 'basket' had increased by 5½ per cent over 1936. Since the real value of male manual workers' wages is calculated to have risen by only 4½ per cent between 1936 and 1950, the two poverty lines can be seen to bear a very similar value.

The weakness of Rowntree's method remains that it depended, in the end, on his personal judgement. His poverty line was, nevertheless, widely accepted and was highly influential on official policy. But it is not possible, 30 years after his last study, to replicate his work to define an up-to-date poverty line. Allowing only for rising prices, his 'basket of goods' of £5.00 (excluding housing costs) would now cost £37.65 per week. But allowing for the conventional element by indexing the value in line with rises in male manual workers' wages, Rowntree's poverty line would now be £68.78.[23] The state's minimum subsistence level provided by National Assistance in 1950 was £3.67 (for a family of the same composition as Rowntree's standard); in 1980, the basic rate of supplementary benefit for the same family is £52.10. The state minimum will be discussed later (p. 17) but it should be noted that it was below Rowntree's poverty line in 1950, and it is still well below his poverty line indexed according to wages.

An alternative poverty line would be based on an empirical measure of a level of income below which people were unable to maintain the conventions of the society in which they lived. An attempt to define a *relative deprivation* poverty line has been made by Townsend,[24] based on his observation that average participation in a sample of conventional behaviours varied little between income groups across most of the range of inequality, but that below a certain level of income, participation fell off rapidly. He defined this group as poor, according to the concept of relative deprivation. It can be estimated, from Townsend's data, that this cut-off point between normal and reduced participation lies about 38 per cent above the (basic) rate of supplementary benefit (exclusive of housing costs).

An instinctive reaction to this analysis is to criticise individual items within the sample of conventional behaviour as failing to provide a reliable index of poverty. While such criticisms are misapplied, it has yet to be established that the list as a whole was a valid sample of behaviour. It remains a first attempt. In general, it is to be doubted whether so sophisticated an analysis can expect to gain wide public acceptance as a measure of poverty, even if the difficulties that have been observed in the methodology were to be ironed out. What the analysis does show clearly, however, is that there is an identifiable normal convention of social behaviour in which those on low incomes cannot participate. Perhaps the most important conclusion is that the state's social security provisions leave families well within the poverty bracket, since the relative deprivation threshold lies at a level of income well above the (basic) supplementary benefit scales.

A third approach has received little attention in this country. A *public perception* poverty line could be derived by asking the general public to define what it considers a minimum level of participation in social conventions. The only data in this context are derived from the European Economic Community's multinational survey of the perception of poverty in Europe.[25] UK respondents reported on average that 'the absolute minimum income for a family of two adults and two children to make ends meet' would be £55 per week in 1976. This was 78 per cent higher than (basic) supplementary benefit rate at that time. The public appears to be saying that the state (on behalf of the public) has determined to maintain its dependants at an income on which they could not nearly make ends meet. The approach might be valuable if it was researched more thoroughly.

The most commonly used approach to defining poverty in the United Kingdom is the *state's minimum* poverty line, often referred to as the 'official' poverty line. Any family whose head is not in full time work can apply for supplementary benefit. 'Needs' are calculated from scale rates according to the number and ages of family members; housing costs are usually allowed in full; if the family's income is less than its 'needs', supplementary benefit makes up the difference. This calculable level of needs constitutes the state's minimum poverty line, on the ground that the state, in setting the scale rates, is expressing the current national convention of a minimum tolerable level of income.

A minor problem associated with this definition is that supplementary benefit is itself commonly paid at a level slightly higher than the scale rates because weekly or occasional payments may be made to meet special needs. Although both of these additions are frequent, the amount of money involved is very small in relation to total calculated needs,[26] and this problem is a blemish, rather than a major drawback, in using scale rates as a poverty line.

The fundamental problem of using this poverty line, which is often ignored by analysts who employ it, is concerned with the level at which the state has set the rates. This poverty line completely begs the question of whether the state has decreed that its dependants should live in poverty or out of poverty.

The question is thrown into sharper focus by the development, since 1966, of not one but two scale rates.[27] The basic rate is the direct successor of the pre-1966 national assistance rates. Over the years, these rates have maintained a roughly constant relationship with male manual workers' wages.[28] The long-term rate is available immediately to the elderly, and to other claimants (excluding the unemployed) after one year at the basic rate (two years prior to November 1980). As will be explained in Chapter 5, this differential was originally intended to cover small exceptional needs of the sick and elderly, but since 1966 the two rates have gradually diverged, and in 1980 the long-term rate is 27 per cent higher than the basic rate.

It is essential for poverty analysis to interpret this divergence between the two state minima. There is no evidence, nor logic, for the suggestion that certain types of people have 'needs' that are 27 per cent higher than others. One interpretation would be that the basic rate constitutes the poverty line; in that case, the state has decided to raise some of its dependants to a position well above the poverty line. The alternative interpretation is that the basic rate was always below the poverty line, and that the long-term rate represents a better estimate of a family's minimum needs. On that interpretation, the introduction of the long-term rate can be considered as a decision by the state to raise some of its dependants up to the poverty line, leaving only the unemployed, and temporary claimants, in poverty. The following evidence suggests that the basic rates are below the poverty line.

(a) When national assistance (the precursor of the basic rates of supplementary benefit) was introduced in 1948, the rates were set in relation to Rowntree's 1936 study, but deliberately set below his poverty line. Current basic rates are no higher, in relation to wages, than they were in 1948.
(b) Medical estimates of the actual cost of an adequate diet suggest that the majority of children require an expenditure greater than their scale rate, even without taking account of the cost of clothing and other items,[29] and a study of the costs of children similarly suggests that their scale rates are insufficient.[30]
(c) The Supplementary Benefits Commission has, in recent years, consistently argued that the basic rate leaves claimants in poverty. Its research supports its contentions.[31]
(d) Townsend's study of relative deprivation clearly indicates lack of participation among those living at or near the basic rates.[32]

Within the framework of the scale rates, there are four possible poverty lines: households' income can be compared with the basic rate; with their 'potential' rate (that is, the long-term rate for the elderly and the basic rate for others); with the actual long-term rates; or with long-term rates adjusted to the needs of children.[33] Table 1.1

Table 1.1 Extent of poverty according to successive variants of the supplementary benefit poverty line: households in Great Britain, 1975

	Households below this level	Proportion of households below this level
	000s	*Per cent*
Basic rate	880	4.4
Potential rate	2,220	11.1
Actual long-term rate	2,560	12.9
Long-term rate adjusted for children	2,890	14.6

Source: General Household Survey 1975 (Special tabulations).

illustrates the differing results.

There remains, therefore, a choice as to the poverty line to be adopted for this study. On the evidence presented, the basic supplementary benefit rate can be rejected as too low. Both the 'potential' rate and the actual long-term supplementary benefit rate retain elements of the basic rate and it is more appropriate to concentrate on the adjusted long-term rate. This implied poverty line lies 4 per cent lower than Rowntree's minimum consumption poverty line (adjusted for the increase in wages) and 8 per cent lower than Townsend's relative deprivation poverty line. The three poverty lines are very close to each other, but the adjusted long-term state minimum is the most conservative.

The fundamental problem of judging where supplementary benefit rates lie in relation to some independently determined poverty line has made it difficult to decide which rate to use. It is also essential that measures of improvement or deterioration can be taken. If the scale rates as such are used to define a poverty line, then it follows that any attempt by the government to improve their relative value will appear to increase poverty and vice versa. This is both theoretically predictable and actually observable; the scale rates as such are worse than useless as a means of measuring changes over time. The only solution is to take a sight on the relative value of the (adjusted) long-term rate at a particular point in time, and then to measure changes in the income distribution about that relative value. In the following chapter, poverty will be defined in terms of the adjusted long-term supplementary benefit rate, but the analysis of recent changes will use an inequality measure derived from that definition.

This definition of poverty would not be applied appropriately to people who do not live in private households. There is, in any case, no information about non-householders' incomes, and all the analysis in Chapter 2 is confined to private households. The 1971 census showed that there were 910,000 permanent residents of institutions, including 552,000 (excluding staff) in hospitals, children's and old people's homes and prisons;[34] most of these would have very little cash income, but at least a moderate income in kind. There are no good data on the homeless and rootless, but there is little doubt that there are some thousands of them, and that they include the poorest of the poor.

Notes

1 Office of Population Censuses and Surveys, *Population Projections 1977–2017*. (HMSO, London, 1978).
2 Ibid.
3 Office of Population Censuses and Surveys, *Population Trends*, No. 20, Summer, 1980, (HMSO, London).
4 Office of Population Censuses and Surveys, *General Household Survey 1978*, (HMSO, London 1980).
5 *Department of Employment Gazette*, (HMSO, London), monthly.
6 Ibid.
7 Ibid.
8 Central Statistical Office, *Economic Trends*, (HMSO, London), monthly.
9 Central Statistical Office, *Social Trends*, (HMSO, London), annual.
10 Department of Health and Social Security, *Social Security Statistics*, (HMSO, London), annual.
11 *Economic Trends*, op. cit.
12 Central Statistical Office, *National Income and Expenditure*, (HMSO, London), annual.
13 *The Government's Expenditure Plans 1980–81 to 1983–84*, Cmnd. 7841, (HMSO, London, 1980).
14 Quoted in George Victor, *Social Security and Society*, (Routledge and Kegan Paul, London, 1973).
15 Rowntree, Seebohm, *Poverty: A Study of Town Life*, (Macmillan, London, 1901).
16 Lewis, Oscar, *The Children of Sanchez*, (Penguin Books, Harmondsworth, 1965).
17 Discussed in Holman, Robert, 'Poverty: concensus and alternatives', in Fitzgerald, M. (ed) *Welfare in Action*, (Open University, London, 1977).
18 For fuller discussion of these theories, see Townsend, Peter, *Poverty in the United Kingdom*, (Penguin Books, Harmondsworth, 1979); and George, Victor, *Social Security and Society*, (Penguin Books, Harmondsworth, 1979).
19 Townsend, Peter, op. cit.
20 Rowntree, Seebohm, *Poverty: A Study of Town Life*, op. cit.
21 Rowntree, Seebohm, *Poverty and Progress*, (Longmans Green, London, 1941).
22 Rowntree, Seebohm, and Lavers, G. R., *Poverty and the Welfare State: A Third Social*

Survey of York, Dealing only with Economic Questions. (Longmans Green, London, 1951).

23 Upton, Michael 'Reviewing Rowntree: poverty lines and levels of social security benefits for the unemployment, 1950–1978' *Social Policy and Administration* Vol. 14, No. 1, 1980.

24 Townsend, Peter, *Poverty in the United Kingdom*, op. cit.

25 Commission of the European Communities. *The Perception of Poverty in Europe*, (Brussels, The Commission, 1977).

26 Department of Health and Social Security. *Social Security Statistics 1977* (HMSO, London, 1979).

27 From 1966, there was a 'long-term addition' to the basic rates; in 1973, this was consolidated into a 'long-term rate'. See Chapter 5.

28 *Social Security Statistics*, Ibid.

29 Walker, C. L. and Church, M., 'Poverty by administration: a review of Supplementary Benefits, nutrition and scale rates', *Journal of Human Nutrition*, Vol. 32, No. 1, 1978, 5–18.

30 Piachaud, D. *The Cost of a Child: A Modern Minimum*. (Child Poverty Action Group, London, 1979).

31 Supplementary Benefits Commission. *Annual Reports* 1976, 1978 (HMSO, London).

32 Townsend, Peter. op. cit.

33 Much of the evidence on the poverty of those living at the basic rate refers to the difficulty of bringing up children. But when the long-term rate was introduced, it applied to adults only; children continue to have their needs assessed on the basic scale. The 'long-term rate adjusted for the needs of children' upgrades the children's basic rate in line with married couples' long-term rate.

34 Royal Commission on the Distribution of Income and Wealth *Report No. 6, Lower Incomes*, Cmnd 7175, (HMSO, London, 1978).

2 The Distribution of Income and the Extent of Income Poverty*

BEFORE the poverty line defined at the end of the previous chapter is applied to the measurement of poverty in the United Kingdom, it will be useful to consider the whole range of inequality in incomes. Most people depend on earnings from work, but there are millions of households with no worker to provide earnings. Many of these would have hardly any income at all, if it were not for the substantial transfers of money effected by the state, which tends to tax those with relatively high incomes, and to provide cash benefits to people with little or no earning power. In addition, the state provides free services, especially in the fields of health and education, which can also be shown to have a slight effect of reducing the gap between rich and poor. But in spite of these activities of government, the poorest tenth of all households experience a standard of living at about half the national average; at the other extreme, the richest tenth live at nearly twice the national average.

It is generally held that some degree of inequality is acceptable, even desirable, in any complex society. Inequality is so abstract a concept that it is not possible objectively to identify a point at which incomes become excessively unequal. That point will have been reached, however, if it can be shown that those with least resources are unable to participate in the normal activities of society, and it is here that the analysis turns to the concept of poverty. In spite of the responsibility accepted by the state for income maintenance, just over one household in seven in the United Kingdom reports an income below the poverty line defined in Chapter 1, and there is little evidence of much change in this proportion in the years since the welfare state was introduced.

Much of the detailed analysis of poverty in this chapter is designed to indicate the size and nature of the tasks faced by policy makers –

* This chapter has been drafted mainly by Richard Berthoud.

tasks which are discussed in each of the following chapters. Perhaps the most important analysis focusses on families' economic activities. The majority of the poor do not work at all; they include pensioners, the permanently sick and disabled and lone parents. These people are chiefly dependent on social security payments, policy on which is assessed in Chapter 5. Poverty is relatively rare where at least one member of the family has a secure full-time job, but, as discussed in Chapter 3, policies on low pay and on the taxes and benefits of the low paid are of critical importance not only to the working poor, but also to those not in work. In between the working and the non-working population lies a group of families with an insecure economic position. The unemployed, especially the long-term unemployed, are highly likely to experience poverty, and policies in this field are reviewed in Chapter 4.

The direct link between poverty and the three other main fields of social policy (housing, health and education, which are covered by Chapters 6, 7 and 8) is much less clear. However, the concluding section of this chapter suggests that there is a tendency for the poor to suffer problems in each of these three areas more often than those with adequate incomes. Moreover, there is clear evidence of multiple deprivation, in which poor households suffer a number of other disadvantages in combination. Thus although poverty may be defined for measurement purposes in terms of spending power, low incomes form only part of the general pattern of disadvantage.

Original income, cash transfers and net income[1]

Nine-tenths of the original income available to private households in the United Kingdom consists of earnings from employment or self-employment.[2] Since one quarter of all households consist entirely of people who are not members of the labour force,[3] the outstanding characteristic of the distribution of original income is the presence of a large group who receive virtually no income at all. The lowest one-fifth of households share between them only one per cent of total original income (Table 2.1). The highest income within the bottom one-fifth is only 20 per cent of the median, or 18 per cent of the average.[4]

Since the war, there have been substantial increases in the numbers of elderly people, of lone-parent families, and of the unemployed (see Chapter 1). All these groups tend to have low original incomes. At the same time, the increasing proportion of married women at work has added to the number of two-earner households in the middle and upper income ranges. These trends have led to a substantial widening in original inequality. Table 2.1 shows that some 5 per cent of original income has, in effect, moved from the lower half of the distribution to the upper half over a 17-year period.

The state deducts about one-fifth of original income by direct taxation – income tax (17 per cent of original incomes) and National Insurance contributions (3 per cent).[5] The state also makes cash payments of social security benefits equal to 14 per cent of original incomes.[6] Since 94 per cent of direct taxation is paid by households in the top six-tenths of original incomes, while 71 per cent of cash benefits are received by households in the bottom four-tenths,[7] the effect of the state's transfers is redistributive. Some 10 per cent of income is transferred by the state from the top six-tenths to the bottom four-tenths.

Over the period when original incomes were becoming more unequal, the state increased both the percentage of original income taken in taxes and the percentage paid out in benefits.[8] Increasing

Table 2.1 Percentage shares of original and net incomes, 1961 and 1978: households in the United Kingdom

Percentages

	Original income		Net income	
	1961	1978	1961	1978
Lowest 10 per cent	0.2	0.05	2.4	2.7
2nd 10 per cent	2.7	0.96	4.3	4.1
3rd 10 per cent	5.6	3.2	6.1	5.5
4th 10 per cent	6.5	6.1	6.8	6.9
5th 10 per cent	8.3	8.4	8.2	8.4
6th 10 per cent	9.3	10.3	9.5	9.8
7th 10 per cent	11.7	12.2	10.9	11.3
8th 10 per cent	13.2	14.5	13.2	13.1
9th 10 per cent	15.7	17.6	15.2	15.6
Highest 10 per cent	26.7	26.5	23.5	22.6
Lowest 40 per cent	15.0	10.3	19.6	19.2
Highest 60 per cent	85.0	89.7	80.4	80.8

Sources: Royal Commission on the Distribution of Income and Wealth, *Report No. 5, Third Report on the Standing Reference* (HMSO, London, 1977).
Central Statistical Office, 'The effects of taxes and benefits on household incomes in 1978' *Economic Trends,* January, 1980, (HMSO, London).

inequality in original incomes has nearly been balanced by increased redistribution: a balancing act remarkable in view of the changes in the structure of the population, changes in the economy as a whole, and changes in policies. Nevertheless, the long-term trend over the period for which data are available is towards very slightly wider inequality in net incomes.

Although the state's assumption of responsibility for those without their own sources of income – especially the provision of pensions – has largely eliminated total destitution among the poorest households, and although better-off households are net losers from taxation, redistribution still leaves a wide range of income inequality. The average net incomes of the top one-tenth of households are more than eight times those of the bottom one-tenth and there are, of course, richer households in the top category and poorer households in the bottom category.

'Equivalent' incomes

A household's actual income is not the best measure of its income standard of living. Clearly, a single person with a given income is better off than a household which has to spread the same income between four people. There is a general tendency for large households to have higher net incomes than do small households, for a number of reasons. First, because retired people, often with very low incomes, usually live on their own or with their spouse; second, where there are two or more adults under retirement age, there is a probability of two or more workers; and, third, because taxation and benefit arrangements are geared to take less from, or to give more to, larger households. Indeed, it has been calculated that two-fifths of the reduction in inequality effected by redistribution is 'horizontal' (reducing inequality in standards of living between different types of household); the remaining three-fifths is 'vertical' (reducing inequalities in incomes within each type of household).[9]

Households' net incomes can be recalculated in relation to the number of household members, to indicate relative standards of living. This measure is known as 'equivalent' income.[10] Because of the tendency for large households to receive relatively large incomes, there is less inequality in equivalent incomes than in unadjusted incomes: the standard of living of the top one-tenth is now measured at five times the standard of living of the lowest one-tenth (Table 2.2). The distribution of equivalent incomes has been essentially stable

Table 2.2 Percentage shares of equivalent net incomes, 1968 to 1976: households in the United Kingdom

Percentages

	Equivalent net incomes			Unadjusted net incomes
	1968	1972	1976	1976
Lowest 10 per cent	4.4	4.0	4.3	2.5
2nd 10 per cent	5.6	5.4	5.6	4.1
3rd 10 per cent	6.5	6.2	6.5	5.4
4th 10 per cent	7.5	7.2	7.3	7.0
5th 10 per cent	8.3	8.3	8.3	8.5
6th 10 per cent	9.3	9.3	9.4	9.9
7th 10 per cent	10.5	10.7	10.6	11.4
8th 10 per cent	11.9	12.3	12.2	13.0
9th 10 per cent	14.2	14.7	14.5	15.5
Highest 10 per cent	21.8	21.9	21.4	22.7
Lowest 40 per cent	24.0	22.8	23.7	19.0
Highest 60 per cent	76.0	77.2	76.3	81.0

Source: Royal Commission on the Distribution of Income and Wealth. *Report No. 5, Third Report on the Standing Reference,* (HMSO, London, 1977).

over the eight years for which data are available, but there was a trend towards greater inequality between 1968 and 1972, followed by a recovery to the former position by 1976.

Another way of showing the distribution of living standards is to compare households' equivalent incomes with the national average (Figure 2.1). As is usual with income distributions, the range of inequality is wider among high incomes than among low incomes. The largest group of households lives at between 65 per cent and 70 per cent of the national average, and 14.4 per cent are below 60 per cent of the average. Very few people (1.02 per cent of households) live below 40 per cent of the average, but there are sizeable groups above twice and even three times the average.

Post-income redistribution

Households' net income represents cash available to be spent. In the course of spending it, households are subject to three further forms of state transfers which affect the value of goods and services which can be bought out of a given income (Table 2.3).[11]

Indirect taxes (such as VAT) on expenditure represent 20 per cent

Proportion of households in Great Britain in each income band 1975, expressed in relation to the Great Britain average

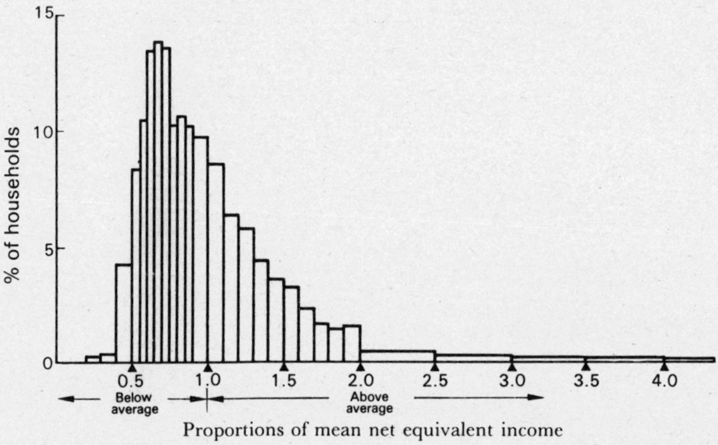

Source: Special tabulations from the General Household Survey, 1975
1 Equivalence scale derived from Supplementary Benefit scale rates
2 The vertical scale shown at the left applies to the medium width columns (e.g. 1.0–1.1). For the narrow columns (e.g. 0.50–0.55) the scale should be halved. For the wide columns (e.g. 2.0–2.5) the scale should be multiplied by five.

Figure 2.1

of total net income. Better-off households pay more in indirect taxes, but these taxes form a slightly lower proportion of high incomes than of low incomes. The distribution of incomes is, therefore, slightly more unequal after indirect taxation than before.

Subsidies (on municipal housing, for example) represent 2.7 per cent of total net income. Low income households benefit more absolutely from subsidies, and much more proportionately, than high income households. Subsidies, therefore, reduce inequality, although the scale of subsidies is too low to have more than a slight redistributive effect.

Rough estimates have also been made of the effects of state benefits in kind – the National Health Service and state education (plus a small element for welfare foods). These benefits represent 43 per cent of services provided by government or 14 per cent of total net household income. Expenditure on the health service is allocated to individual members of households in accordance with the average use

Table 2.3 Post income transfers: households in the United Kingdom, 1978

	Net income	Indirect taxes	Subsidies	Benefits in kind	As a proportion of net income: Indirect taxes	Subsidies	Benefits in kind
	£	£	£	£		*Per cent*	
Lowest 10 per cent of net incomes	1,216	259	197	344	21	16.2	28
2nd 10 per cent of net incomes	1,858	402	181	417	22	9.7	22
3rd 10 per cent of net incomes	2,484	597	142	531	24	5.7	21
4th 10 per cent of net incomes	3,150	706	132	593	22	4.2	19
5th 10 per cent of net incomes	3,825	840	128	665	22	3.3	17
6th 10 per cent of net incomes	4,460	959	95	755	22	2.1	17
7th 10 per cent of net incomes	5,153	1,072	90	735	21	1.7	14
8th 10 per cent of net incomes	5,977	1,200	81	788	20	1.4	13
9th 10 per cent of net incomes	7,098	1,376	86	802	19	1.2	11
Highest 10 per cent of net incomes	10,260	1,808	87	943	18	0.8	9

Source: Central Statistical Office, 'The effects of taxes and benefits on household incomes', *Economic Trends*, January 1980, (HMSO, London).

made of the service by members of each age group; the costs of education are allocated to households containing children attending schools or colleges of each type. These benefits are, therefore, allocated on the unreal assumption that the full cost of health insurance and education would otherwise be borne by the household directly. Allocation of benefits in kind is higher for higher income households, largely because higher income households tend to contain more people; as a proportion of net income, however, benefits in kind fall with rising income, and the net effect of these benefits is a slight reduction in inequality.

Measured against actual incomes, the combined effect of indirect taxes, subsidies and benefits in kind is very slight. The tendency of benefits in kind to help larger households more than small ones, however, means that there is a larger effect on the distribution of equivalent incomes (Table 2.4).

Table 2.4 Percentage shares of net equivalent income, before and after post-income transfers: households in the United Kingdom, 1976

Percentages

	Before post-income transfers	After post-income transfers
Lowest 10 per cent of incomes	4.5	5.0
2nd 10 per cent of incomes	5.7	6.5
3rd 10 per cent of incomes	6.6	7.3
4th 10 per cent of incomes	7.7	8.2
5th 10 per cent of incomes	8.5	8.8
6th 10 per cent of incomes	9.5	9.6
7th 10 per cent of incomes	10.6	10.3
8th 10 per cent of incomes	12.1	11.6
9th 10 per cent of incomes	14.2	13.5
Highest 10 per cent of incomes	20.6	19.4

Source: J. L. Nicholson, *The changing impact of taxes and benefits on household incomes in the United Kingdom, 1957–1976*, Policy Studies Institute, unpublished.

The distribution of assets

Estimates of the ownership of capital assets (or 'wealth') are derived from highly complex calculations based on the size of estate left by people who have died. They are thought, if anything, to underestimate the extent of concentration of assets.[12]

The top 1% of adults own 25% of assets
The top 5% of adults own 46% of assets
The top 10% of adults own 61% of assets
The top 25% of adults own 84% of assets
The top 50% of adults own 94% of assets

It is clear from these estimates that a very small number of people control an enormous amount of wealth, and the power that wealth provides. At the other end of the scale, half the population share only 6 per cent of assets, and most of them can reasonably be assumed to have no wealth at all.

Table 2.5 Ownership of assets by income, United Kingdom, 1968

Percentages

	Household income[1]				
	Below 100%	100 to 139%	140 to 199%	200 to 299%	300% or over
Household assets[2]					
Less than £200	59	36	20	8	14
£200 to £5,000	33	45	49	45	29
Over £5,000	8	19	31	47	57

Source: Townsend, P., *Poverty in the United Kingdom*, (Penguin Books, Harmondsworth), 1979).
[1] Household income expressed in relation to supplementary benefit scale rates plus housing costs.
[2] In 1968, £5,000 was four times mean income; £200 was one sixth of mean income.

The only detailed analysis of asset-holding in relation to incomes relates to 1968,[13] but there is no evidence of any major change in the relationship since then (Table 2.5). The association between assets and incomes was strong: the majority of the poorest group had negligible assets; the majority of the highest income group had substantial assets. The effect, therefore, of combining income with assets to provide a measure of 'income net worth' is substantially to extend the degree of inequality at the upper end of the scale, but to have little effect on the measured purchasing power of the lowest group (Table 2.6).

Table 2.6 The effect of adding assets to income, United Kingdom, 1968

Percentages

Household income[1]	Net disposable income	Income including annuity value of assets
Below 100 per cent	6	4
100 to 139 per cent	22	16
140 to 199 per cent	33	28
200 to 299 per cent	28	31
300 per cent or over	10	22

Source: Townsend, P., *Poverty in the United Kingdom,* (Penguin Books, Harmondsworth, 1979).

[1] Ranges of income expressed in relation to supplementary benefit scale rates plus housing costs.

Counting the poor: variability of the estimates

The general problem of defining poverty was discussed in Chapter 1. The definition of a 'poverty line' is derived from the long-term supplementary benefit scale rates which define the level of income which the state guarantees to certain types of family not in work. A poverty line is far more useful for comparing one group of the population with another or for making comparisons from year to year than for giving a precise and meaningful estimate of the numbers in poverty. There is much room for debate as to exactly where the line should be drawn, and the estimate is very sensitive to this decision. Second, many of those 'in poverty' would be 'out of poverty' if they had only an extra pound or two each week, even though they would still have very low incomes. Third, estimates of the extent of poverty depend on a number of purely technical considerations, so that no one estimate should be considered absolutely correct. In this section, these technical points are summarised.

(i) *Households or families*. The economic unit which is generally assessed for paying income tax or for receiving cash benefits is often referred to as the family or the family unit. This consists either of a non-married adult or of a married couple, plus the dependent children of that adult or couple. Poverty is often calculated with reference to family units, on the ground that supplementary benefit, the basis for the poverty line, is assessed separately for each such unit. Households (defined as a group of people who live together and share at least some of their catering) often contain more than one family unit. Since 82 per cent of these cases involve a parent-child relationship, and 93 per cent involve some blood relationship,[14] it is reasonable to assume that standards of living are shared between the families within a household. Indeed, it is probable that many young adults and elderly people live with their parents or children in order to avoid the poverty that they would experience if they lived on their own. Of all families sharing households, 17 per cent are below the poverty line on their family account; only 6 per cent on their household account.[15]

The estimate of household poverty (14.6 per cent for Great Britain) is therefore lower than the equivalent estimate of family poverty (16.3 per cent).[16] Other analysts have suggested an even larger difference between estimates based on household and family incomes.[17]

(ii) *Treatment of recipients of supplementary benefit.* Official estimates published every year of the numbers of families whose income is below their potential supplementary benefit entitlement are substantially lower than those of independent analysts.[18] The independent analyses calculate the incomes of all families' in exactly the same way, while the official analyses assume that families actually receiving supplementary benefit cannot, by definition, receive incomes below the supplementary benefit level. The difference appears to be substantial: the official estimates suggest that there are only 37 per cent as many poor families as the alternative analyses indicate.[19]

(iii) *Period of income.* The main estimates quoted in this chapter are based on income accumulated over twelve months. An alternative calculates 'normal income': if a family contains individuals who have been out of work, sick or unemployed, for less than three months, their wages or salary when in work are counted, not their social security receipts or sick pay. This will reduce the extent of estimated poverty compared with yearly income. A third option is to calculate income 'this week' so that the short-term sick or unemployed, those on strike, or even those working a short week, can appear to be poor, even though the problem is strictly temporary. Estimates of poverty based on 'last week's' income are 18 per cent higher than those based on 'normal' income.[20]

(iv) *Income or expenditure.* It may be argued that expenditure is a better measure of people's standard of living than is income. It is also noted that low income households report, on average, a higher level of expenditure than their income would appear to support,[21] and this may be interpreted as under-reporting of income. This suggests that income based calculations will over-estimate the extent of poverty. But expenditure does not provide a better estimate: most items of households' expenditure can be measured only over a two-week period and variations in households' expenditure from week to week give the appearance of wider inequality than actually exists. Poverty estimates based on expenditure are 32 per cent higher than those based on 'last week's' income.[22]

The estimates quoted in this chapter are based on the following decisions on these four technical points: households rather than families[23]; reported incomes of all households; annual income rather than normal or last week's income; income rather than expenditure. The estimates for the numbers of poor in the United Kingdom[24] are as follows but, if only because of the sensitivity of the figures to technical considerations, they should not be interpreted as exact figures.

Table 2.7 Incidence of poverty: households in the United Kingdom, 1975

	Thousands	Percentages
Poor households	3,020	14.8
Families in poor households	3,250	13.3
Individuals in poor households	6,140	11.3

Source: General Household Survey, 1975 (Special tabulations)

It will be noted that the proportion of households in poverty according to the state's minimum definition (14.8 per cent in the UK, 14.6 per cent in Great Britain) is very similar to the proportion below 60 per cent of mean net equivalent income (14.4 per cent in Great Britain).[25]

Changes over time in the extent of poverty

Although the poverty line has been derived from the supplementary benefit scale rates as an appropriate indicator of the extent of poverty at any one time, it has been argued (in Chapter 1) that the use of supplementary benefit rates as such are a false indicator when comparison is made from year to year. This is because a relatively large rise in the scale rates, which will actually tend to reduce the amount of poverty, will raise the standard against which incomes are compared and so appear to show an increase in poverty. Measures of inequality are therefore adopted to indicate changes in the extent of relative poverty.

The earliest attempt to count the number of households living in poverty, relating to 1953 and to 1960, yielded estimates that were lower than more recent analyses.[26] There is, however, no collateral evidence for an increase in the extent of relative poverty, and the first attempt was probably an under-estimate. Identical calculations for 1953, 1967 and 1971 suggest a very stable pattern, although there was a very slight widening of inequality over this period (Table 2.8).

Table 2.8 Inequality in equivalent gross incomes; households in the United Kingdom, 1953 to 1971

Percentages

	1953	1967	1971
5th percentile as proportion of median	48.8	48.8	48.5
10th percentile as proportion of median	57.9	57.7	57.4

Source: Fiegehan, G. C. *et al.*, *Poverty and Progress in Great Britain, 1953–1973* (Cambridge University Press, 1977).

A consistent series of analyses is available from 1971 to 1979. Inequality widened slightly and relative poverty increased between 1971 and 1972, but from then on inequality narrowed and relative

Table 2.9 Inequality in equivalent net income: households in the United Kingdom, 1971 to 1979

Percentages

	1971	1972	1973	1974	1975	1976	1977	1978	1979
5th percentile as proportion of median	46.9	46.7	47.4	48.4	48.9	49.4	49.6	n.a.	47.3
10th percentile as proportion of median	55.6	54.6	56.1	56.4	57.0	57.2	56.3	n.a.	55.4
Proportion of households below 50.5 per cent of median	7.0	7.2	6.8	6.2	5.8	5.8	5.7	n.a.	6.5
Proportion of households below 60 per cent of median	12.8	14.1	12.7	12.5	12.0	12.2	12.7	n.a.	13.2

Source: S. Lansley, 'Changes in inequality and poverty in the UK, 1971–1976', *Oxford Economic Papers*, Vol. 32, No. 1, March 1980. Figures for 1977 and 1979 have been calculated by Lansley for this study.

Note: The long-term supplementary benefit rate plus allowance of 30 per cent for housing costs and other needs has ranged between 48 and 55.5 per cent of median equivalent net income during this period.

poverty decreased, through to the middle of the decade. Most recently, however, there has been a reversal of this trend.

The changes in relative poverty through the 1970s can, in part, be ascribed to changes in the level of the supplementary benefit scale rates. The long-term scale rate, for instance, fell by 5 per cent in relation to median net incomes between 1971 and 1973, rose by 16 per cent between 1973 and 1976, and fell again by 6 per cent by 1979.[27] Other factors may have been changes in male manual workers' earnings in relation to male non-manual workers', and changes in women's earnings in relation to men's (see Chapter 3).

Demographic characteristics of the poor

Table 2.10 shows the demographic structure of the families who are in poverty, using household income as the basis for calculation. Poverty is very largely a problem of old age. The elderly are well above average in their risk of poverty, and account for 63 per cent of all poor families. Old couples are less likely to be poor than old men, who in turn are less likely to be poor than old women. Although the calculated needs of couples are, of course, higher than those of single people, they appear to be able to earn more and receive larger occupational pensions.[28] Both of these factors may be associated with the fact that the average elderly widower is older than the average elderly married man. Elderly widows tend to be older still; moreover, many occupational pension schemes have made no provision at all for widows.

Nevertheless, the greatest risk of poverty is not for any group of the elderly, but for lone parents. Only 3 per cent of all families are lone parents, but they constitute 9 per cent of the poor. The number of lone parents has been rising for some years, with the increasing rate of divorce, and as it has become socially more acceptable for single women to raise their own children. Concern for the welfare of lone parent families has also been increasing. Indeed, since the Finer Committee Report on one-parent families,[29] all three of the main family benefits[30] have been revised to give special preference to lone parents, though neither lone parents and their spokesmen nor the government are satisfied that this constitutes a true solution. The real problem lies in the conflict between the double duties of paid work and child care. This conflict is illustrated by the fact that far more lone mothers do paid work than married mothers but nevertheless, only a minority of lone mothers are able to work full-time.[31] The

Table 2.10 Demographic characteristics of the poor; families poor on their household account, Great Britain, 1975

	Total	Pensionable Age			Non-pensionable Age					
					Married			Non-married		
		Couple	Man	Woman	No children	1–2 children	3 or more children	With children	Without children Man	Without children Woman
Numbers (000s)	3,110	400	200	1,370	130	200	220	290	150	150
Risk of poverty, per cent	13	20	26	38	3	4	14	41	5	7
Proportion of poor families, per cent	100	13	6	44	4	6	7	9	5	5

Source: General Household Survey, 1975 (Special tabulations)

problem is then exacerbated by the very low pay available to women (see Chapter 3).

Table 2.10 shows that married couples with three or more children are substantially more likely to be poor than are couples with few or no children. This will inevitably be so, since extra children imply extra needs, so long as the taxation/benefit system fails to ensure adequate extra income for families during their period of child-rearing. Sizes of family have been falling steadily since the mid-1960s,[32] and it cannot be concluded that excessively large families contribute much to the total problem of poverty. Only two per cent of all couples with children have more than four and five per cent have exactly four; these large families contribute only 1.5 per cent and 1.8 per cent to the total number of poor families in Great Britain.[33] Nevertheless, increasing family size had a demonstrable effect on the risk of poverty (Table 2.11, first line). It has also been estimated (Table 2.11, second line) how many families with children would have been poor in 1975 if the then existing structure of family allowances (£1.50 per week, excluding the first child, taxable) and child tax allowances had not existed. Clearly the 1975 system had an effect in reducing child poverty, which was especially valuable for large families, even though there was still inequality between families of different sizes (first line of table). Since 1975, the family/child allowance system has been replaced by child benefit, a flat-rate, non-taxable benefit. The third and fourth lines of Table 2.11 offer examples of the potential of such a benefit to reduce poverty. Child benefit at a rate of £3.50 per child per week in 1975 would have halved child poverty to three per cent. But this still leaves inequality between families of different sizes. A system yielding three per cent poverty, about equal for all family sizes, would be to pay nothing for the first child and £5 for each subsequent child. This formula would have reduced the risk of poverty of all sizes of family to about three per cent, and would have been slightly cheaper than a flat rate of £3.50 per child. (The current rate of child benefit is £4 per week for each child.[34] Table 2.11 is dated 1975: at 1980 prices, £3.50 would be about £7; £5 would be about £10.)

Table 2.10 showed that 63 per cent of all poor families were headed by an elderly man or woman, while 22 per cent contained one or more children. When the comparison is based on individuals, however, the balance shifts considerably because there are never more than two elderly people in a poor family unit, but there are often three

Table 2.11 Poverty and family size; married couples with children, Great Britain, 1975

Percentages

	Number of children					
	One	Two	Three	Four	Five or more	Total
Actual income	3	5	10	21	37	6
Minus 1975 child and family allowances	4	10	23	44	79	13
Minus allowances, plus £3.50 p.w., each child	2	3	5	6	11	3
Minus allowances, plus £5.00 p.w., second and later children	4	3	3	3	2	3

Source: General Household Survey, 1975 (Special tabulations)

or more children. Indeed, nearly one third of all the people in poor households are children: 26 per cent are adults under the age of 60, and 43 per cent are aged 60 or more.

Geographical variations in poverty

On 'mainland' Great Britain, the detailed pattern of regional variation in the extent of poverty is not very wide and is inconsistent between sources of data. A general pattern does emerge, however, of increasing poverty with increasing distance from London and the South-East (Table 2.12). This general pattern of disadvantage in the north of England and Scotland is mirrored in regional analyses of earnings (Table 3.6) and unemployment (Table 4.4).

Northern Ireland, however, is quite outside the range of variation observed within Great Britain. According to two independent sources, low incomes are more than 50 per cent more common in Northern Ireland than in the rest of the United Kingdom. Table 2.13 suggests some of the reasons for the severity of poverty in Northern Ireland. An exceptionally high proportion of Northern Ireland house-

Table 2.12 *Broad regional variations in the extent of poverty; Great Britain*

Percentages

	Households below adjusted long-term SB rate, 1975[1]	Households below lower quartile of UK equivalent incomes, 1976[2]	Households below 140 per cent of basic SB rate plus housing costs, 1968[3]
Scotland, North, North West	16	28	31
Yorks/Humberside, East Midlands, Wales, South West	15	24	28
West Midlands, East Anglia, London & South East	13	23	24

Sources: [1]General Household Survey, 1975 (Special tabulations).
[2]Royal Commission on the Distribution of Income and Wealth, *Report No. 6, Lower Incomes,* (HMSO, London, 1978).
[3]Townsend, Peter, *Poverty in the United Kingdom,* (Penguin Books, Harmondsworth, 1979).

Table 2.13 *Poverty in Northern Ireland, compared with Great Britain*

	Northern Ireland	Great Britain
Households below the lower quartile of UK equivalent incomes, 1976[1] - per cent	38	25
Households below 140 per cent of basic supplementary benefit rates plus housing costs, 1968[2] - per cent	44	27
Proportion of households with no earner (1978)[3] - per cent	34	23
Unemployment rate (June 1980)[4] - per cent	12.7	6.7
Average weekly earnings: full time men (1978)[5] - £s	81.5	89.1
Proportion of households with 6 or more persons (1978)[3] - per cent	11	4

Sources: [1] Royal Commission on the Distribution of Income and Wealth; [2] Townsend, Peter, op. cit.; [3] Family Expenditure Survey; [4] *Department of Employment Gazette*; [5] New Earnings Survey.

holds consist of economically inactive people. Moreover, the province suffers from very high unemployment and low wages, and the average household is larger in Northern Ireland than in Great Britain.

Low incomes tend to be slightly more common in the large cities (apart from London)[35] and there is some evidence to suggest that the inner areas of the big cities (including London) are worst off in this respect.[36] Although there are, of course, local variations in the extent of poverty, it would be a mistake to think that poverty is a mainly local phenomenon, to be tackled by locally-based initiatives. It is far more widespread.

Economic characteristics of the poor

Table 2.14 shows the incidence of poverty among non-married individuals and among married couples, according to whether they are economically active.[37] Not surprisingly, economic activity has a major influence on the incidence of poverty.

Where both husband and wife are economically active, there is very little poverty. Only one per cent of these couples are poor; they constitute 29 per cent of all family units, but only 2.3 per cent of poor family units.

Table 2.14 Economic characteristics of the poor; families in Great Britain, 1975

	Family account			Household account		
	Numbers	Risk of poverty	Share of poverty	Numbers	Risk of poverty	Share of poverty
	(000s)	*Per cent*		*(000s)*	*Per cent*	
Couple, both economically active	80	1	2	80	1	3
Couple, one active	420	8	11	400	8	13
Single person, active	560	10	14	310	6	10
Couple, neither active	550	31	14	470	27	15
Single person, inactive	2,280	51	59	1,850	41	59
Total	3,890	16	100	3,110	13	100

Source: General Household Survey, 1975 (Special tabulations)

Poverty is common among those who do not work. Calculated purely on the basis of their own net incomes, 51 per cent of non-working individuals and 31 per cent of non-working couples would be poor. To a certain extent, this problem is alleviated by sharing a household with other family units; on the household account, poverty is reduced to 41 per cent for non-working individuals, and to 27 per cent for non-working couples.

Very nearly three-quarters of poor families have no economically active member; they are almost entirely dependent on social security benefits (see p. 45). Any argument that these benefits need to be kept low to maintain work incentives cannot possibly apply to them: they are not expected to work, and most of them could not work if asked to. In the course of this century, the state, to its credit, has removed these people from destitution. Their poverty, however, remains the state's direct responsibility.

The analysis of those family units consisting of one worker – either a non-married individual, or one member (usually the husband) of a couple – is more complex. For them, poverty is much more common than among working couples, but much less common than for the economically inactive. As can be seen from Table 2.14, many single

Table 2.15 Detailed working status and poverty: single economically active people, and married couples where the husband is economically active, the wife is not, Great Britain, 1975

	Numbers	Household account Risk of poverty	Household account Share of poverty
	(000s)	Per cent	Per cent
Full-time full-year employee	190	3	6
Part-time full-year employee, Employee, 40–51 weeks, Self-employed	250	9	8
Employee, 25–39 weeks	60	15	2
Employee, 1 to 24 weeks	100	35	3
Others	100	67	3
Total	700	7	23

Source: General Household Survey, 1975 (Special tabulations)

Note: The small number of married couples where the wife is economically active, but the husband is not, are excluded from the table.

workers who are poor on their own account are not poor on their household account; these would largely be young people on low wages living with their parents, and the analysis focusses on those who are poor on the household calculation.

Table 2.15 analyses this group according to the details of their position in the labour force. Starting at the bottom of the table, two-thirds of those who, although part of the labour force, had not worked at all during the preceding year were calculated to be in poverty. (On their own 'family' calculation, the figure is 80 per cent.) The great majority of these had been unemployed (the others had been off work sick), and it is clear that long-term unemployment almost certainly spells poverty. The unemployed differ from the retired in having no occupational pensions,[38] their social security benefits are set at a lower rate than the state pension and they are not entitled to the long-term rate of supplementary benefit. As long-term unemployment grows (it has already grown since 1975, the date on which these figures are based),[39] poverty will grow with it and will demand either a solution to unemployment or improved income support for the unemployed or, preferably, both.

Poverty is, of course, less for those who had been unemployed for less than the whole of the 12 months preceding the survey from which these figures are derived. It can also be seen from Table 2.15 that those with a good, if not perfect, employment record average a 9 per cent poverty risk – part-time workers, those out of work for less than three months of the preceding year, and the self-employed.[40] Sole workers who were in full time employment for the full year were relatively unlikely to be measured as poor: only 2.7 per cent of them.

Although the incidence of poverty is low among families supported by the full-year earnings of a single worker, this does not mean that such poverty should be dismissed lightly. First, the absolute numbers of such poor families are not negligible – nearly 200,000 of them – 6 per cent of all poor families and 24 per cent of poor families containing any economically active person. Second, this group is largely poor because of taxation: as a group, these working poor families pay about 2½ times as much in tax[41] as they receive in benefit[42]; 46 per cent of them would cease to be poor if there were neither taxes nor benefits and 73 per cent of them would cease to be poor if they paid no tax, but continued to receive their modest benefits.[43]

The third, and perhaps the key point that needs to be stressed in relation to poverty in families supported by one full-year earner is the

Table 2.16 Unemployment, according to weekly earnings when employed: heads of household with any employment in the preceding year, Great Britain, 1975

	£10 to £20	£20 to £25	£25 to £30	£30 to £35	£35 to £40	£40 to £45	£45 to £50	£50 to £60	£60 to £75	£75 or more
Proportion not employed throughout year	36	37	34	25	24	18	21	16	12	8
Average number of weeks not employed	7.3	6.8	5.7	4.5	3.8	2.4	2.8	1.7	1.3	0.8

Source: General Household Survey, 1975 (Special tabulations)

relation between earnings levels and full employment. Table 2.16 shows a very clear relationship: those who receive low earnings when they are working are much more likely to experience unemployment. One of the reasons for the relatively low incidence of poverty among full-year workers is that the great majority of them enjoy reasonably rewarded as well as full employment. The working poor tend to suffer both low wages and unemployment. A similar relationship exists between poverty, employment and occupational status: only 3 per cent of professional and managerial workers (without a working spouse) are poor; 19 per cent of unskilled workers are poor, not so much because they risk poverty while in work, but because two-thirds of them were not full-time, full-year employees.[44]

Taxes, benefits and poverty[45]

Table 2.17 shows, overall, how taxes and benefits have redistributed income between the poor and the non-poor. Twenty-nine per cent of families would be poor if only their original income were taken into account. After taxes and benefits, this figure falls to 16 per cent, a reduction of 44 per cent. The poverty deficit – the gap between the incomes and needs of the poor – falls from £5.12 billion to £0.65 billion, a reduction of 87 per cent. These estimates of the poverty deficit are of the same order as those of Beckerman, whose basis for calculation was somewhat different.[46] Redistribution therefore goes a long way towards reducing poverty.

Table 2.17 The incidence of taxes and benefits; families in Great Britain, 1975

Family's position *before* redistribution	Poor	Poor	Not poor	Not poor	
Family's position *after* redistribution	Poor	Not poor	Poor	Not poor	
Number of families (000s)	3,600	3,370	290	16,530	23,790
	£ million				Total
Original income	810	1,460	470	58,000	60,740
+ Benefits	2,550	2,910	10	1,640	7,110
− Taxes	90	190	80	15,180	15,540
Net income	3,270	4,180	400	44,460	52,310
'Needs' (including housing costs)	3,900	3,490	420	22,720	30,530
Original deficit	−3,090	−2,030			−5,120
surplus			+50	+35,280	+35,330
Net deficit	−630		−20		−650
surplus		+690		+21,740	+22,430

Source: General Household Survey, 1975 (Special tabulations)

On the other hand, while nearly half of the originally poor rise out of poverty as a result of net benefits, 7 per cent of the net poor have fallen into poverty as a result of net taxes – 290,000 families. Taxation of families who are still poor after redistribution seems pointless: the total of £170 million is only one per cent of the total tax take, but it contributes 26 per cent of the total net poverty deficit. Eleven per cent of the poor would be eliminated if they paid no income tax; 6 per cent if they paid no National Insurance; 14 per cent if they were relieved of both payments.[47] Raising the tax threshold would, therefore, be an obvious means of reducing poverty.

Table 2.17 gives the total surplus of net incomes over needs as £22.43 billion; this represents the source out of which the remaining poverty deficit of £0.65 billion would have to be found; the deficit is 3 per cent of the surplus. Among the non-poor there is a large group whose net incomes exceed twice their requirements (not shown in the table). The surplus of their incomes over twice their needs totals £8.11 billion; the poverty deficit is 8 per cent of this reserve.

The general effect of the redistribution system is to tax higher incomes at a relatively high rate, and to give cash benefits to those with low incomes. This, indeed, is how the tax system actually works, but the benefit system as a whole does not operate in this way. This can be illustrated by comparing the income sources of two extreme groups: families with no earners on the one hand, and families with a single full-time, full-year employee on the other (Table 2.18). In both groups, income tax represents a rising proportion of original income as incomes rise, although employees' National Insurance contributions are a roughly fixed proportion of original incomes. But, in both groups, cash benefits are received at roughly the same rate, whatever the family's original income. The difference between the two groups is that those outside the labour force receive substantial benefits, while those in work receive very little, since most of the

Table 2.18 Average taxes and benefits for two types of family, Great Britain, 1975

	Income below 100% of needs	Income 100 to 139% of needs	Income 140 to 199% of needs	Income 200% needs or over
	£	£	£	£
(i) *Families with no economically active person*				
Original income	90	290	960	2,940
+ Benefits	790	850	770	660
– Taxes	10	30	180	950
Net income	870	1,110	1,550	2,650
(ii) *Families supported by full-time, full-year employee*				
Original income	1,530	2,090	2,550	3,830
+ Benefits	100	70	60	60
– Income Tax	160	330	510	1,050
– National Insurance	80	110	130	150
Net income	1,390	1,720	1,970	2,690

Source: General Household Survey, 1975 (Special tabulations)

benefit system is based on contingencies (which give rise to low incomes), such as retirement or unemployment, and not on low incomes as such.

Poverty and other disadvantages

Finally, it is possible to compare poverty with crude measures of

Table 2.19 Poverty and other disadvantages; families in Great Britain, 1975

Percentages

	Non-elderly families		Elderly families	
	Poor (6)	*Non-Poor* (94)	*Poor* (31)	*Non-Poor* (69)
Proportion with a:				
health problem	38	24	59	55
housing problem	37	18	20	17
work problem	41	23	n.a.	n.a.
education problem	64	42	n.a.	n.a.
family problem	35	5	n.a.	n.a.
Proportion with:				
none of these problems	5	33	32	39
one	21	35	57	51
two	37	22	11	10
three	26	8	n.a.	n.a.
four or five	10	2	n.a.	n.a.

Source: General Household Survey, 1975 (Special tabulations)

Note: The figures in brackets at the head of the table indicate the proportion of the non-elderly and of the elderly who are poor and non-poor respectively.

Definitions *Elderly*: head of family and man aged 65 and over or a woman aged 60 and over

Health problem: head of family temporarily or permanently out of work due to sickness *or* reports limiting long-standing illness

Housing problem: household has more persons than rooms *or* lacks exclusive use of kitchen or bathroom or inside WC

Work problem: head of family in semi-skilled or unskilled manual occupations *or* currently unemployed *or* employed less than 40 weeks in past year

Education problem: head of family left school at minimum age *and* reports no educational qualifications

Family problem: lone parent *or* four or more children

disadvantage in other fields. Among the non-elderly, there is a positive association between poverty and each of the other social problems included in Table 2.19. The strongest association is with family problems: one third of the non-elderly poor have an unbalanced family structure, compared with only one in twenty of the non-elderly non-poor. The poor also show a relatively high risk of each of the other problems, in work, health, education and housing, although it is clear that these difficulties do not invariably coincide with poverty.

This analysis can be continued a step further by counting (among the non-elderly) how many of these five social disadvantages is experienced by each family. It then becomes clear that, while a majority of the non-poor suffer none or only one of these problems, a majority of the poor suffer two or more of them. Thus while poverty is not closely associated with any particular form of social disadvantage, it is associated with the general structure of disadvantage. Multiple deprivation is closely linked with poverty. Indeed, these estimates suggest that there may be as many as 100,000 non-elderly families in Great Britain who suffer poverty in combination with four or five of these other disadvantages.

Among the elderly, no sensible analysis of the problems identified under work, education or family is possible. There is only a weak direct association between poverty in old age and either sickness or substandard housing. On the other hand, there is a strong indirect link between them, in that the elderly are at greater risk of each of these three problems than the non-elderly.

Notes

1 *Original income*: earnings, occupational pensions and other private unearned income before subtraction of direct taxes and before addition of cash benefits. *Net income*: original income, minus direct taxation, plus cash benefits.

2 Department of Employment. *Family Expenditure Survey*, 1978, (HMSO, London, 1979).

3 Ibid.

4 The effects of taxes and benefits on household incomes in 1978, *Economic Trends*, No. 315, January 1980, (HMSO, London).

5 Ibid.

6 Ibid.

7 Ibid.

8 Royal Commission on the Distribution of Income and Wealth. *Report No. 5 Third Report on the Standing Reference*, Cmnd. 6999 (HMSO, London, 1977).

9 Layard, R., Piachaud, D. and Stewart, M., *The Causes of Poverty*, Royal Commission on the Distribution of Income and Wealth, Background Paper No. 5. (HMSO, London, 1978).

10 The Royal Commission on the Distribution of Incomes and Wealth adopted an equivalence scale as follows: 2 adults = 100; 1 adult = 61; each extra adult = 39; each child = 27. This is roughly derived from empirical estimates of the relative costs of maintaining a given standard of living. The National Institute of Economic and Social Research study by Fiegehan *et al.* and work by Lansley, whose data are quoted in this chapter, adopt a very similar variant of this scale. Nicholson uses another, but still very similar, variant. The supplementary benefit scales are different, mainly because they allow for increasing needs with rising age of children. The Royal Commission has shown that the precise equivalence scale adopted makes little difference to the analysis of poverty. Royal Commission on the Distribution of Income and Wealth. *Report No. 6: Lower Incomes*. Cmnd. 7175, (HMSO, London, 1978).

11 The effects of taxes and benefits on household incomes in 1978, *Economic Trends*, op. cit.

12 Royal Commission on the Distribution of Income and Wealth. *Report No. 7: Fourth Report on the Standing Reference*, Cmnd. 7595, (HMSO, London, 1979).

13 Townsend, P. *Poverty in the United Kingdom*, (Penguin Books, Harmondsworth, 1979).

14 Special tabulations from the General Household Survey 1975. This survey is described in OPCS, *General Household Survey 1975*, (HMSO, London, 1977). The analysis was based on the working tape of the Centre for Labour Economics at the London School of Economics; the tape is described in Layard *et al.*, op. cit.

15 Ibid.

16 Ibid.

17 Fiegehen, G. C., Lansley, P. S. and Smith, A. D., *Poverty and Progress in Great Britain, 1953–73*. National Institute of Economic and Social Research Occasional Paper No. XXIX, (Cambridge University Press, 1977).

18 Department of Health and Social Security estimates. Published annually by Central Statistical Office in *Social Trends*, (HMSO, London).

19 Fieghen, G. C., Lansley, P. S. and Smith, A. D., op. cit.

20 Ibid.

21 *Family Expenditure Survey 1978*. op. cit.

22 Fiegehen, G. C., Lansley, P. S. and Smith, A. D., op. cit.

23 Some of the analyses later in the chapter are derived from family incomes, because more detailed data are available on that basis. In other cases, it is appropriate to treat the family as the analytical unit, but to categorise each family as poor or not poor according to the income of the household of which it is a part.

24 The *General Household Survey*, on which the majority of the poverty analyses in this chapter are based, covers Great Britain only. For the purpose of these total UK estimates, the small population of Northern Ireland is assumed to suffer poverty at a rate of 50 per cent higher than Great Britain; see Table 2.13.

26 Abel-Smith, B. and Townsend, P. *The Poor and the Poorest*. (Bell and Sons, London, 1964).

27 Lansley, P. S., 'Changes in inequality and poverty in the UK, 1971–76', *Oxford Economic Papers*, Vol. 32, No. 1. Mar. 1980. The figures for 1977 and 1979 have been calculated by Lansley for this study.

28 Special tabulations from the *General Household Survey*, 1975.

29 Department of Health and Social Security, *Report of the Committee on One-Parent Families (Finer Report)*, Cmnd. 5629, (HMSO, London, 1974).

30 Child benefit, supplementary benefit and family income supplement.

31 Office of Population Censuses and Surveys, *Census 1971*, (HMSO, London).

32 Department of Health and Social Security, *Social Security Statistics 1975*, (HMSO, London, 1976).

33 Special tabulations from the *General Household Survey 1975*. op. cit.

34 Rising to £4.75 in November, 1980.

35 Royal Commission on the Distribution of Income and Wealth. *Report No. 6:* op. cit.

36 Berthoud, R., 'Where are London's Poor?' *Greater London Intelligence Quarterly*, No. 36, September 1976.

37 Economically active includes those who work, and also those who would work if they could – unemployed or temporarily sick. The inactive are the permanently disabled, the retired, housewives, non-working lone parents and those in full time education.

38 Apart from some older unemployed.

39 Unemployment figures published monthly in *Department of Employment Gazette*.

40 The incomes of the self-employed are difficult to measure accurately but show wide variation. Self-employment is the normal status for some very prosperous occupations such as the law; on the other hand, it is also used as a fall-back or temporary expedient by those unable to find secure employment and it would be the latter who risk poverty.

41 Two-thirds of this is income tax, one-third national insurance contributions.

42 Special tabulations from the *General Household Survey*, 1975, op. cit.

43 Ibid.

44 Ibid.

45 This section is based on the income of family units since that is the basis for the taxation/benefit system. It will be remembered that not all families who are poor on their family account are also poor on their household account.

46 Beckerman, W., The impact of income maintenance payments on poverty in Britain, 1975, *The Economic Journal*, Vol. 89, No. 354, June 1979.

47 Special tabulations from the *General Household Survey*, 1975, op. cit.

3 Low Pay and Poverty*

POVERTY is most clearly associated with being excluded from the labour force, whether permanently or on a temporary basis. Only a small proportion of full-time full-year workers are in poverty directly due to low pay. Most full-time workers earn sufficient to maintain their households above the poverty line including many low-paid workers who share a household where there are other workers or have few or no persons dependent upon them. Nevertheless, low pay is an important poverty issue.

The absolute numbers involved are quite substantial: 200,000 families in poverty who are dependent on a full time, full-year worker; some 790,000 families in poverty where at least one family member works; and over 3 million full-time workers earning wages below the defined low-pay line. However, the relationship between work and poverty goes deeper than even these figures suggest. Industries which pay low wages are frequently characterised by poor working conditions and high labour turnover. Low-paid workers are highly vulnerable to unemployment, have less access to fringe benefits and receive less benefit from official schemes where these are related to pay, length of service and contribution record. Low pay prevents savings and thus the accumulation of a buffer against times of adversity.

For women workers, low pay may mean poverty in female-headed one-parent families. It reduces the contribution married women can make to raising their families out of poverty and ultimately produces a poor level of wage-related pension in old age. Perhaps the most important reason for concern about low pay is the influence of low pay levels on income available to the social security population, particularly the unemployed, whose income is depressed to ensure that it does not 'compete' with low-paying jobs.

Governments have been slow to recognise low pay as an important poverty issue and still have not developed coherent policies to deal

* This chapter has been drafted mainly by Joan Brown.

with it. Broadly speaking, the development of policy can be divided into two periods. From 1950–1970, apart from the payment of increasingly marginal family allowances, the policy-makers assumed that the problem must be tackled within the labour market. After 1970, although labour market approaches were maintained and even strengthened, policy-makers increasingly looked to the social security system as the answer to poverty due to low pay.

Labour market policies have been, with few exceptions, tentative and often weak throughout the period. Dependence was placed on individual effort to climb out of low-pay poverty, through changing jobs or seeking promotion, through the efforts of working wives and through training. Little support was offered for this individual effort and training schemes were poorly oriented to the low paid. Much dependence has been placed on the extension of collective bargaining. While the numbers of low-paid workers who are unionised has increased, the most vulnerable workers in the secondary labour market remain under-unionised and the union movement as a whole has been slow to develop effective policies on low pay. Anti-discrimination legislation (on race, religion and sex) had as one objective the reduction of job segregation but has had only limited effects on this. Women in particular continue to be segregated in low-paying employment. Some intervention in wage-setting has operated through equal pay legislation, wages councils and boards and the various incomes policies, but with the exception of equal pay, these have proved unsatisfactory programmes and the option of establishing a minimum wage was rejected in 1969.

The labour market policies in the main have assisted individual low-paid workers to better themselves and have prevented excessive discrimination and exploitation of vulnerable workers. With the exception of the equal pay legislation and to a certain extent support for collective bargaining, they have done little to eliminate low-paying jobs. The social security approach adopted after 1970, including child benefit, family income supplement (FIS) and various means-tested programmes, have similarly been directed to supporting families of low-paid workers. In the case of FIS and the other means-tested benefits they may indirectly have reduced the pressure to upgrade low-paying jobs as well as extending the phenomenon known as the poverty trap. In addition, taxation thresholds have been allowed to fall well below the poverty line so that some workers are actually being taxed into poverty and those already poor forced into greater dependence on means-tested benefits. The child benefit scheme, on the other hand, is and will remain of key importance, since however much improvement can be achieved in wage-setting policies, it can never be expected that wages can fully take into account the number of individuals dependent upon them.

Recognition of the problem

Low pay as a cause of poverty has been slow to become a political and public issue in the United Kingdom. The main thrust of the major anti-poverty legislation of the 1940s was directed at assisting those whose poverty arose from interruption or loss of earning power. Low pay as a cause of poverty was not entirely ignored. Since wages were set without taking into account the number of dependants the worker had to support, it was recognised that low earners with large families could be in poverty. To counter this, a modest system of family allowances was introduced in 1945 to assist with the cost of supporting dependent children other than the oldest. In addition, the Wage Councils Act 1945 and the Fair Wages Resolution of 1945[1] provided some machinery to protect the most vulnerable of workers from exploitation. Thereafter the problem of low wages was, it seems, expected to respond to a combination of full employment and a steadily strenthening trade union movement.

The report, *The Poor and the Poorest*, by Brian Abel-Smith and Peter Townsend, published in 1965, marks the 're-discovery' of poverty in the UK after the apparently affluent 1950s.[2] In their analysis of two surveys undertaken by the Ministry of Labour in 1953–54 and 1960, and using a poverty line derived from national assistance rates in the relevant years, the authors found that, of those in poverty in 1953–54, 19.6 per cent of households were headed by a full-time worker and, with dependants, comprised 34.6 per cent of all those in poverty.[3] In 1960, 41 per cent of persons in poverty were living in households primarily dependent upon earnings.[4]

Although it was considered that the finding that over one-third of those in poverty were in households whose head was employed was 'one of the most interesting and important results to emerge from the analysis'[4, 5] the recommendations of the report did not directly address the issue of low pay. Instead they called for a radical review of the whole social security system including, for the benefit of the low paid, the family allowance scheme.[6]

By 1965, the problem of low pay had at least entered official thinking. Throughout the period of prices and incomes policies, 1965–1971, special account was supposed to be taken of cases 'where there is general recognition that existing wage and salary levels are too low to maintain a reasonable standard of living'.[7] However, the National Board for Prices and Incomes, which had the task of supervising the policy, found the concept of low pay extremely difficult to handle. There was no generally accepted definition of low pay, and data which would facilitate the development of a policy was not readily available.[8]

From 1967 onwards, concern about low pay gathered pace. In that year, the Trades Union Congress adopted for the first time a minimum earnings goal (of £15 per week).[9] A key development took place in 1968[10] when the Department of Employment and Productivity introduced the New Earnings Survey. The detailed information provided by this survey, conducted annually since 1970, showed for the first time the extent and nature of low pay. At the same time, the poverty lobby (i.e. non-government agencies which focussed attention on poverty issues) which had, in the 1960s, concentrated mainly on pressing the need for better social security support for the low paid, now turned to a more direct attack on low pay itself. This was formalised in 1974, with the establishment of the Low Pay Unit, a voluntary organisation which uses research and information on earnings in the campaign against poverty.

In another development, the increased presence of women in the labour force together with the growing strength of the women's movement has produced, among other things, a questioning of the wage system and labour force structure which allocates women to the lowest levels of pay and status in the labour market. Finally, the rapid growth in union membership among low paid workers, in particular among national and local government employees, has produced strong unions in key sectors which became increasingly militant during the 1970s. This militancy reached a peak in 1978/79 with a series of low pay strikes by local authority and health service workers.

Defining low pay

While the issue of low pay and poverty is now clearly on the map, the task of reaching a generally agreed definition of low pay has proved a difficult one. In 1967, the National Board for Prices and Incomes, reporting on the implementation of the low pay provisions in the prices and incomes policy, said:

> 'We have found this criterion extremely difficult to apply. Clearly anyone whose pay is scarcely above the level of national assistance is low paid. By and large, however, the concept of the low paid is a relative rather than an absolute one; the most that can be said in most cases - and even this is difficult - is that pay is too low or alternatively too high, in relation to somebody else's. What is at issue therefore is the question of differentials.'[11]

A 1969 report of an Inter-departmental Working Party on a National Minimum Wage simply sidestepped the problem of defining low pay, though it appeared to waver towards relating the definition to basic benefit rates for unemployed persons.[12] During the 1970s, a number of definitions have emerged. Originally separate bases were used for men and women, but since the Equal Pay Act 1970 began to take effect, this differentiation by sex has been largely dropped. Earnings in the definitions were taken to include overtime, shift pay and payment by results. The most common conventional definitions are as follows:-

(a) Earnings at or below the lowest decile of full-time male manual workers aged 21 and over in the New Earnings Survey whose earnings were not affected by absence in the survey pay period. This definition was adopted by the National Board for Prices and Incomes in 1971, and by the Royal Commission on the Distribution of Incomes and Wealth in 1977-78.[13]
(b) Earnings below two-thirds average weekly earnings. This most commonly refers to average earnings of male manual workers. The Trade Union Congress for a time used this definition as one of the criteria for their low pay targets.[14]
(c) Earnings below two-thirds of median weekly earnings of all male workers (manual and non-manual) working full-time. This definition appeared in the poverty reports produced by the Institute of Community Studies in 1974 and 1975.[15]
(d) Earnings below those required to achieve a standard of income equal to the income of a man, wife and two children on the long-term rate of supplementary benefit (SB), including SB rent and rates allowances and less child benefits. This is the definition currently supported by the Low Pay Unit, but it has been around for some time, with variations. Some have used the short-term supplementary benefit level[16] as a base and the number of children in earlier versions was one and not two.

Certainly the first three of these conventions are not objective definitions of low pay in relation to poverty. Since there will always be a lowest ten per cent of wage earners, the setting of a low pay level at earnings below the lowest decile ensures that some workers will always be defined as low paid. Definitions related to average or median earnings are similarly criticised as being more definitions of inequality than of poverty.

The last definition is generally seen as the most valid of the four, since the SB rate to which it is linked is regarded as an official poverty line. (This shift from the short-term SB rate to the long-term rate as a basis for calculation accords with the current view that the short-term can no longer be regarded as a reasonable level of living – see Chapter 1). However, since the SB rates are, by policy, maintained in a fairly steady relationship with average earnings, this is a somewhat circular argument. In any case, the difference between the outcomes of the various definitions are suprisingly small and reflect the basically unchanging nature of the earned income distribution in the UK for at least a century.[17] Table 3.1 shows the position in Great Britain under the four definitions. It may also be noted that the poverty line adopted in Chapter 2 contains an adjustment for the long-term needs of children which would, in 1979, have raised the wages required to keep a couple with two children out of poverty under definition (d) from £58.10 to £62.82 per week.

Table 3.1 Outcome of various definitions of low pay in selected years in mid year, Great Britain, 1971–1979

£

Year	a Lowest decile earnings manual men 21 years and over	b Two-thirds average earnings manual men 21 years and over	c Two-thirds median earnings all men 21 years and over	d Wage before deductions equivalent to supplementary benefit plus rent & rates[1]	e Entry point for family income supplement[2]
1971	19.2	19.40	19.66	n.a.	20.00
1977	48.1	47.19	47.70	49.03	45.00
1978	53.4	53.26	54.12	54.98	47.80
1979	60.3	61.38	61.97	58.10	50.00[3]

Sources: *Department of Employment, New Earnings Survey* (different years)
Department of Health and Social Security, *Social Security Statistics 1977* (HMSO, London, 1980).
Hansard 22.11.77, 30.11.78, 7.11.79.

[1] Long-term rate, man, wife and 2 children. [2] Two-child family. [3] Moves to 58.50 later in the year. (This column is included for later reference only.)

How many low paid?

Given the similarity in the outcome of the definitions as far as Great Britain is concerned, it may be seen as reasonable for present purposes to select £60 per week as the low pay level for 1979, and £19 per week for 1971. The New Earnings Survey is conducted independently in Northern Ireland, and many analyses are available for Great Britain only. But because of the smaller numbers in Northern Ireland the differences between Great Britain and the UK as a whole are usually very slight.

Table 3.2 Full time workers with low pay, Great Britain, 1971 and 1979.

Percentages, millions

	1971 Under £19 p.w.		1979 Under £60 p.w.	
	Per cent	*Million*	*Per cent*	*Million*
Male (21 years and over)				
Manual	9.5	0.7	9.6	0.6
Non-manual	5.5	0.2	6.1	0.3
All	7.9	0.9	8.1	0.8
Female (18 years and over)				
Manual	83.2	1.4	66.6	0.8
Non-manual	55.2	1.8	48.4	1.6
All	71.3	3.2	53.3	2.5
Male and female		4.1		3.3

Source: Department of Employment *New Earnings Surveys* 1971 and 1979.

Table 3.2 shows the position in Great Britain in 1971 and 1979. Table 3.3 shows Northern Ireland figures. The proportion of workers earning less than the defined low-pay level is greater in Northern Ireland than in Great Britain and much greater among women than among men. In 1979, about 3.4 million full time workers in the UK were low paid although, largely because of a relative improvement in women's wages, this is a substantial reduction since 1971. Table 3.4 gives a further breakdown of the figures for Great Britain in 1979. It shows the number of workers earning considerably less than the low pay level of £60 per week and gives some indication of the influence of overtime. Some 500,000 more men and 100,000 women would fall into the low pay group were it not for working hours in excess of the normal working week. In addition to these low paid workers, it may be noted that a large number of part-time workers are being paid at wage levels which, if they worked a full week, would leave them below the low earnings level of £60 for 1979. The Low Pay Unit calculates that in this category there are 126,000 men and 1.7 million women.[18]

It should not be assumed from the figures given here that upwards of 3.4 million persons with their dependants are in poverty because of low pay. Many factors operate to reduce this figure considerably though, as will be shown later, the numbers are still significant.

Table 3.3 Full time workers with low pay, Northern Ireland 1971 and 1979.

Percentages, thousands

	1971 Under £19 p.w.		1979 Under £60 p.w.	
	Per cent	*000s*	*Per cent*	*000s*
Male (21 years and over)				
Manual	22.5	36	20.5	26
Non-manual	7.6	5	11.4	10
All	17.9	42	16.7	36
Female (18 years and over)				
Manual	86.3	43	73.6	32
Non-manual	69.1	43	50.6	47
All	73.6	87	58.1	80
Male and female		129		116

Source: Department of Manpower Services (Northern Ireland), *New Earnings Surveys*, 1971 and 1979.

Note: Estimates of numbers obtained by application of crude grossing factors to survey results. Comparison of the figures for women are affected by a large shift from manual to non-manual employment over the period.

Who are the low paid?

Low pay by sex

As Tables 3.2 and 3.3 showed, three times as many women as men were low paid. The difference appears more stark expressed in

Table 3.4 Estimated number of adults[1] with earning below lowest decile male manual earnings, April 1979, Great Britain.

Weekly earnings	Number with gross weekly earnings below specified amounts						Number with gross weekly earnings excluding over-earnings below specified amounts					
	Men 21 years and over			Women 18 years and over			Men 21 years and over			Women 18 years and over		
	Manual	Non-manual	All	Manual	Non-manual	All	Manual	Non-manual	All	Manual	Non-manual	All
Under £25												
Under £30						0.1						0.1
Under £35				0.1	0.1	0.2				0.1	0.1	0.2
Under £37				0.1	0.1	0.3			0.1	0.1	0.1	0.3
Under £40			0.1	0.2	0.2	0.4			0.1	0.2	0.2	0.4
Under £42			0.1	0.2	0.3	0.6				0.3	0.3	0.6
Under £45	0.1		0.1	0.3	0.5	0.8				0.4	0.5	0.9
Under £47	0.1	0.1	0.2	0.4	0.7	1.1	0.1	0.1	0.2	0.4	0.7	1.1
Under £50	0.2	0.1	0.2	0.5	0.9	1.4	0.3	0.1	0.3	0.6	0.9	1.5
Under £52	0.2	0.1	0.3	0.6	1.0	1.0	0.4	0.1	0.5	0.6	1.1	1.7
Under £55	0.3	0.1	0.5	0.7	1.2	1.9	0.6	0.2	0.7	0.7	1.3	2.0
Under £60	0.6	0.3	0.8	0.8	1.6	2.5	1.0	0.3	1.3	0.9	1.7	2.6

Source: Department of Employment *New Earnings Survey*, 1979.

[1]Full time men aged 21 and over and full time women aged 18 and over, whose pay for the survey period was not affected by absence.

percentage terms. While in 1979 8.1 per cent of men were low paid, for women the proportion was 53.3 per cent. If the 18–20 age group of women are excluded to provide a more straightforward comparison with male workers 21 years and over, the percentage of low paid women would be reduced by about five per cent (see Table 3.5). The numbers and percentage of low paid women, while still excessive, have improved since 1971, falling in Great Britain from 3.2 million in 1971 to 2.5 million in 1979, with a proportionate fall in Northern Ireland. The number of men earning less than the defined low pay level decreased only slightly between 1971 and 1979.

Low pay by age

Table 3.5 shows the distribution of low pay by age in 1979 in Great Britain. Leaving aside those aged under 21 years and over retirement age, whose wages can be expected to be lower, the lowest paid age groups for both men and women are 21–24 years and the five years immediately preceding retirement age (65 for men and 60 for women).

Table 3.5 Percentage with weekly earnings less than £60 by age,[1] *Great Britain, 1979.*

	Males			Females		
Age Group (years)	Manual	Non-manual	All	Manual	Non-manual	All
Under 18	91.2	97.3	92.5	95.5	99.3	98.2
18 to 20	47.2	70.2	54.3	79.8	87.0	85.4
21 to 24	15.7	22.1	18.3	68.0	57.0	58.8
25 to 29	8.9	5.4	7.3	58.6	33.9	38.0
30 to 39	6.4	3.0	4.8	61.8	35.8	42.5
40 to 49	6.8	3.0	5.2	63.4	38.7	46.8
50 to 59	9.8	5.2	8.0	66.8	41.1	51.1
60 to 64	16.9	10.5	14.8	75.9	48.8	60.6
65 and over	45.9	32.1	40.2	92.0	64.1	77.7
18 and over	12.3	9.1	10.9	66.6	48.4	53.3
21 and over	9.6	6.1	8.1	65.0	41.9	48.3
All ages	15.0	10.3	13.1	68.3	51.0	55.7

Source: Department of Employment, *New Earnings Survey*, 1979.

[1] Full time males anu females whose pay for the survey period was not affected by absence.

For some of the 21–24 years age group, low earnings, especially (but not only) among non-manual workers, reflect the stage they have reached in the career structure and the problem will cure itself in time. However, depending on their commitments, they may nevertheless suffer real hardship during this period. The higher percentage of low wage earners among the pre-retirement group of manual and non-manual workers is the result of a number of factors. Among these are a reduction in overtime working, declining physical abilities, a tendency for higher paid workers to retire early, leaving the lower paid behind, and the fact that younger workers may be promoted ahead of older workers. Women who return late to the labour force may have few promotion opportunities.

Outside these age groups, substantial numbers of prime age female workers and not insignificant numbers of prime age male workers are low paid.

Low pay by region

Table 3.6 shows the proportion of workers in each region who are low paid. For males, Northern Ireland stands out as the lowest paid for both manual and non-manual workers in spite of an improvement in

Table 3.6 Full time workers earning less than £60 per week by region: UK 1979

Percentages

	Males		Females	
	Manual	Non-manual	Manual	Non-manual
South East	8.4	4.4	60.3	36.8
East Anglia	13.1	6.7	70.6	54.9
South West	14.4	8.4	73.8	56.1
West Midlands	7.5	6.0	65.1	52.6
East Midlands	9.9	5.6	68.9	54.4
Yorks./Humberside	9.3	7.4	71.8	56.3
North West	9.7	7.2	67.7	54.1
North	8.6	7.3	72.1	56.0
Wales	10.2	9.2	64.0	53.8
Scotland	10.8	6.9	68.6	55.6
Northern Ireland	20.5	11.4	73.6	50.6

Source: Department of Employment, *New Earnings Survey*, 1979.
Department of Manpower Services (Northern Ireland), *New Earnings Survey*, 1979.

average Northern Ireland wages relative to Great Britain in the 1970s. The South West and East Anglia are also low paid areas for manual men. All the women are disadvantaged, but the South West, Northern and Northern Ireland manual women more than most. The lowest decile male manual worker earned 17 per cent more in the South East of England than in Northern Ireland (£61.5 compared with £52.5). But lowest decile female manual workers earned much less – between £35.7 (South West) and £38.5 (South East).

Low pay by industry and type of work place

Tables 3.7 and 3.8 show the industrial distribution of low earning

Table 3.7 The industrial distribution of low earners; women 18 years and over in full time work, April 1977, Great Britain

Percentages

	Manual women		Non-manual women	
	Percentage in industry who were low-earning	Percentage of low-earning women in the industry	Percentage in industry who were low-earning	Percentage of low-earning women in the industry
All industries and services	67.9	100.0	46.3	100.0
All manufacturing industries	64.2	53.1	56.8	19.0
Food, drink and tobacco	60.6	6.2	58.0	2.3
Textiles	76.0	8.5	78.0	1.4
Clothing and footwear	84.3	11.2	75.3	0.9
Bricks, pottery and glass	59.5	1.8	67.8	0.7
All other manufacturing	55.6	24.4	54.5	13.4
Construction	na	na	75.3	2.3
Gas, electricity and water	na	na	29.0	0.9
Transport and communication	32.7	1.4	29.0	3.0
Distributive trades	84.9	6.8	83.4	27.9
Insurance, banking and finance	na	na	53.7	12.3
Professional and scientific services	72.4	18.1	26.2	17.5
Miscellaneous services	79.3	16.0	52.9	7.0
Public administration and defence	53.7	2.2	32.3	9.2

Source: Royal Commission on the Distribution of Income and Wealth, *Report No. 6 Lower Incomes*, Cmnd. 7175, (HMSO, London, 1978).

Table 3.8 The industrial distribution of low earners; men 21 years and over in full time work, April 1977, Great Britain

Percentages

	Manual men		Non-manual men	
Industry	Percentage in industry who were low-earning	Percentage of low-earning men in the industry	Percentage in industry who were low-earning	Percentage of low-earning men in the industry
All industries and services	9.7	100.0	6.7	100.0
All manufacturing industries	5.6	28.0	4.2	17.9
Agriculture	35.1	8.8	17.5	1.2
Mining and quarrying	0.8	0.3	1.4	0.2
Coal and petroleum	0.5	0.0	2.2	0.1
Clothing and footwear	24.7	2.0	14.2	0.9
All other manufacturing	5.3	25.7	4.0	16.7
Construction	6.0	7.1	5.8	4.3
Gas, electricity and water	1.8	0.5	1.9	0.7
Transport and communication	4.4	6.0	3.4	3.3
Distributive trades	26.6	15.5	18.8	29.5
Insurance, banking and finance	20.5	2.1	7.9	10.5
Professional and scientific services	22.8	7.6	4.9	12.1
Miscellaneous services	31.9	15.9	16.0	12.9
Public administration and defence	19.2	7.2	3.2	7.0

Source: Royal Commission on the Distribution of Income and Wealth, *Report No. 6 Lower Incomes*, Cmnd. 7175, (HMSO, London, 1978).

workers in 1977 in Great Britain. In certain industries, low paid workers, both men and women, occur in sizeable percentages, while in others low pay principally affects one sex; for example, males in agriculture and females in textiles, clothing and footwear. One can also distinguish between low-paying industries, i.e. those industries where a substantial proportion of all the employees are low paid, for example miscellaneous services, and the industries where the general level of wages is adequate, but a minority of workers are low paid, for example transport and communications for men.

Insufficient information is available about industry as a whole to determine whether small firms have proportionately more low paid workers than large firms. However, it is clear enough that when an industry group is made up of large numbers of very small establishments, it is frequently a low-paying industry. Wages Councils and Boards have been established to protect about 3 million workers in these kinds of industries through the setting of minimum wage levels (see p. 75).

An estimated 100–150,000 persons (mainly women) are employed as homeworkers[19]; that is, they carry out work, usually for manufacturing industries, in their own homes. Of these, approximately 27,000 are covered by Wages Councils.[20]

Information on the wages and conditions of homeworkers is inadequate, but studies undertaken by the Advisory, Conciliation and Arbitration Service (ACAS)[21] indicate a high incidence of earnings below the minimum Wages Council rates, and note that homeworkers may have to pay for collecting and delivering work, the cost of machinery and electricity, as well as providing work space in their homes. They have no job security and are subject to fluctuations in available work. Homeworkers may be seen as the extreme end of the low pay spectrum.[22]

Other groups

The problem of employment discrimination on the grounds of religion in Northern Ireland (but not elsewhere in the UK) will be discussed in Chapter 4. Figures from the 1971 Census (the most recent available) suggest that, while the proportion of Roman Catholics in low paid jobs in 1971 was probably higher than the proportion of low paid Protestants, the distribution of opportunities has not produced a simple division into low paid Roman Catholics and well paid Protestants. Both groups suffered from low paid employment in 1971. However, discrimination does hamper mobility.

Separate low pay figures by race are not available. Ethnic minority workers are more highly concentrated in unskilled and semi-skilled work than their white counterparts. However, studies indicate that they tend to do more shift work than white workers, thus attracting shift premiums which helped to upgrade their wages. Figures available from a 1976 PEP report[23] on racial disadvantage do not suggest an excessive concentration of low pay as a result of racial factors. As with the majority population, sex appears to be a more important determinant of wage levels.

Migrant workers entering the UK on work permits are thought to suffer very low pay. Although no figures are available on their levels of pay, a large proportion of them work in catering and domestic service, and migrant workers, whose job mobility is restricted by the terms of their permits, often occupy the worst jobs in these industries, which are in any case badly paid and with poor conditions of service. In 1969, nearly 68,000 work permits were granted; by 1978, this figure (including EEC residence permits) had fallen below 24,000.

Low pay tends to be related to a poor level of skills and educational qualifications, to poor health and to disability. Individuals with these characteritics are not necessarily low paid, but will be vulnerable to both low pay and unemployment.

Poverty, low pay and the development of low pay policies

Poverty is measured by comparing net household incomes with household 'needs', while low pay is measured on the basis of gross individual earnings without considering household needs; there is not a direct and simple relationship between low pay and poverty. Table 3.2 showed some 3.3 million individuals in Great Britain on low pay in 1979, and the numbers would have been similar in 1975.

The analysis in Chapter 2 (Table 2.14) showed 790,000 families living in poor households (Great Britain, 1975) where at least one family member (husband or wife) was economically active. Although only 190,000 of these were supported by a full-time, full year employee, and were therefore in poverty purely as a result of low wages, it was shown that inability to obtain full-time, full-year employment was itself directly related to wage levels. The official DHSS estimates[25] for the numbers in poverty relate to the 'normal' income of those who are 'normally' in work. These show only 230,000 families below the basic rate poverty line (in 1977, the latest available, Great Britain), but it has been argued in Chapter 1 that the long-term rate provides a better valuation of the poverty line. In that case, the number of working families in poverty in 1977 would be about 790,000; exactly the same figure, by coincidence, as the differently calculated estimate quoted at the beginnng of this paragraph. It may be suggested, therefore, that poverty and low wages coincide in about three-quarters of a million families in Great Britain. Thus, many of the low paid are not in poverty either because their household's 'needs' are less than those of the average couple with two children used to define the low pay line, or because the household has extra income – social security/assistance payments such as family income supplement, or a second earner.[26] It should be noted that these figures do not include Northern Ireland, where a larger proportion of low earning families are in poverty.[27]

Given this much lower set of figures of those actually in poverty because of low pay, is low pay an issue of importance in the discussion of poverty? There are a number of reasons for believing that it is, quite apart from asking whether it is acceptable that a full week's work, often with overtime, should result in a poverty level wage, and the particular severity of the problem in Northern Ireland.

Industries which pay low wages are also frequently characterised by poor working conditions and high labour turnover. A low paid worker is all too often a worker highly vulnerable to unemployment and, as already indicated, low pay combined with part-year unemployment brings families into poverty. Moreover, low pay has a flow-on effect into unemployment. Certain benefits, for example, earnings-related supplement[28] to unemployment benefit, and redundancy pay, because they are based on pay, are of less benefit to a low paid worker and particularly a worker subject to intermittent unemployment. There are also longer term effects. Low paid workers have less access to fringe benefits than higher paid workers and where these are available, for example, occupational pensions, these are frequently wage-related. The lower the wage, the lower the pension in retirement.[29]

Low pay will also result in an inability to save and to accumulate material resources, factors which make unemployment, sickness and retirement a harsher experience for low earners than for those with some cushions for times of adversity.

Low pay for women workers cannot be lightly dismissed either. Married women are making a significant contribution to the reduction of poverty through their earnings, a contribution which could be more effective if women's full-time wages and, as a consequence, part-time wages, were not so depressed. In addition, wages are of key importance to women heads of households with dependent children, a group, as indicated earlier, which is growing substantially and is very vulnerable to poverty. Low-earning single women living alone may also be found in poverty.

Perhaps the most important reasons for concern about low pay is the influence of low pay levels on the levels of income available for those outside the labour force, particularly the unemployed. In the setting of social security and supplementary benefit rates, one factor taken into account is the desirability of maintaining a gap between benefit rates and wages. This is partly intended to maintain an incentive to work, but it also reflects a sense that it is 'unfair' that someone who puts in a full week's work on a regular basis should have a lower income than someone who is not working, but is capable of work. But other factors (for example, subsistence levels) have to be taken into acount in setting benefit rates and, as a result, overlap between low pay and the benefit rate can occur. Should this gap be widened by lowering the rate of benefit for the unemployed or by tackling the problem of low pay?

The Supplementary Benefits Commission and an official team which reviewed the supplementary benefits scheme, have maintained that if there is a problem, the solution does not lie in cutting benefit for the unemployed, which both groups regard as inadequate. Rather, attention should be given to the unacceptably low level of some wages and to support programmes such as child benefit.[30] Nevertheless, there is pressure to cut benefits. There are echoes here of the old Poor Law principle of 'less eligibility'. This principle could be seen operating as late as 1975, through a mechanism called the wage stop, which maintained the gap between wages and benefits by down-grading benefits (see Chapter 5).

Although the wage stop was abolished in 1975, the unemployed have consistently been denied the progression from the short-term to the higher long-term rate of supplementary benefit available after two years[31] to other types of beneficiaries, and this year (1980) steps have been taken to hold back price-related increases in the benefit rates for the unemployed.

Low pay has now been recognised as an issue which must be tackled, but it cannot be said that clear policy lines have been developed. There are still more questions than available answers. Are women workers low paid because of their (alleged) marginal attachment to the labour market or are they suffering from discrimination? Are male low wage earners in this position because of personal characteristics (low educational levels, physical handicaps, poor health, age) which justify employers paying them low wages and, if so, should policies be directed to 'correcting' these adverse characteristics, where possible, and accepting the inevitability of low wages where it is not? Ought the labour market be left to sort itself out with perhaps (modest) state intervention only on behalf of the most vulnerable workers, or ought employers to be encouraged, pressed or even required to pay a living wage for a full week's work? If the former, how can the vulnerable worker be effectively protected? If the latter, who is to do this – the unions or the state – and will it lead to fewer jobs? How is a living wage to be set and maintained? Is is reasonable to expect workers to put in excess or unsocial hours simply to achieve a living wage?

Alternatively, should means be found through the social security system to supplement the income of low wage earners? If so, should this be by means of means-tested benefits directed specifically to low wage earners (and others on low incomes) or through universal benefits such as allowances for all dependent children? These and other questions lie behind the various approaches to the problem of low wages currently operating in the UK. Broadly speaking, the development of policy can be divided into two periods. From 1950–70, apart from the payment of increasingly marginal family allowances, the policy makers asumed that the problem must be tackled within the labour market. After 1970, though labour market approaches were maintained and even extended, policy makers increasingly looked to the social security system as the means of tackling poverty caused by low pay.

Policies on low pay – the individual approach

Individual effort

The workers with earnings below the low pay level are not a static group. Young workers obtain age-related wage increases, workers are promoted and low earners seek and find better jobs. Many workers, especially in the manual sector, experience 'natural' fluctuation in their wage levels depending, for instance, on the amount of overtime available. Year to year analyses suggest that just over one-third of the lowest 10 per cent of earners will have moved out of that group the following year. Although half of these will be found only in the second lowest 10 per cent, some experience a substantial increase in relative earnings.[32]

However, as Table 3.2 showed, while the numbers and proportion of low paid women fell during the 1970s, the numbers and proportion of low paid men has not varied a great deal since 1971. Thus as some male workers climb out of the low pay bracket, others join it or slip back into it. In other words, the number of male low paid jobs does not change a great deal, though the individuals who occupy them do.[33] The effect of this process is that, while in any one year 10 per cent of male manual workers will be low paid, over a period of five years a much larger group have experienced low pay. This is illustrated by an analysis over a five-year period of the same sample of male manual workers: 3 per cent of them were low paid in all five years, 21 per cent were low paid in at least one of the five years.[34] The pattern for women is not likely to be different except that, since a higher proportion of female jobs are low paid, more difficulty will be experienced in getting out of the low pay group. Thus, while individual effort and the workings of the labour market can have a beneficial effect on some workers, the pool of low paid jobs, and thus the low pay problem, remains largely unaffected.

Working wives

One route out of poverty for a family dependent on the low wage of the male head of household is the introduction of a second wage – that of the wife. Research has shown the key importance of the working wife in combating poverty due to low pay. In 1975 in Great Britain, among couples where the man's earnings were below 140 per cent of the supplementary benefit level, some 63 per cent of the wives were working. The effect of this on all couples in this group (with or without children) was to reduce the percentage of those below the poverty line from 37 per cent to 13 per cent; and on families with children, to reduce those in poverty from 38.8 per cent to 17.4 per cent.[35]

Although working wives make such an effective contribution to reducing poverty due to low wages, it cannot be said that this role has been fully recognised or that substantial policies have been developed to support families who attempt to take this route out of poverty. Frequent reference is made by labour market commentators to the 'marginal attachment' of married women to the labour force and, as 'second earners', the incidence of unemployment among married women is not seen as of great significance. At the same time, adequate provision of day care for under-fives and after school and holiday care for school age children of working mothers has not been developed. Surveys and studies undertaken during the 1970s consistently show that demand for these forms of care exceeds supply by far and, moreover, that those families with the lowest income have the least access to the available provision.[36]

Training to improve skills

Since low pay in many instances is the result of lack of skills or the possession of skills no longer in demand, skill training to enable low paid workers to move up the occupational scale may be seen as an appropriate element of the individual approach to the low pay problem.

Employment training in the United Kingdom is provided by industry itself, often in co-operation with educational establishments, and by the Manpower Services Commission (MSC) through the Training Opportunities Scheme (TOPS) and other MSC programmes. TOPS provides preparatory courses for unskilled workers aimed at improving their standards of literacy and numeracy, and for groups vulnerable to low paid employment – disabled persons and persons unemployed for a prolonged period – the MSC provides courses at Employment Rehabilitation Centres.[37]

These special programmes excepted, the training system is more geared to the needs of industry than to the low paid. Industry training in fact is more likely to be available in the higher paying industries and TOPS will as cheerfully train workers for low paid jobs as for high paid if the demand for such workers exists. The proportion of women among TOPS trainees has increased from 3.5 per cent in 1971 to 43 per cent in 1977, but for the most part these have been trained for traditionally female occupations which almost by definition are poorly paid.[38]

The potential of training for enhancing the skills of low paid or potentially low paid workers certainly exists, though studies suggest that training does not necessarily produce higher pay.[39] However, as currently operated, it does little to alter the pool of low paid jobs.

Policies on low pay – the collective bargaining approach

It was suggested at the beginning of this chapter that major reliance had been placed on the combination of full employment and increased unionisation as the means of eliminating low pay. Full employment no longer operates in the UK, but there is still a strong body of opinion that holds that the only effective means of combating low pay is through the extension of collective bargaining.

It is correct to say that many of the lowest paid industries are under-unionised or have active unions only in the larger units. A clear example of this is the catering industry, where in 1974 only 5.2 per cent of its workers were union members (mostly in the industrial and staff canteen sector), compared with an all industries and services percentage of 51 per cent.[40] On the other hand, some low paying industries are highly unionised, for example education and local government, with an 85.6 per cent density, health with 60 per cent and clothing and footwear with 79 per cent.[41] While a low level of unionisation leaves the door wide open to low pay, other factors also operate to depress wages or raise them, for example whether an industry is declining or expanding. In some cases, the fact that the employer is government, combined with the government's desire to hold or decrease public expenditure, leads to the persistence of low pay in spite of a high level of unionisation. However, it can be said that the presence of large and active unions ensure that low pay does not descend to the abysmal levels prevailing in the under-unionised Wages Council sector.

Some unions have always given a high priority to low paid workers. The Trades Union Congress, on the other hand, was somewhat slow in making low pay a central issue. Concern over government wages policies and attention to differentials has tended to dominate union thinking, and the record of some unions at the local level on equal pay and anti-discrimination legislation has been less than admirable. However, since the mid-1960s, the TUC has pursued a fairly steady policy of pressing for the setting of minimum targets for low pay and urging its member unions to give priority to low paid workers. It also argues that in so far as low pay results from inefficient industrial organisation and low productivity, collective bargaining is the best means to negotiate improved output while protecting the jobs of the workers as far as possible.

It seems clear that the claim that the extension of collective bargaining has an important role to play in combating low pay is justified, but to rely solely on the union movement to eliminate low pay would be less than wise. It is not a problem which will respond to a single approach.

Policies on low pay – the anti-discrimination approach

Race

Legislation to combat racial discrimination, particularly (but not only), in employment was passed in 1968 and reinforced in the 1976 Race Relations Act. These Acts apply to Great Britain, but not Northern Ireland, where the racial minority population is very small.

Briefly, the legislation outlaws discrimination on the grounds of colour, race, ethnic or national origin or nationality in the hiring, conditions of employment, training or dismissal of workers. Theoretically then, minority workers should have access to the full range of employment opportunities and if they are low paid it should be for reasons which would affect the working population at large and not for reasons of race. Research carried out on the functioning of the Acts suggests that, while discrimination in recruitment and promotion has decreased, it is not yet eliminated and continued pressure is necessary to enforce the legislation.[43]

Religion

Job discrimination on the grounds of religion is confined mainly to Northern Ireland. After an investigation in 1973, the Fair Employment (Northern Ireland) Act was passed in 1976. This established a Fair Employment Agency with the task of promoting equality of employment opportunity in Northern Ireland. So far, only limited progress has been reported by the Fair Employment Agency.[44]

Women

As indicated earlier, three times as many women are low paid as men. Three factors are at work here; first, the hours worked by women, second, equal pay and third, job segregation.

Women work fewer hours of overtime than men and benefit less from shift premiums. This pattern is in part the result of legal restrictions under protective legislation dating from the 19th century, and the more recent 1961 Factories Act affected the hours of work of about 900,000 million women in 1979.[45] However, even if such restrictions were removed, other considerations would probably prevent women from increasing their income through shift work and overtime, since married women have to combine work with domestic commitments.[46]

Low pay among women prior to 1970 was further depressed by the absence of equal pay legislation, though some employers (in particular, national and local government) had introduced equal pay for their employees. The Equal Pay Act of 1970, which came into full operation in the UK on 29th December 1975, required employers to give equal treatment in pay and terms and conditions of employment to men and women employed (a) on work of the same or broadly similar nature and (b) on work which, though different, had been given an equal value under a job evaluation scheme. Table 3.9 shows the changes in women's hourly earnings in Great Britain in relation to male earnings over the period 1970–1979.

Table 3.9 Average gross hourly earnings excluding the effects of overtime hours of employees aged 18 and over, 1970–1979, Great Britain

Pence per hour

	1970[1]	1974	1975	1976	1977	1978	1979
Men	67.4	104.8	136.3	162.9	177.4	200.3	226.9
Women	42.5	70.6	98.3	122.4	133.9	148.0	165.7
Differential	24.9	34.2	38.0	39.5	43.5	52.3	61.2
Women's earnings as per cent of men's	63.1	67.4	72.1	75.1	75.5	73.9	73.0

Source: Department of Employment, *New Earnings Surveys*, 1970–79.
[1] 1970 figures converted from shillings per hour.

In spite of progress for which the Equal Pay Act can take much of the credit, a considerable differential in basic rates remains and indeed some falling off has occurred since 1977. The Equal Opportunities Commission reported in 1977 that 'there is a continuing and widespread tendency to segregate jobs in order to retain lower rates of pay for women' and, in 1978, expressed concern about problems arising from the rigidity of the Equal Pay Act 'which insists on the existence of a definite male comparison, will not allow comparisons of equal value in the absence of a job evaluation scheme, and does not recognise the concept of indirect discrimination.[47]

Job segregation has always been a characteristic of women's employment and studies indicate that the overall pattern of both horizontal and vertical job segregation has hardly changed at all in almost three-quarters of a century.[48] Three forms of segregation may be distinguished. First is the concentration of women in certain industry groups. In 1976, almost 71 per cent of women were employed in five industry groups, all of which were low paying industries for both sexes. Second is the over-representation of women in certain industries where they are paid low wages, though male workers in these industries are not. Textiles, and clothing and footwear are typical examples of this. Third, throughout other industries the majority of women occupy the lower status and lower paid jobs. Part-time women suffer the same forms of segregation, but to a greater extent than full-timers.

Although the choice of work for married women in particular is influenced by domestic factors, such as the need to work close to home and to have convenient hours and, although some women may emphasise job satisfaction over higher pay, the extent of job segregation and resultant low pay among women is considered to be more the result of discrimination than of choice. To combat this, the Sex Discrimination Act was enacted in 1975 with the object of opening up a fuller range of work opportunities for women. Research so far indicates that the Act appears to be having little effect on the occupational distribution of women. In many firms, little effort has been made to reduce job segregation for fear of causing difficulties with male workers. Assumptions that women are best fitted for certain types of work and that they are not interested in promotion still prevail in personnel policy. Career paths and training arrangements still militate against women, especially in relation to broken career patterns because of childbearing and child-rearing.[49]

The Equal Opportunities Commission is continuing to press for full implementation of both the Equal Pay Act and the Sex Discrimination Act.[50] It should be noted that while improvements in the equal pay field and access to overtime and shift premiums actually reduce the number of low paid workers, the ending of job segregation will not necessarily have the same effect. It may instead distribute low paid jobs more equally between the sexes. This is justice of a sort, but it will leave a bitter taste.

Policies on low pay – state intervention

Fair wages resolutions

Fair wages resolutions of the House of Commons (requiring government contractors to pay fair wages) date back to 1891, when the first was adopted to prevent sweated labour being used in competing for government contracts. This was strengthened in 1909 to include penalties for government contractors whose employees' rates of pay or hours of work were less favourable than those commonly 'recognised' by employers or unions, or than those adopted by 'good employers' in the district. In the years up to 1945, similar provisions were adopted by local authorities and they became standard practice for statutes dealing with particular industries decreeing that wages and conditions must not be less favourable than those which would have to be observed under the fair wage resolution.[51] The resolution currently operating was passed in 1945.

The nature of the Fair Wages Resolution makes it almost impossible to identify its influence on wages, but no doubt it has helped to prevent grossly exploitive wages. The present government is questioning the usefulness of the 1945 resolution, which it believes interferes unnecessarily with normal pay bargaining. However, it recognised that some such arrangement is required by the International Labour Organisation (ILO) Convention 94 (1949), which has been ratified by the UK. The government has, on the other hand, repealed a provision in the Employment Protection Act of 1975 which, from 1977, had allowed an application by an employers' organisation or a trade union to the Central Arbitration Commission if it was considered that an employer was not observing recognised terms and conditions of employment (as established by agreements or awards) or, where there are no such recognised conditions, then the general level of terms and conditions in the trade, industry or sector.

Incomes policies

In the period 1965–70, the various phases of the incomes policy (of the Labour Government) usually provided for exceptional pay increases where 'there is general recognition that existing wage and salary levels are too low to maintain a reasonable standard of living'.[52] The National Board for Prices and Incomes (NBPI), reviewing the low pay situation in 1971 said:

> 'It is apparent from our studies that what little improvement took place in the relative position of the low paid in the earlier years of the prices and incomes policy was later lost. This does not mean that another attempt to help the low paid in the context of a prices and incomes policy would inevitably fail. There are many factors which contributed to the lack of success of this aspect of the policy in 1965–70, including for example, the intrinsic difficulty of the task, the shortage of experience in tackling it, the lack of concensus as to what constitutes low pay and the difficult economic circumstances in which the policy was operating.'[53]

After a two-year gap, an incomes policy was revived by the then

Conservative Government. It also set down as one of its principles: 'to facilitate an improvement of the relative position of the low paid'.[54] This policy, which lasted until 1974, again produced little long-term improvement in the position of the low paid. The principles were believed to be good, but the practice unsatisfactory. The Pay Board (the monitor of the 1972–74 policy) commented in 1974 that 'the factors which were largely responsible for their low pay in the first place militated against their securing maximum advantage from the permissive concessions in the Codes'.[55] Later versions of the incomes policy between 1974 and 1979 showed the same pattern of early gains followed by the re-establishment of traditional wage patterns.

This experience should not necessarily lead to the conclusion that the low paid cannot be helped by an incomes policy, but it has shown that an incomes policy which operates without clear government policies on low pay is likely to be ineffective in the longer term for low paid workers. This inherent weakness in all the programmes of state intervention in wage setting as they affect low paid workers can be seen most clearly in the operation of the Wages Council system.

Wages Councils and Boards

The most important and long-lasting form of state intervention on low pay is through the Wages Council system. Statutory minimum wage legislation was introduced through the Trade Boards Act of 1909 as a means of dealing with the evils of 'sweated labour.' Subsequent legislation has modified the system from time to time. The most recent Act was passed in 1979.

The principal object of the Wages Councils (and the Agricultural Wages Board) is to protect those who work in traditionally low paying industries, usually composed of large numbers of small firms where the level of unionisation, and therefore the opportunity for collective bargaining, is low. The Wages Councils set minimum wage rates, holidays and holiday pay and, since 1975, certain other conditions of employment. Enforcement procedures are available through a Wages Inspectorate. Broadly speaking the industries covered are hotel and catering, retail distribution, sections of clothing manufacture, laundries, hairdressing, toy making, agriculture and other miscellaneous industries. In 1979, almost 3 million workers in the United Kingdom were supposed to be protected by the system of 55 Councils and Boards.

A secondary object of the Wages Councils system is to encourage the development of collective bargaining machinery on the understanding that if and when this develops, the Wages Council concerned may be abolished.

The Wages Council system has come under a steady hail of criticism in the last 10–15 years, directed at the failure of the Wages Councils to achieve both their primary and their secondary goals. Indeed, it is difficult to find commentators with a good word to say about the system.

Table 3.10 shows the distribution of the minimum rates fixed for the lowest paid adult workers for a 40-hour week in Wages Council industries in 1979 in Great Britain, at a time when the low pay level was £60 per week. Rates set by Northern Ireland Wages Councils, in some cases, are lower than for the equivalent industry in Great Britain.[56] Table 3.11 shows the actual wage distribution in 1979, which reflects the higher wages paid to older workers and by employers who pay above minimum rates.

Table 3.10 Wages Councils[1] minimum rates for lowest paid categories of adult workers 18–22 years for 40-hour week, Great Britain, 1979

	Wage range (£'s)			
	25–29	30–34	35–39	40–44
Number of Wages Councils	1	6	7	27

Source: Incomes Data Services Report 321, (January 1980).
[1] Not including Agricultural Wages Board.

Table 3.11 Distribution of earnings for full time workers covered by Wages Councils and Boards, Great Britain, 1979

	Percentage of workers earning per week less than:						
	£30	£35	£40	£45	£50	£55	£60
Manual men	–	–	–	5.8	12.0	22.4	33.5
Non-manual men	–	–	–	5.8	8.5	14.2	22.5
Manual women	4.1	13.9	27.7	48.0	63.9	75.7	83.8
Non-manual women	1.6	6.3	20.0	45.3	63.7	76.3	83.0

Source: Department of Employment, *New Earnings Survey*, 1979.

Table 3.12 compares the position of Wages Councils and Board workers with all low paid workers and shows clearly the disadvantaged position of the former compared with other low paid workers.

Table 3.12 Percentage of workers paid less than £60 per week, Wages Councils and Boards[1] and others, Great Britain, 1979

Percentages

	All workers	Wages Councils and Boards
Manual men	9.6	33.5
Non-manual men	6.1	22.5
Manual women	66.6	83.8
Non-manual women	48.4	83.0

Source: Table 3.3 and Table 3.11
[1] Including agriculture.

There appear to be a number of reasons for the failure of the Wages Councils and Boards even to attain reasonable parity with low paid workers in general. The Wages Councils have not established any minimum wage goal, either in general or in relation to average wages in related industries nor, except for a brief period in the mid-1970s, has any goal been proposed to them by government. Moreover, the Wages Councils and their predecessors took few steps to collect information about wages in the industries for which they were responsible.[57]

Wages Council workers did not fare particularly well as a result of incomes policies. While the private sector as a whole could often find means of evading the most stringent restrictions of the incomes policies, Wages Councils had far less leeway. On the other hand, they did not always take advantage of opportunities to advance the interests of their workers within the incomes policy provisions for low paid workers. The Wages Councils have not always made annual determinations, even in times of high inflation. While there has been some catching up in 1980, when a wages order is made, there is no guarantee that it will be paid in all establishments, because of the difficulty in understanding the complexities of wage determinations and the fact that some employers and many workers are unaware of the functions (and sometimes even of the existence) of the Wages Council which covers them.[58]

Enforcement of Wages Council orders in Great Britain is the responsibility of the Wages Inspectorate of the Department of Employment where, in 1978, 150 outdoor inspectors were employed. In Northern Ireland, in the Department of Manpower Services, there are two Wages Inspectors. The Inspectorate undertakes a programme of routine visits to selected establishments together with investigation of complaints. On average, between 7 per cent and 9 per cent of establishments are visited each year. Since late 1976, an additional inspection technique has been used in Great Britain – the low pay blitz. Certain towns were selected for a 1–3 weeks' intensive inspection programme. The average amounts by which each worker is underpaid are not usually high, but are a further reduction of already inadequate pay.[59]

More serious attention has been given to homeworkers in recent years. In 1978, a special homeworking unit was established within the Wages Inspectorate and 18 inspectors were designated as homeworking inspectors. An Advisory Committee on Home working has also been established. Homeworkers are now to be covered by Health and Safety legislation and efforts are being made to establish a registration system to overcome the problem of identifying homeworking inspectors. An Advisory Committee on Home working whether these various steps will reduce underpayment of homeworkers.

In spite of persistent dissatisfaction with the functioning of Wages Councils, there appears to be no pressure towards the abolition of this system. The consensus appears to be that some system is essential to protect the most vulnerable workers and that Wages Councils are better than nothing. At the same time, while a number of official bodies have produced reports on the functioning of individual Councils, no total review of the system has been undertaken.

There are, however, several proposals for providing more effective protection for Wages Council workers. These include more active efforts to unionise them in order to bring about the restructuring of low paid industries.[60] Such an extension would include greater unionisation of homeworkers.

The Low Pay Unit has urged upon government the need to set minimum targets for low pay which Wages Councils would be required to reach over a period of 3–5 years,[61] and a number of groups have recommended the strengthening of the Wages Inspectorate. All parties appear to be agreed about the necessity of increasing and simplifying the information about Wages Council orders and their other activities. So far no substantial changes have been proposed by government and, in fact, the inspection system has been weakened by the termination of the 'blitz' programme.[62]

A national minimum wage

The UK has no national minimum wage. In late 1967, the government established an inter-departmental working party to examine 'the social, industrial and economic consequences of introducing a national minimum wage'.[63] The report concluded that there would be no serious administrative difficulties in introducing, policing and periodically up-grading a minimum wage, but believed that there could be undesirable economic consequences, the impact of which would depend on the level at which the minimum wage was set, the way it was phased in and the extent to which the rest of the labour force acted to maintain existing differentials.

The working party noted that a national minimum wage, as an anti-poverty measure, 'has the merit that it would help certain categories of the poor who are not adequately covered by the government's existing methods for relieving poverty'. However, it seemed to regard it as a counter-argument that such a measure would only help the one-third of the poor who were in poverty due to low earnings and not the two-thirds who were outside the labour force. The report stressed the difficulty of setting a minimum wage which could overcome the problem of variations in the number dependent on the wage, and concluded that 'a national minimum is likely to be a less efficient means of relieving poverty than selective social benefits related to individual needs'.

Since the publication of this rather inadequate report in 1969, there has been no serious move by government (of either party) towards a national minimum wage. The subject is not quite dead, but the worsening economic situation in the 1970s, together with the somewhat tepid support given to the proposal by the TUC, has ensured that it has received little consideration.[64]

On the other hand, one of the major unions for low paid workers, the National Union of Public Employees (NUPE), has continued to press for a national minimum wage,[65] taking the view that in the end a statutory national minimum wage will be found to be the only solution to low pay, just as the Equal Pay Act was in the end found to be the only solution to the problem of discriminatory wage levels for women. By combining a realistic national minimum wage with adequate levels of child benefit and a taxation system which did not penalise the low paid, the problem of poverty due to low wages could, in the view of NUPE, be seriously tackled.[66] In 1979, the Irish Congress of Trade Unions (which covers Northern Ireland), at the insistence of the Northern Ireland Committee, adopted as policy the need for a statutory minimum wage.

Policies on low pay – the social security approach

By 1970, there was sufficient concern about poverty due to low pay to lead government to seek a solution to the problem. At the same time, official reports were tending to stress the difficulty of a direct attack on low pay itself and were pointing out the advantages of a selective social benefits approach. It was not, therefore, surprising that in 1970 the newly elected (Conservative) government decided to try the social security route to reduce poverty due to low wages.

Family income supplement

The Family Income Supplement Act 1970 (1971 in Northern Ireland) established a system of supplementation of low wages. This supplement is available to two-parent families whose head works 30 hours a week or more, and to lone parents who work 24 hours a week or more and who have a gross weekly income below a 'prescribed amount' in relation to the number of dependent children (see Table 3.1). Half the difference between actual earnings and the prescribed amount is paid as family income supplement. Benefit runs for 52 weeks, even though earnings may change during that period. In 1978, nearly 90,000 families in the UK received this benefit.[67] In Great Britain, 46 per cent were lone parent families; in Northern Ireland, only 10 per cent. Recipients of family income supplement also have automatic entitlement to other benefits which are normally subject to separate means tests including free school meals, free NHS prescriptions, dental care etc., and legal aid. Although the take-up rate for FIS is estimated to have risen from 50 per cent in 1972 to 75 per cent in 1974,[68] it will be noted that the number of claimants, at 90,000, is well below the minimum estimates of the numbers of families of wage earners who are in poverty – approximately 200,000, though some of the short-fall would consist of families without children.

Few commentators have proposed the abolition of FIS without its replacement, but most are uneasy or frankly critical of the scheme. It blurs the distinction between earning one's living and depending on social assistance. At best, it is felt to lead to complacency about the problem of low pay, without solving working poverty; at worst, it may directly perpetuate low pay, effectively subsidising low paying employers. Moreover, it does not provide a minimum income guarantee above the poverty line. Only half the difference between gross wages and the prescribed amount is made up and the greater the original difference, the greater the gap will remain after FIS is paid. Finally, it has exacerbated a problem which has become known as the poverty trap.

The poverty trap

The poverty trap arises as a result of the relationship between three factors: an increase in pay, the ensuing increase in tax and national insurance deductions, and the reduction in the level of, or the eligibility for, various means tested benefits, including such items as rent and rate rebates and allowances (discussed in Chapter 6), free school meals, free welfare milk, and a number of other benefits.

Table 3.13 serves as an illustration of the process for a notional two-child family at a time when the defined low income level was £60 per week. As wages rise, so do tax and national insurance deductions, while FIS and the four major means tested benefits decrease and eventually cut out. The example shows that to achieve less than £1 per week increase in net weekly spending power, the worker must earn £30 per week more and to achieve less than £9 increase, he must earn £50 per week more.

The reality is not quite so clear cut. Family income supplement is granted for 52 weeks and may continue in payment for some time after the wage rise. Take-up of the four means tested benefits used in the illustration, is by no means 100 per cent. Whilst these factors may mitigate the effects of the poverty trap, the overall effect remains. On the one hand, the existence of FIS and the growing number of means tested benefits markedly improve the spending power of the low paid worker and, on the other hand, the struggle to attain complete independence of means tested support schemes and to gain full benefit from increased wages or longer overtime work can be very prolonged and, for some, never achievable. Since even with the full range of benefits the low paid family has little or no margin for expenditure on other than essentials or little hope of saving except to

Table 3.13 Illustration of the poverty trap for a married couple with two children aged 4 and 6 years,[1] 1979

£

Normal earnings	Tax	National Insurance Contributions	Family Income Supplement	Rent rebate	Rate rebate	Free school meals	Free welfare milk	Net weekly spending power
35	0.02	2.28	12.80	6.44	2.49	1.50	1.05	53.23
45	2.52	2.93	7.80	5.19	2.09	1.50	1.05	53.43
55	5.31	3.58	2.80	3.94	1.69	1.50	1.05	53.34
65	8.31	4.22	–	2.70	1.26	1.50	–	54.18
75	11.31	4.87	–	1.00	0.66	–	–	56.73
85	14.31	5.53	–	–	0.06	–	–	61.47
95	17.31	6.13	–	–	–	–	–	67.76
105	20.31	6.82	–	–	–	–	–	72.12
115	23.31	7.48	–	–	–	–	–	80.46

Source: Hansard, 7.11.79.

[1] Rent – £6.50; rates – £2.80; work expenses – £2.45; child benefit – £8.00; husband employed.

pay regular bills, this becomes a very grey and dispiriting existence While those who are concerned about poor people criticise the poverty trap for its effect on their lives, those who are mainly concerned about work incentives view the process with equal dismay.

Low paid workers simultaneously suffer from the operation of the general tax system. The sliding scale for national insurance contributions set at 6½ per cent of earnings began to operate at £19.50 per week in 1979, well below the low pay level, and it is unrelated to the number of dependants. In addition, the income tax threshold, the point at which the worker becomes liable to tax, has been steadily falling for a number of years. In the case of a two-parent, two-child family, it has fallen from 103.4 per cent of average male manual earnings in 1952–53 to 43.4 per cent in 1979–80.[69] The defined low pay level is roughly two-thirds of average male manual earnings. The effect of the whole process of the poverty trap is that during the period when means-tested benefits apply, the government is giving with one hand and taking back with another.

Although there is almost universal agreement about the need to reduce the effects of the poverty trap, recent moves by the present government are having the effect of increasing the problem. Various means tested schemes which formerly extended to low paid workers not receiving FIS are now being restricted to supplementary benefit and FIS recipients. For example, discretion has been given to local authorities in the provision of school meals and milk for pupils with the exception of provision for recipients of supplementary benefits and FIS; provision in these cases remains mandatory. The result may be that when wages increase sufficiently to take a family off FIS, certain other benefits will cut out immediately, instead of partially and at staggered intervals as at present. A wage increase in this case may bring an actual loss of income.

Child benefits

Dissatisfaction with a means-tested approach to low pay problems re-activated the discussion of universal methods of dealing with poverty among working families with children.

Poverty among low-earning families with a number of children to support had been recognised in the 1942 Beveridge Report. The solution then recommended was a scheme of family allowances to be given to families with two or more children, on the assumption that a full week's wage ought to be able to support a married couple and one child. Family allowances were first paid in 1946, though at a lower rate than recommended by Beveridge. At the same time, families with children, including the first child, could claim a child tax allowance, thus reducing the amount of income tax to be paid. While family allowances were paid at a flat rate for all children, regardless of family income, child tax allowances varied in their impact from being of no benefit at all to families below the tax threshold to being of maximum benefit to taxpayers in the highest tax brackets.

Changes in the rates of family allowance in the first 30 years were quite small, rising from £0.25 in 1946 to £1.50 per child in 1975. As a percentage of average gross male manual earnings, the allowance for 2 children together with child tax allowance, fell from 9.3 per cent in 1946–47 to 6.3 per cent in 1973–74.[70] In 1975, a new Child Benefit Act provided for a staged increase in family allowances, now to be called child benefit. Stage one was the extension of benefit to the first child of one-parent families in 1976, together with an increase in the general benefit rate. Stage two, in 1977, provided benefit for the first child of all families and subsequent stages increased the rates to the present level of £4.75 per child per week. Simultaneously, child tax allowances have been progressively phased out and the new child benefit is tax-free. A child benefit increase is also available as an additional benefit for one-parent families. An indication of the possible effects of child benefit was given in Chapter 2.

The new child benefit scheme has commanded all-party support and appeals to a diversity of groups in the community. The poverty lobby welcome the higher universal payments to families with children and those concerned with work incentives note with satisfaction that the fact that child benefit is paid to unemployed and employed alike tends to widen the gap in income between employed and unemployed families with children. There has been fairly continuous political and public pressure to index the benefits against inflation and to improve the value of child benefit as a proportion of average earnings. For a 2-child family, this proportion in 1978–9 was 7.5 per cent, which was still below the 1946 level. The fact that child benefit payments are not differentiated by age as are the allowances for children under National Insurance and supplementary benefit is also seen as a deficiency of the present scheme.

Future directions for low pay policy

Of the wide range of measures directed at the problem of poverty due to low pay, only a few stand out as really effective. These are equal pay, child benefit and, up to a point, increased unionisation. It is clear that, given the complexity of the problem, no one programme is likely to be able to deal with it effectively. The recommendations emerging from various official and unofficial bodies suggest a multi-faceted programme on the following lines:–

(a) Concentrated union attention on the needs of the lowest paid, combining the extension of unionisation among the 'hard to organise' and the development of means to up-grade the pay of the lowest earners without triggering off a readjustment process across the whole pay structure, together with union assistance to improve company and worker efficiency. There were signs that the TUC was moving towards such a programme in the early and mid-1970s, but a great deal of thinking and worker education will be needed if such a programme is to have any success.
(b) Active pursuit of anti-discrimination legislation particularly (but not only) to implement fully the Equal Pay Act and to tackle questions of job segregation.
(c) Either a serious attempt to make the Wages Council system workable and adequate, including the setting of minimum targets for low pay, or a full re-examination of the potential of a national minimum wage and how it could be phased in to ensure the least possible adverse economic effects.
(d) Improved and indexed child benefits.
(e) The raising of the tax threshold to exclude the low paid from tax liability.

Of these proposals, only the last fits comfortably into present government policies. The government has already shown some reluctance to index and upgrade child benefit and its stated dislike of intervention in industry would lead it to reject the idea of minimum wages and to be somewhat lacklustre about tough anti-discrimination policies. The government instead appears to prefer to strengthen the means tested support programmes for the low paid and it has over the last 18 months improved both the family income supplement and the rent and rates allowance schemes.

At the same time, workers across the country are experiencing intense economic insecurity and fear of unemployment, and the effects of a high inflation rate. At times such as these, the willingness of workers to stand back while others less advantaged move forward is very limited. Nevertheless, an effective anti-poverty programme must include a coherent set of proposals to deal with poverty caused by low pay.

Notes

1 See p.
2 Abel-Smith, Brian and Townsend, Peter, *The Poor and the Poorest*, (Bell and Sons, London, 1965).
3 Ibid.
4 Ibid.
5 Ibid.
6 Ibid.
7 *Prices and Incomes Policy*, Cmnd. 2639, (HMSO, London, 1965).
8 National Board for Prices and Incomes, *Second General Report*, July 1966–August 1967, (HMSO, London, 1967).
9 Fisher, Alan and Dix, Bernard, *Low Pay and How to End It*, (Pitmans, London, 1974).
10 1971 in Northern Ireland.
11 National Board for Prices and Incomes. op. cit.
12 Department of Employment and Productivity, *A National Minimum Wage: an Inquiry*, (HMSO, London, 1969).
13 National Board for Prices and Incomes, *General Problems of Low Pay*, (HMSO, London, 1971); Royal Commission on the Distribution of Income and Wealth. *Lower Incomes*, Cmnd. 7175, (HMSO, London, 1978).
14 Fisher and Dix. op. cit.
15 Young, Michael (ed.), *Poverty Report, 1974* and *Poverty Report, 1975*, (Temple Smith, London, 1974 and 1975).
16 See, for example, the *Low Pay Unit Bulletin*, December 1979 and Atkinson, A. B., *Poverty in Britain and the Reform of Social Security*, (Cambridge University Press, 1969).
17 In 1886 lowest decile male manual earnings were 68.6 per cent of median earnings. In 1979 they were 68.3 per cent; see *Department of Employment Gazette*, May 1978, and *Low Pay Bulletin*, December 1979.
18 *Low Pay Bulletin*, December 1979.
19 Townsend, Peter, *Poverty in the United Kingdom*, (Penguin Books, Harmondsworth, 1979).
20 Royal Commission, *Lower Incomes*. op. cit.
21 Advisory Conciliation and Arbitration Service, *Toy Manufacturing Wages Council*, (London, 1978); and *Button Manufacturing Wages Council*, (London, 1978).
22 Crine, Simon, *The Hidden Army*, (Low Pay Unit, London, 1979).
23 Smith, David J., *The Facts of Racial Disadvantage: a National Survey*, (PEP, London, 1976).
24 See *Department of Employment Gazette* for annual work permit figures.
25 Department of Health and Social Security, *Social Security Statistics, 1977*, (HMSO, London, 1979).
26 Layard, R., *et al., The Causes of Poverty*, Royal Commission on the Distribution of Incomes and Wealth, Background Paper No. 5, (HMSO, London, 1978).
27 Evason, Eileen, *Family Poverty in Northern Ireland*, (Child Poverty Action Group, London, 1978).
28 This benefit is discussed in more detail in the chapter on Unemployment.
29 Ibid.

30 Department of Health and Social Security, *Social Assistance: A review of the supplementary benefits scheme in Great Britain*, (London, 1978); Supplementary Benefits Commission, *Response of the Supplementary Benefits Commission to Social Assistance: a review of the Supplementary Benefits Scheme in Great Britain*, (HMSO, London, 1979).

31 After one year from November 1980.

32 Sanders, C. *et al.*, *Winners and Losers – Pay Patterns in the 1970s*, (PEP, London, 1977).

33 It should be emphasised that the lowest decile male manual earnings line is being used here as a low pay level, not because it represents the lowest 10 per cent of earners, but because it is roughly the same as the low pay line calculated under definition (d) – p. 55 – and as the poverty line used in the rest of this study. Thus conclusions drawn which may appear to be simply the result of the use of an inequality definition are in fact reasonable because the low pay level being used is also a poverty line.

34 How individual people's earnings change, *Department of Employment Gazette*, January, 1977.

35 Layard *et al.*, op. cit.

36 Equal Opportunities Commission, *I Want to Work... but what about the Kids?*, (EOC, Manchester, 1978); Bone, Margaret, *Pre-School Children and the Need for Day Care*, (HMSO, London, 1977).

37 Manpower Services Commission, *TOPS Review 1978* and *Annual Report 1978–79*.

38 *TOPS Review*. op. cit.

39 Berthoud, R., *Training Adults for Skilled Jobs*, (Policy Studies Institute, London, 1978).

40 Royal Commission on Trade Unions and Employers' Associations, 1965–1968, *Report* (Donovan Report), (HMSO, London, 1968); *Report of the Committee of Inquiry on Industrial Democracy* (Bullock Report), (HMSO, London, 1977), Brown, Marie and Winyard, Steven, *Low Pay in Hotels and Catering*, (Low Pay Unit, London, 1975).

41 Donovan Report, op. cit.

42 Ibid, and Trades Union Congress, *Low Pay, TUC General Council Discussion Document*, (TUC, London, 1970).

43 Smith, David J. op. cit.

44 *Fair Employment Agency Annual Reports* 1976–77, 1978–79 and 1979–80, (HMSO, Belfast).

45 Equal Opportunities Commission, *Health and Safety Legislation: Should we Distinguish between Men and Women?* (EOC, London, 1979).

46 Ibid, Table 6.9.

47 Equal Opportunities Commission, *Second Annual Report*, 1977, (HMSO, London, 1978); and *Third Annual Report*, 1978, (HMSO, London, 1979).

48 Hakim, Catherine, Sexual divisions within the labour force: occupational segregation, *Department of Employment Gazette*, November 1978.

49 Glucklich, P. *et al.*, Equal Pay Experience in 25 Firms, *Department of Employment Gazette*, December 1976; and Glucklich, P. *et al.*, Equal Pay and Opportunity, *Department of Employment Gazette*, July 1978, and Equal Opportunities Commission, *Equality Between the Sexes in Industry, How Far Have We Come?*, (EOC, Manchester, 1978).

50 Fox, Alan, Labour law between two wars, *New Society*, 22.2.79.
51 *Department of Employment Gazette*, September, 1979.
52 *Prices and Incomes Policy*, Cmnd. 2639, op. cit.
53 NBPI, *General Problems of Low Pay*. op. cit.
54 Pay Board, *Report 2nd April–31st May 1973*, (HMSO, London, 1973).
55 Pay Board, *Experience of Operating an Incomes Policy*, (HMSO, London, 1974).
56 Low Pay in the three nations, *Low Pay Bulletin*, February, 1979.
57 Donovan Report. op. cit.
58 ACAS, *Button Manufacturing Wages Council*, and *Toy Manufacturing Wages Council*, op. cit.
59 *Department of Employment Gazette*, February, 1977.
60 TUC, *Low Pay*. op. cit. and NBPI, *General Problems of Low Pay*, op. cit.
61 Winyard, Steve, *From Rags to Rags*, (Low Pay Unit, London, 1977).
62 Crine, Simon, Pick Pocketing the Low Paid, *Low Pay Report*, August, 1980.
63 Department of Employment and Productivity, *A National Minimum Wage. An Inquiry*, (HMSO, London, 1969).
64 TUC, *Low Pay*. op. cit.
65 Fisher and Dix. op. cit.
67 Ibid.
68 Supplementary Benefits Commission, *Annual Report 1978*, (HMSO, London, 1979); Supplementary Benefits Commission (Northern Ireland) *Annual Report 1979* (HMSO, Belfast, 1979).
69 Department of Health and Social Social Security. *Social Security Statistics*, 1977 (HMSO, London, 1979).
70 Commons *Hansard*, 27.7.79.
71 *Social Security Statistics*, op. cit.

4 Unemployment*

CHAPTER 2 showed that the risk of poverty was directly related to the extent and duration of unemployment so that the overwhelming majority of families whose supporter had not worked at all during the previous year had failed to aggregate a yearly income adequate to reach the poverty line. Moreover there is a close link between low pay, unemployment and poverty. Families of low-paid workers who experience part-year unemployment will also be in poverty. While not all unemployed persons are in poverty (and especially those who experience short-term unemployment after a reasonable period of regular well-paid employment), unemployment and particularly long-term unemployment - is a major indicator of deprivation. It is therefore a matter of serious concern that the level of unemployment in the UK has risen inexorably over the last three decades and very rapidly in the past few years, including a very large increase in the numbers of long-term unemployed.

In recent years, governments have shifted the priority from full employment to the reduction of inflation. The present government is prepared to accept a substantial increase in unemployment in order to pursue its other economic goals. If unemployment is to be reduced, the key role must be played by the macro-economic policies of government and other policies related to the unemployed cannot substitute for this. In the meantime, there are two other kinds of policies, which may be described as managing unemployment and managing the unemployed, which are of importance to unemployed people and to their standard of living. This chapter focuses on these policies.

The management of unemployment is undertaken through various manpower policies and through selective labour market interventions. In the 1950s and 1960s when unemployment ranged between the quarter and half a million, policies tended to be framed in relation to the individual characteristics of the unemployed (their age, health,

* This chapter has been drafted mainly by Joan Brown.

skills, work history and attitudes) and to factors which impeded labour mobility. As unemployment moved further upwards, and throughout the period in regions where unemployment was always high, additional policies were developed for selective intervention in the labour market. Thus the list of programmes includes the re-organisation of the employment services, expansion of training for adults and young people, special grants to enable workers to move to jobs, anti-discrimination legislation and special assistance for disabled people and persons with special needs. Regional policies focused on long-term job creation while other programmes aimed to protect existing jobs, to subsidise new jobs and to create short-term job opportunities.

The period has been notable for a willingness to experiment and innovate and the programmes had some success in the limited objective of containing unemployment and challenging various forms of discrimination. However, more than two million persons are now unemployed in the UK and significant proportions of the labour force in some towns and regions are out of work. Even if existing programmes had been expanded, they would have been hard-put to cope with such large numbers. As it is, the present government has cut back many of these programmes and so reduced the resources of the Manpower Services Commission that it is seriously handicapped in the task of developing policies to deal with large-scale unemployment.

The management of the unemployed is undertaken through the differential use of social security beyond its relatively neutral role of basic financial support for families temporarily without wage income. For example, some benefits may be kept low to deter people from remaining unemployed and remove disincentives to accept low-paid employment, while higher benefits may be paid to encourage change-over from declining to growing industries. As the level of unemployment has increased, the main issues have become the nature of the benefit arrangements and the level of benefits. When the social security system for the unemployed was re-organised in 1948, it was assumed that the majority of the unemployed would be supported by national insurance and only a residual group by national assistance/supplementary benefit. This system has been overtaken and outclassed by the inexorable growth in unemployment so that a very large proportion of the unemployed are now supported by supplementary benefits. Claims that the level of benefits causes loss of work incentive have been influential in holding general benefits for unemployed persons below the poverty line and this applies no matter how long they have been unemployed and whatever their realistic chances of re-employment.

Thus the unemployed are being adversely affected by a combination of government policies. First, a macro-economic policy which has contributed to a very sharp increase in unemployment; second, cuts in public expenditure on manpower and job creation programmes; and, third, decisions on social security arrangements which are at best holding down and at worst reducing the income of the unemployed.

The registered unemployed – numbers and distribution

The annual unemployment figures published by government represent only one segment of much larger-scale movement in the UK labour force. In 1978, the estimated size of the United Kingdom labour force was 26.4 million males and females, aged 16 years and over. Between 1950 and 1978, the labour force had grown by almost 3 million (mainly female workers) and is expected to grow by a further 2 million persons by 1989. An unusually large number of young people is likely to enter the labour force in the late 1970s and early 1980s, stemming from the high birth rates of the late 1950s and early 1960s.[1]

An average of 9½ million people change jobs each year and almost half of these experience some unemployment.[2] Not all unemployed persons register. The Manpower Services Commission estimates the 1977 figure for unregistered unemployed as 400,000. The General Household Survey in 1977 found that 11 per cent of unemployed males were not registered, 24 per cent of non-married females and 53 per cent of married females.[3]

It is necessary to distinguish between the total number of registered unemployed in any one year and the annual average figures of unemployed persons. For example, in 1978 the annual average number of unemployed in the United Kingdom was 1,475 thousand, while the number registering as unemployed during the year was about 4,500 thousand. The difference in part is the result of different methods of counting. The total registered unemployed represents a person by person count of everyone registering and is known as the unemployment flow. The annual averages are drawn from counts of those registered on a single day each month averaged over 12 months.

The unemployment flow figures give a better picture of the extent of short-term unemployment, while the monthly and annual averages represent with reasonable fairness medium and long-term unemployed persons. The bulk of the available data relates to workers caught in the monthly counts and the analysis which follows relates principally to these men and women.

Table 4.1 shows the annual average of the registered unemployed and the unemployment rate for the period 1950–79. The most striking feature of the table is the inexorable increase in unemployment over the three decades (Figure 1.3 also illustrated this). Table 4.2, in which the temporarily stopped are excluded for the whole period (instead of from 1967 onwards as in Table 4.1), further emphasises the deterioration in the employment situation. Not only is peak unemployment higher in each successive decade, but the low point is higher for each of the ten-year periods. Unemployment in August 1980 stood at 2 million, and is still rising.

A characteristic of unemployment in the last decade has been an increase in the average length of time it has taken for an unemployed person to find a new job and a marked growth in the number of

Table 4.1 Number of registered unemployed persons and rate of unemployment, United Kingdom 1950–1979

Annual averages

Year	No.	Rate	Year	No.	Rate	Year	No.	Rate
	(000s)	*Per cent*		*(000s)*	*Per cent*		*(000s)*	*Per cent*
1950	341.1	1.6	1960	392.8	1.7	1970	612.2	2.6
1951	281.4	1.3	1961	376.8	1.6	1971	792.1	3.5
1952	462.5	2.2	1962	499.9	2.1	1972	875.6	3.8
1953	380.0	1.8	1963	612.3	2.6	1973	618.8	2.7
1954	317.8	1.5	1964	413.4	1.7	1974	614.9	2.6
1955	264.5	1.2	1965	359.7	1.5	1975	997.6	4.2
1956	287.1	1.3	1966	390.9	1.6	1976	1358.8	5.8
1957	347.2	1.6	1967[1]	556.7	2.3	1977	1483.6	6.2
1958	500.9	2.2	1968	583.3	2.5	1978	1475.0	6.2
1959	512.1	2.3	1969	576.2	2.4	1979	1390.5	5.7

Sources: *Department of Employment and Productivity, British Labour Statistics Historical Abstract 1886–1968*, (HMSO, London, 1971).
Department of Employment, British Labour Statistics Year Book 1976. (HMSO, London, 1978).
Department of Employment Gazette, January 1979 and May 1980.
[1] Figures from 1967 onwards exclude the temporarily stopped. If included in 1967 and 1968, the figures would be 599.1 and 601.3 respectively.

persons unemployed for over 52 weeks, as Table 4.3 shows. In July 1979, of 268.8 thousand males unemployed for more than 52 weeks, 54.4 thousand had been unemployed for 104–155 weeks and 88.5 thousand for more than 156 weeks. The equivalent figures for females were 71.7 thousand, 14.3 thousand and 14.2 thousand respectively.[4] In Northern Ireland, in December 1977, of 61.1 thousand (male and female) unemployed, 6.3 thousand had been unemployed for more than 3 years.[5]

Table 4.2 Annual average unemployment, United Kingdom, best and worst years by decade 1950–1979

	Best year (000s)	Worst year (000s)
1950s	243.2 (1955)	480.2 (1959)
1960s	346.5 (1960)	558.0 (1963)
1970s	612.2 (1970)	1483.6 (1977)

Source: As Table 4.1

Note: The figures exclude the temporarily stopped for the whole period and thus differ from the previous table.

Neither unemployment nor the duration of unemployment is distributed evenly over the United Kingdom. Table 4.4 shows the employment rate by region for the period 1950–79 (see Map 1 for regions). The most notable feature of the table is the consistently high unemployment in Northern Ireland over the whole three decades. Scotland and Wales, which have also suffered persistently higher unemployment rates than the rest of the country, were joined by the North region in the 1960s and the North West in the 1970s. These regions also have the highest proportion of long-term unemployed. While, in absolute numbers, unemployment must be seen as largely an urban phenomenon, many rural areas are also severely affected by unemployment.

Both unemployment and long-term unemployment fall most heavily on manual workers and, in particular, on the semi-skilled and unskilled. In 1979, for example, while approximately 53 per cent of the labour force were manual workers, they constituted 72 per cent of

The United Kingdom: National boundaries, standard regions, and principal urban centres

REGION	*AREA* Sq. Km.	*POP.* M's
North	15,401	3.09
North West	7,331	6.49
Yorks. and H/side	15,402	4.87
East Mids.	15,630	3.75
West Mids.	13,013	5.15
East Anglia	12,573	1.84
South East	27,222	16.83
South West	23,833	4.29
Scotland	77,171	5.17
Wales	20,768	2.76
N.I.	14,147	1.53
U.K.	242,510	55.83

Map 1

the unemployed.[6] A Manpower Services Commission survey of the long-term unemployed in 1979 found that almost three-quarters of their sample had previously been manual workers, the majority of whom had done semi-skilled or unskilled jobs.[7] This problem must be viewed in the context of a general shift in the available employment from manual to non-manual and in relation to a very substantial loss of jobs in major industrial sectors. In the period 1950 to the end of the first quarter in 1980, in Great Britain some 2¼ million jobs have been lost from agriculture, fisheries and food (441.2 thousand), mining and quarrying (521.5 thousand), metal manufacturing (117.9 thousand), construction (114.3 thousand), textiles (674.9 thousand), shipbuilding (128.1 thousand) and vehicles (273.9 thousand). More losses can be expected in both metal and vehicles, because of the contraction of the steel and motor industries. In Northern Ireland, serious job loss has occurred in agriculture, shipbuilding and linen.[8]

Table 4.3 Persons unemployed for more than 52 weeks June/July in selected years 1957–1979, Great Britain

	Males			Females		
Year	Total unemployed	No. over 52 weeks	Per cent over 52 weeks	Total unemployed	No. over 52 weeks	Per cent over 52 weeks
	(000s)	(000s)		(000s)	(000s)	
1957	170.3	21.9	12.9	76.7	4.0	5.2
1960	214.3	49.6	23.1	82.9	8.8	10.6
1965	243.4	48.9	20.1	82.6	7.8	9.4
1970	508.3	89.9	17.7	85.2	8.4	9.9
1975	753.0	129.2	17.2	191.3	13.9	7.3
1976	1030.7	201.8	19.6	371.8	28.0	7.5
1977	1087.3	254.5	23.4	466.2	52.6	11.3
1978	1038.8	264.1	25.4	473.7	64.2	14.7
1979	933.7	268.8	28.7	458.3	71.7	15.6

Source: *Department of Employment Gazette*, June 1978, and January and August 1979.

Unemployment is also unevenly distributed by age group (Table 4.5). Males over 60 years suffer disproportionately from unemployment. At the other end of the age scale, both males and females under 25 years have excessive unemployment rates, even after discounting the July rates for the under-18s, which reflect the immediate impact of school leavers each year.

Table 4.4 *Unemployment rates of registered unemployed persons, by region, United Kingdom 1950–1979.*

Annual averages, Percentages

Standard regions[1]	1950	1952	1954	1956	1958	1960	1962	1964	1966	1968[2]
United Kingdom	1.6	2.2	1.5	1.3	2.2	1.7	2.1	1.7	1.6	2.5
Great Britain	1.5	2.0	1.3	1.2	2.1	1.6	2.0	1.6	1.5	2.4
England	1.2	1.8	1.1	1.0	1.8	1.3	1.6	1.4	1.3	2.1
South East }									1.0	1.6
East Anglia }	1.1	1.3	1.0	0.8	1.4	1.0	1.3	1.0	1.4	2.0
South West	1.5	1.5	1.4	1.3	2.2	1.7	1.7	1.5	1.8	2.5
West Midlands	0.5	0.9	0.6	1.1	1.6	1.0	1.8	0.9	1.3	2.0
East Midlands }									1.1	1.8
Yorkshire & Humberside }	0.8	1.5	0.8	0.7	1.8	1.1	1.5	1.1	1.2	2.5
North West	1.6	3.7	1.5	1.3	2.7	1.9	2.5	2.1	1.5	2.4
North	2.8	2.6	2.3	1.5	2.4	2.9	3.7	3.3	2.6	4.6
Wales	3.7	2.8	2.4	2.0	3.8	2.7	3.1	2.6	2.9	3.9
Scotland	3.1	3.3	2.8	2.4	3.8	3.6	3.8	3.6	2.9	3.7
Northern Ireland	5.8	10.3	7.0	6.4	9.3	6.7	7.5	6.6	6.1	7.1
	1970	1971	1972	1973	1974[3]	1975[3]	1976[3]	1977	1978	1979
United Kingdom	2.6	3.5	3.8	2.7	2.6	4.2	5.8	6.2	6.2	5.7
Great Britain	2.5	3.4	3.7	2.6	2.6	4.1	5.7	6.1	6.0	6.0
England	2.3	3.0	3.4	2.3	2.4	3.9	5.4	5.6	5.5	5.6
South East	1.6	2.0	2.2	1.5	1.5	2.8	4.2	4.5	4.2	3.6
East Anglia	2.1	3.2	2.9	1.9	1.9	3.4	4.9	5.4	5.1	4.4
South West	2.8	3.3	3.4	2.2	2.6	4.7	6.4	6.9	6.7	5.5
West Midlands	1.9	2.9	3.6	2.2	–	4.1	5.9	5.8	5.6	5.6
East Midlands	2.2	2.9	3.0	2.0	2.2	3.6	4.8	5.1	5.1	4.6
Yorkshire & Humberside	2.8	3.8	4.2	2.8	2.6	4.0	5.6	5.8	6.0	5.7
North West	2.7	3.9	4.8	3.6	3.5	5.3	7.0	7.4	7.5	7.1
North	4.5	5.7	6.3	4.7	4.6	5.9	7.5	8.4	9.0	8.6
Wales	3.8	4.4	4.8	3.4	3.7	5.6	7.4	8.0	8.5	7.9
Scotland	4.2	5.8	6.4	4.5	4.0	5.2	7.0	8.2	8.3	7.8
Northern Ireland	6.8	7.9	8.0	6.1	5.7	7.9	10.3	11.1	12.0	11.4

Sources: Department of Employment and Productivity, *British Labour Statistics Historical Abstracts 1886–1968*. (HMSO, London, 1971); *British Labour Statistics 1977*. (HMSO, London, 1979); and *Department of Employment Gazette*, January 1978 and 1979, May 1980.

[1] Regions as defined in 1965. Prior to 1965, combined employment rates only can be compiled for (a) South East and East Anglia, and (b) East Midlands and Yorkshire & Humberside.

[2] Percentages from 1967 onwards exclude the temporarily stopped.

[3] Industrial action affected collection of figures in 1974–1976. Averages are based on 10, 11 or 12 months in different regions.

Table 4.5 Estimated unemployment rates by age: Great Britain, 1977–1980

Percentages

	January 1977	July 1977	January 1979	July 1979	January 1980
Males					
Under 18	12.9	28.7	11.4	24.6	10.8
18–19	10.9	11.3	10.6	10.0	10.8
20–24	10.1	9.6	9.4	7.9	9.6
25–34	7.0	6.5	6.6	5.3	6.3
35–44	5.7	5.4	5.4	4.4	5.2
45–54	4.9	4.7	4.7	4.1	4.6
55–59	5.4	5.5	6.2	5.8	6.4
60 and over	10.3	9.5	10.0	9.2	9.8
All ages	7.3	7.6	7.0	6.6	7.0
Females					
Under 18	14.3	29.8	12.3	24.2	12.4
18–19	9.7	11.1	10.1	10.4	10.2
20–24	7.0	7.6	8.3	7.7	8.9
25–34	3.4	3.6	4.2	4.1	4.9
35–44	1.7	1.8	1.9	1.8	2.1
45–54	1.9	2.0	2.1	1.9	2.1
55–59	2.4	2.4	3.0	2.9	3.2
60 and over	0.2	0.2	0.2	0.2	0.3
All ages	3.8	4.9	4.3	4.8	4.5

Source: *Department of Employment Gazette*, March 1979, April 1980.

Notes: (1) While the figures are presented to one decimal place, they should not be regarded as implying precision to that degree.
(2) The rates for those under 20 are subject to the widest margins of error.

Table 4.6 looks at the distribution of prolonged unemployment by age in Great Britain. The most disadvantaged group is males aged 60-64 years who not only experience excessive unemployment, but have the greatest difficulty in getting back to work. However, the problem of excessive long-term unemployment is not confined to this age group. Males aged 55–59 years, while having a below average unemployment rate, nevertheless are becoming increasingly disadvantaged in the search for re-employment and there has also been a substantial increase in the number of females 55–59 years who are unemployed for more than 52 weeks. In addition, there is a striking increase in long-term unemployment across the whole range of prime

Table 4.6 Persons registered as unemployed for more than 52 weeks in selected years, Great Britain by age and sex

	Age group												
	Under 18	18–19	20–24	25–29	30–34	35–39	40–44	45–49	50–54	55–59	60–64	65 & over	Total
July 1970													
Male	150	675	2,468	2,810	3,627	4,489	6,108	7,866	8,017	14,157	37,929	320	88,616
Female	82	254	520	357	291	418	634	1,198	1,712	2,613	80		8,159
July 1975													
Male	420	1,760	7,321	7,922	7,405	8,202	9,237	10,579	13,686	15,344	46,506	809	129,191
Female	258	769	1,521	920	660	665	910	1,493	2,746	3,187	851		13,850
July 1979													
Male	2,334	7,542	24,380	23,865	22,974	40,057		22,790	27,250	34,880	60,541	1,588	244,336
Female	2,344	6,720	13,845	7,648	5,083	9,008		6,835	8,665	11,933	509		72,590

Source: *Department of Employment Gazette*, August 1970, September 1975, August 1979.

age workers, both male and female, as well as a considerable increase in the number of long-term unemployed young people.

Certain other population groups suffer from above average unemployment. Among these are workers from ethnic minorities. A 1977–78 survey showed that unemployment rates of registered and non-registered unemployment in that year were over 11 per cent of those of minority ethnic origin born in the UK, and over 7 per cent for those born abroad, compared with 4–6 per cent of those of white ethnic origin. The high rates of the first group reflect in part their age (80 per cent under 30 years).[9]

In Northern Ireland, local factors have produced an uneven distribution of unemployment between the two main religious groups, Protestant and Catholic. Up-to-date figures on this are not available, as information on religion is not collected in the regular unemployment data. Census data from 1971 reveals the following pattern.

Table 4.7 Unemployment rates for Protestants and Roman Catholics, Northern Ireland, 1971

Percentages

	Males	Females	All	Northern Ireland rate
Protestants	6.6	3.6	5.6	8.5
Roman Catholics	17.3	7.0	13.9	

Source: Second Report of the Fair Employment Agency for Northern Ireland 1977/78 (drawn from 1971 Census data). (HMSO, Belfast, 1979).

Roman Catholics are disproportionately represented in occupations and industries which are most vulnerable to employment. They also have a larger share of their population in areas with high unemployment rates. However, 1971 Census data shows that, even in areas where unemployment was low, Roman Catholic unemployment rates were twice those of Protestants.[10]

A third disadvantage group is disabled workers. Under the Disabled Persons (Employment) Act of 1944 (Great Britain) and 1945 (Northern Ireland), persons may be registered as disabled if they have a substantial handicap, on account of injury, disease or congenital deformity, in obtaining or keeping employment or work on their own account, suited to their age, qualifications and experience, and if the disablement is likely to last 12 months or more from the date of application. Registration is voluntary and it is estimated that less than half disabled workers register.

The unemployment rate for registered disabled people has always been higher than the general unemployment rate. In January 1977, it stood at 13 per cent compared with a rate for Great Britain of 6.1 per cent. Disabled persons, once unemployed, experience acute difficulties in achieving a return to work. The Manpower Services Commission estimated in 1979 that 60 per cent of registered disabled unemployed were out of work for 52 weeks or longer, compared with 24 per cent of the general unemployed population.[11]

In addition to the groups just described, and overlapping with them, are individuals with employment problems relating to their physical and mental condition (short of registrable disability), prison record, poor qualifications and poor command of English. Numbers are difficult to pinpoint because of the element of overlap, but they crop up as a minority with problems in every survey of the unemployed, even when general unemployment rates are fairly low.[12]

During the later 1970s, there has been considerable debate in the UK on how the unemployment figures should be interpreted. On the one hand, there were those who argued that the unemployment figures exaggerated the problem in a number of ways, by including in the figures persons who, in the current labour market, are 'unemployable', older unemployed workers under official retirement age but in receipt of an occupational pension, and alleged fraudulent claimants of benefit. It was also claimed that unemployment figures have been inflated by the availability of high benefits, particularly during the first six months of unemployment. On the other hand, others considered that these arguments were based on a misinterpretation or exaggeration of the evidence and that, in fact, official unemployment figures understated true unemployment because they excluded the unregistered unemployed.

In addition to these general arguments, a common response to the high unemployment figures in Northern Ireland is to suggest that these are the natural result of the continuing violence in the province. However, it is important to remember that unemployment in Northern Ireland was disproportionately high for at least 20 years before the present disturbances began (see Table 4.4).

Even taking into account the partial truth of some of these propositions, the United Kingdom unemployment situation remains a matter of deep concern. In the first nine months of 1980, over half a million additional workers became unemployed and in May 1980, when the monthly average unemployed had reached 1.5 million and the national unemployment rate was 6.2 per cent, a number of towns had male unemployment rates of over 15 per cent. This large-scale unemployment, the sharp rise in the number of company closures and work force reductions, and steady fall in vacancy rates, together with serious concern about the health of major industries, particularly steel and the motor industry, has challenged public complacency about unemployment. The gloomy prospects for the future tend to reinforce this. In 1979, the worst forecast for 1980 unemployment was 2 million. Forecasts made in 1980 for 1981–82 range from 2.5 million to 3 million unemployed.[13]

The relationship between unemployment and poverty

In the calculations of the incidence of poverty in Chapter 2, it was shown that the risk of poverty was directly related to the extent and duration of unemployment, so that the overwhelming majority of families whose supporter had not worked at all during the previous year had failed to aggregate a yearly income adequate to reach the poverty line.

It would be incorrect to suggest that all unemployed workers are in poverty. Short-term unemployment after a reasonable period in a job which commands satisfactory wages can be weathered fairly successfully with the aid of income such as holiday pay, tax rebates, unemployment benefit, earnings-related supplement and redundancy payments, where these are applicable. Single young workers living at home with families who themselves are in reasonable financial circumstances will not suffer great financial hardship. Older workers drawing the higher levels of occupational pension and unemployment benefit can also survive a not too lengthy period of unemployment without too many financial problems.

The position of unemployed married women is more complex. Where the husband earns an adequate wage, unemployment for the wife will mean a drop in the family's standard of living, but not poverty. Where the husband is a low wage earner, and the wife's earnings are the means by which the family has moved out of poverty, then her unemployment will mean a return to poverty for that family. Where both partners become unemployed, then they are in the same position as other unemployed families.

There are two reasons for the poverty of the unemployed. It will have been observed that, with the exception of women, every type of person known to suffer social and economic disadvantage is disproportionately represented among the unemployed. Unemployment may, therefore, be considered to be a principal indicator of deprivation. In particular, the strong correlation between unemployment, occupation, and earnings is symptomatic of a socio-economic position in which unemployment and low pay alternate to produce chronic poverty.

Second, both the supplementary benefit scale rate assigned to the unemployed, and unemployment benefit itself, are set at a rate lower than the long-term scale rate which, as discussed in Chapter 1, is considered to be on the margin of poverty. The majority of the medium and long-term unemployed who depend solely or principally on state benefits are therefore automatically poor during that period.

In a reference to the group dependent upon the supplementary benefit short-term rate, the Supplementary Benefits Commission said in its 1977 Annual Report:[14] 'Life is hard for everyone who depends on supplementary benefit, but it is hardest of all for the unemployed'. The Northern Ireland Supplementary Benefits Commission endorse this view and in its 1977 report[15] expressed concern about the effect of prolonged unemployment on men and women and their families.

A national survey of unemployed men on supplementary benfits undertaken by the Social Research Branch of Department of Health and Social Security (DHSS) in 1974[16] found that the combination of the level of wages in previous employment and the need to support dependants meant that nearly two-thirds of the men had no savings when they first became dependent on supplementary benefit. In order to make ends meet, normal expenditure was cut, savings were drawn upon (where available) and, in addition, half the men had resorted to borrowing money since they had become unemployed or in the last 12 months where they were long-term claimants. Both savings and borrowed money were, in the main, used for essential items such as food, clothing, heating and rent.

Other studies confirm the findings of the DHSS survey. A study of unemployed men on Tyneside in 1976 found the same pattern of cutting expenditure, using up savings, selling items of furniture or household equipment, cashing in insurance policies and borrowing to make ends meet.[17]

These financial problems can be experienced by all those on short-term supplementary benefit. After two years on Supplementary Benefit (one year from November 1980), recipients, other than the unemployed, are moved to a higher long-term rate because it is not considered reasonable to expect an individual or a family to subsist indefinitely on the short-term rate. Unemployed persons are never entitled to the long-term rate.

Policies on unemployment – some background

In the last three decades, policies towards unemployment as a national problem can be divided into four main periods. In the 1950s and for most of the 1960s, the prevailing policy was a commitment to full employment. This policy was modified somewhat in the late 1960s, when there was a deliberate promotion of a manpower shake-out for the purpose of industrial reconstruction. However, full employment remained the major goal. Since 1975, when inflation reached over 26 per cent, the major policy priority has been reduction of inflation, even if this meant increased unemployment in the short term. The Labour Government, which first shifted the over-riding priority of economic policy to one of combatting inflation, attempted to combine this with policies which restrained the growth of unemployment, as far as possible. From mid-1979, the present government, in giving priority to reducing inflation, has been prepared to accept a substantial increase in unemployment and regards many of the steps to restrain its growth of the type taken by the previous government as either too costly in public expenditure or counter-productive in the long term.

The key role in the reduction of unemployment must be played by the macro-economic policies of government. However, in addition to these, there are other policies which are aimed at managing unemployment and the unemployed. These are mainly manpower and social security policies and, as they have operated in the UK, regional development policies. Macro-economic policies are outside the brief of this report and this chapter will describe the second category of policies. While it is important to emphasise that these policies are no substitute for policies which substantially reduce unemployment, nevertheless they play an important role in relation to poverty. Even when unemployment has been at its lowest in the last 30 years, that is in 1955, when 1.2 per cent of the labour force were unemployed, this figure still represented over a quarter million of individuals (many with dependants) whose standard of living was endangered by unemployment. When a government adopts economic policies which, however justified for other reasons, produce a substantial rise in unemployment, the related policies which it adopts towards the unemployed become of key importance to the living standards of an increasing proportion of the population.

Concurrent with changes in broad policy priorities, since the mid-1970s, the nature of unemployment has changed and periodic re-assessment of unemployment policies has been necessary. When the numbers unemployed ranged between one quarter and half a million, policies tended to be framed in relation to the individual characteristics of the unemployed (their age, health, skills, work history and attitudes) and in relation to some of the factors which impeded labour mobility. As unemployment moved further upwards, and especially in regions where unemployment was always high, additional policies were developed for selective intervention in the labour market, as well as maintaining and strengthening earlier policies.

Unemployment in the UK now stands at two million and significant proportions of the labour force of some towns and regions are now unemployed. In these circumstances, many of the policies described in later sections have been outstripped by recent events. They still have a role to play and will be of increasing significance as and when unemployment is reduced and the problem of the long-term unemployed has to be dealt with. In the meantime, policies to deal with large-scale unemployment have yet to be developed.

Policies for the management of unemployment have, for the most part, been motivated by economically-based theories of poverty, that is, they have assumed that the problem lies not with the unemployed worker, but with the operation of the economic system and of the labour market. Policies for the management[18] of the unemployed have always had a much more confused base combining, in an unhappy mix, economically-based theories and theories which focus on individual deficiencies or see the unemployed as needing to have pressure put on them to return to the labour force.

Managing unemployment – job creation and job protection

Job creation through regional development

As Table 4.4 showed, the unequal distribution of unemployment in the UK has been a matter for concern throughout the whole period

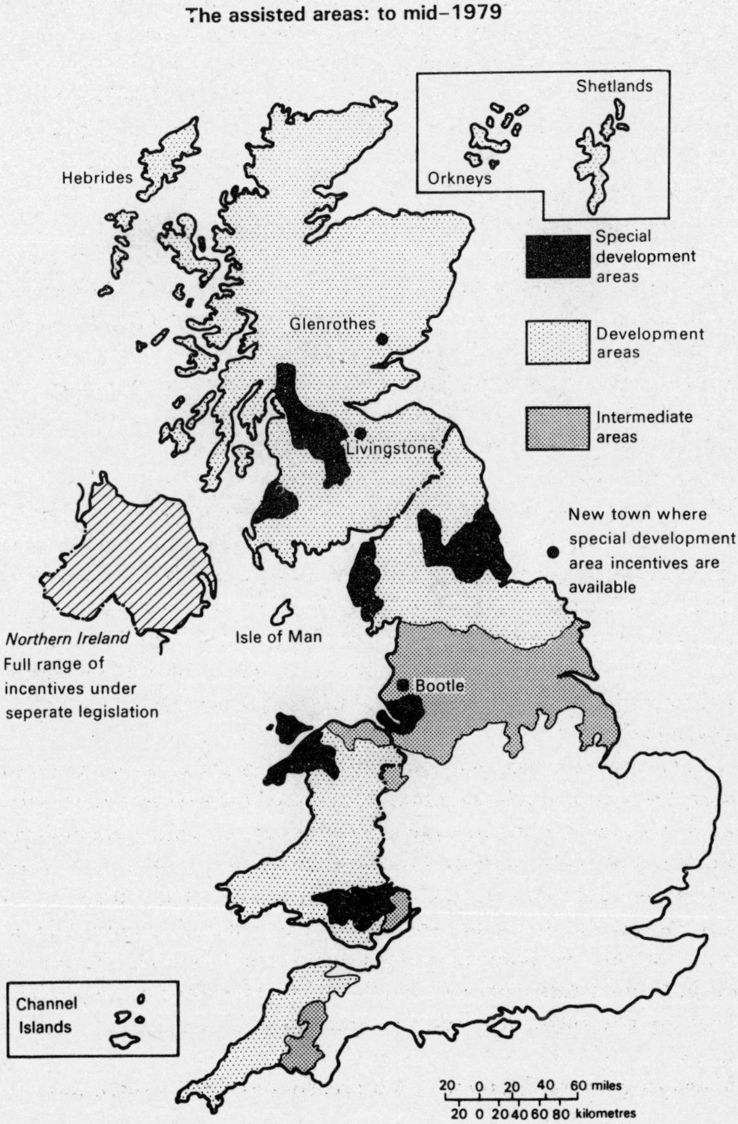
The assisted areas: to mid–1979
Shetlands
Orkneys
Hebrides
Special development areas
Development areas
Intermediate areas
Glenrothes
Livingstone
New town where special development area incentives are available
Northern Ireland
Full range of incentives under seperate legislation
Isle of Man
Bootle
Channel Islands
20 0 20 40 60 miles
20 0 20 40 60 80 kilometres

Map 2

The assisted areas: Designated to take effect from August 1st, 1982.

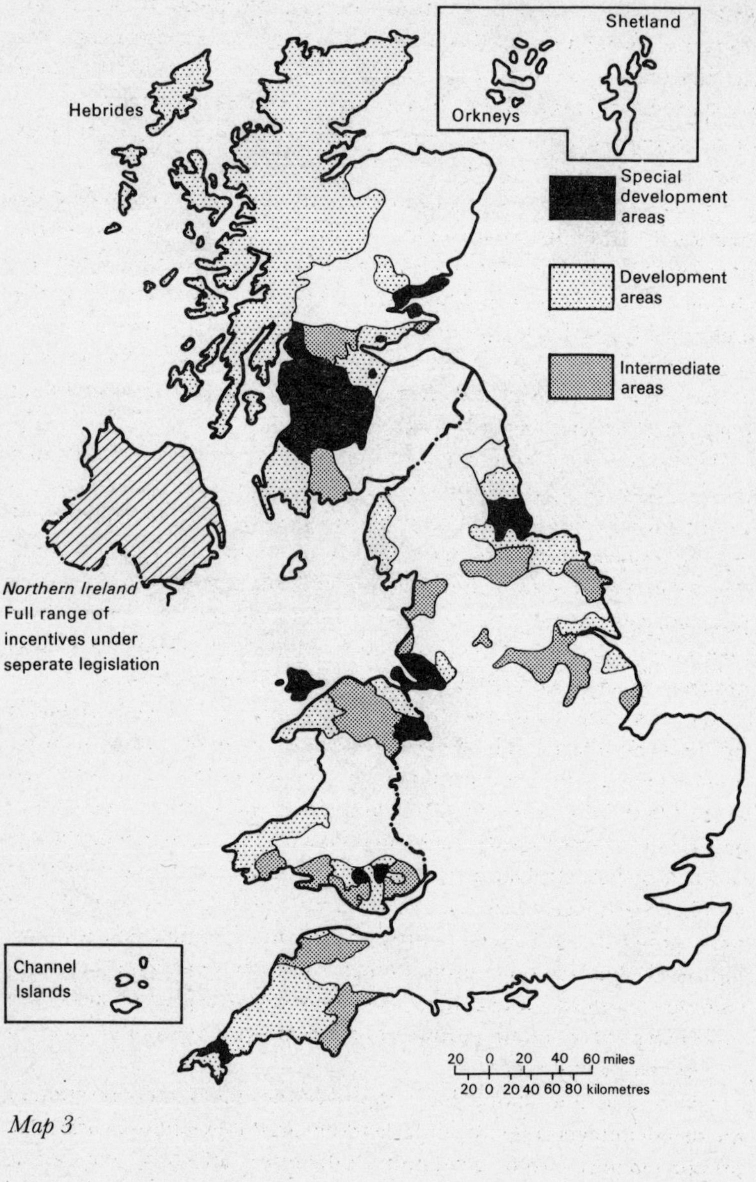

Map 3

1950–1980. Policies to combat unemployment through regional development have existed since the depression years in Great Britain and since the immediate postwar years in Northern Ireland. The objective throughout has been the reduction of unemployment rates in disadvantaged regions to levels similar to those in the most prosperous regions and, for the most part, policies have concentrated on bringing jobs to workers rather than encouraging migration from high unemployment regions.

By early 1979, regional assistance at varying levels was available to two-thirds of the surface area of Great Britain (with 40 per cent of the population) and the whole of Northern Ireland (see Map 2). After the change of government in May 1979, a cut in regional spending was announced which is expected to save £233 million by 1982–83; regional aid is now to be concentrated on areas covering 25 per cent of the population of Great Britain (see Map 3). Smaller cuts are being made in Northern Ireland development aid.

Briefly, the effect of the legislation is to operate a carrot and stick policy. Positive assistance is available through grants and loans to industrial enterprises, provision of advance factories and industrial estates, relocation and settlement aids and, until 1977, a Regional Employment Premium which assisted with the cost of staff. Negative programmes include controls on location of industry and office development, designed to divert development from prosperous to less prosperous areas and from crowded areas to the new towns.

The consensus of opinion is that regional programmes have had a job creation effect.[19] The Assisted Areas net employment gain from inter-regional and overseas moves by companies has been estimated at 512,000 jobs between 1945 and 1971, with more movement occurring in periods when regional policy was active than when it was weak. Northern Ireland's relative success in attracting new jobs has also been ascribed to the generous additional assistance available to firms going to the Province. Studies of firms' location policies have indicated that regional programmes were an important factor in coming to a decision and there is evidence of a degree of success in producing self-sustaining growth in the regions at acceptable levels of income and employment.[20]

All of this activity should have improved the employment position of the disadvantaged regions, or at least ensured they did not suffer disproportionately from economic difficulties affecting the whole country. Unfortunately, parallel changes in the same regions have led to large job losses. Judged solely by the unemployment rates shown in Table 4.4, regional policy has not succeeded in its goals. However, most commentators, critical and favourable, seem to accept the view expressed in a 1977 OECD report that 'the situation of the disadvantaged regions would have been much worse without the continuous effort devoted to rectifying regional imbalance'.[21]

Short-term job creation programmes

During the 1970s, a series of direct job creation programmes were established, aimed at specific categories of the unemployed. The earliest was *Community Industry* (CI), established in Great Britain in 1972. It aims to prepare socially and personally disadvantaged young people for permanent employment through worthwhile work in the community. Originally catering for about 2,000 young people, it has been gradually expanded and reached 6,000 in 1979; it has remained at about that level since that time.[22]

From 1975 to 1978, a *Job Creation Programme* (JCP) operated in both Great Britain and Northern Ireland. It aimed to provide temporary (up to 52 weeks) worthwhile jobs for persons who would otherwise be unemployed. Emphasis was placed on young people under the age of 25 years, but recruitment of unemployed workers over 50 years, usually in supervisory capacities, was encouraged. Projects were to be of benefit to the community, could be sponsored by both public and private employers and voluntary organisations and, where possible, were to offer training and further education opportunities in order to improve the long-term employability of the workers involved. At the close of programme, the Manpower Services Commission reported that in Great Britain approximately 140,000 new temporary jobs had been created, benefitting about 230,000 people. About two-thirds of former JCP employees had entered full-time employment within six months of leaving the programme.[23]

As the Job Creation Programme was being phased out, a new *Special Temporary Employment Programme* (STEP) was established. Starting in April 1978, it aimed to provide temporary jobs for a maximum of 52 weeks. Projects under STEP must be of benefit for the community and ones which would not otherwise be carried out. Priority for recruitment would go to persons aged 19–24 years who had been continuously unemployed for more than 6 months and persons 25 years and over continuously unemployed for more than 12 months. Resources were to be concentrated on areas of high unemployment. The original intention was to provide 25,000 places in Great Britain by March 1979 and, although that number were approved by the due date, only 13,000 people were actually employed. STEP is to continue for a further period under the present government, but funding is to be cut and intake maintained at 12–14,000.[24]

A different type of job creation scheme operating in Northern Ireland is *Enterprise Ulster*. Beginning on a small scale as Enterprise Young Ulster, the main scheme was established in 1972. It uses direct labour on schemes with environmental, amenity, cultural, community or social value. By the end of 1977, it was employing 1,800 unskilled labourers and it has remained at this level. It offers both training and continuous employment, but encourages the employees to seek better paid work elsewhere. Most of the projects are situated in or near areas of particularly high unemployment.[25]

Job creation through recruitment subsidies

A third form of job creation has operated through recruitment subsidy schemes. The earliest was the *Regional Employment Premium*, which ran from 1967–77 and paid employers a subsidy for workers in manufacturing industry in development areas.[26]

In October 1975, the *Recruitment Subsidy for School Leavers* (RSSL) was introduced to encourage employers to provide more opportunities for unemployed school leavers and, in the one year of its operation, 29,000 applications were received. A review of the scheme by the Department of Employment found that additional recruitment, i.e. those young people who would not have been taken on were it not for the payment of the subsidy, was at most 15–20 per cent of the whole and concluded that 'a general subsidy of this type for school leavers has very little effect in terms of the additional recruitment it brings about'.[27]

In October 1976, a *Youth Employment Subsidy* (YES) was substituted for RSSL. This subsidised for 26 weeks newly recruited young persons under 20 years who had been continuously unemployed for six months or more. The scheme was evaluated in February 1978, when some 38,000 applications for subsidy had been approved. Like RSSL, a large proportion of recruits under YES would probably have been taken on without the payment of a subsidy. However, about 25 per cent constituted additional recruitment (40 per cent in small firms) and only about 10 per cent of all recruits were dismissed when their subsidies expired. The scheme was terminated in March 1978.[28]

Another subsidy programme was directed to small firms (less than 200 workers) in certain special development areas. The *Small Firms Employment Subsidy Scheme* offered subsidies for up to 26 weeks. The original scheme ran for an experimental period from July 1977–March 1978, during which time 5,928 new jobs were subsidised. Evaluation of the scheme showed that 60 per cent of these jobs would probably have been created without a subsidy, but a record of 2 out of 5 jobs induced by the subsidy was regarded as sufficient reason to maintain the scheme and to widen the area of elegibility. Total jobs subsidised by the end of 1979 was over 143,000. After the change of government in mid-1979, the scheme was closed for new applications from 31st March 1980.[29]

Finally, an *Adult Employment Subsidy* was established in August 1978 in a few high unemployment areas to encourage the employment of those over 19 years of age who had been unemployed for 12 months or more. It was terminated in July 1979. In all, 1,386 workers were assisted by the scheme.[30]

One scheme officially included in lists of job creation measures is the *Job Release Scheme*. It is, however, based on the principle of robbing Peter to pay Paul. Introduced in January 1977, the scheme offered workers within a certain number of years of retirement a tax-free allowance if they agreed to withdraw from the labour market and the employer agreed to recruit someone from the unemployment register to replace them (though not necessarily in the same job). Unemployed persons were also eligible, but were later exluded, since they did not have a job to vacate.

From January 1977 to March 1978, 24,303 persons applied, including 11,053 unemployed persons at the stage of the scheme when they were eligible. A survey by the Department of Employment in 1978 found that the major reason for the relatively low take-up by employed persons was that the allowance offered was regarded as inadequate.[31] The allowances was subsequently increased and, by February 1979, a total of 48,000 persons in Great Britain had retired under the scheme. A separate, but similar, scheme exists in Northern Ireland. This scheme has been continued by the present government.

Job protection policies

Job protection in the United Kingdom has taken a number of forms. First is the allocation of large-scale funds under the Industry Acts to major industries undergoing temporary difficulties or to industries in decline where restructuring is being undertaken. Usually only a proportion of the jobs have been protected and the remainder made subject to orderly redundancy arrangements. In most cases, the industries involved have been of major national importance and successive governments have played a strong interventionist role. Under the present government, this policy has been severely restricted, though not wholly abandoned.

A second form of job protection is aimed at reducing the number of unfair dismissals and giving the worker greater job security. Protection against unfair dismissal dates from 1971 and was strengthened in 1975. Originally, workers were eligible for protection only after completing two years continuous employment with the employer. Later this was reduced to twelve months and then six months. The present government has restored the twelve-months rule for large firms and the two-year rule for small firms.

Third, are subsidy programmes designed to overcome temporary crises and so avoid redundancies, while preserving manpower and equipment for anticipated economic upturn. The first programme of this type was the *Temporary Employment Subsidy* (TES), introduced in August 1975. From August 1975 to October 1979, over half a million workers were subsidised under this scheme (see Table 4.8). Because of the flow back to the Treasury (in reduced need for unemployment benefit plus continuation in payment of tax and contributions), it was regarded as a cost effective scheme. It was phased out from early 1979.

The *Short Time Working Compensation Scheme* was introduced in April 1978 to encourage employers to adopt short time working instead of making workers redundant. Employers are re-imbursed 75 per cent of normal wages paid to staff on short time plus the total National Insurance contributions for the workless days. The subsidy was originally to apply for twelve months, but this has been reduced to six months by the present government.[32] In July 1980, some 200,000 workers were covered by this scheme.

Managing unemployment – improving access to jobs

Employment Services

From the late 1960s onwards, a series of programmes were established in the United Kingdom to improve the access of workers to jobs. The provision by government of services to bring workers and potential employers together dates back to the establishment of Labour Exchanges by the Liberal Government in 1910. In the early 1970s, the careers service for young people and the adult employment service were re-organised to provide more effective service.

The Employment and Training Act of 1973 paved the way for reorganising the careers service, which was to operate as a bridge between education and work. The careers service has three roles: the provision of career teaching in schools, the placement of school and college leavers in their first jobs, and assistance to unemployed young people. In its early years, the first two tasks consumed most of the time of the careers service.

The substantial rise in youth unemployment from 1975 onwards directed much of the attention of the careers service to unemployed young people. The government allocated an extra 230 unemployment specialist officers in 1975 to careers offices in areas of particularly severe unemployment and a further 90 posts were created in 1977–78.[32]

Of particular concern was the position of young black workers, who have been experiencing disproportionate levels of unemployment. Because they and their families often lacked the wealth of local contacts available to longer-established white families and because of concern about possible discrimination, the careers service was seen as particularly important to them. Special guidance and training in helping ethnic minority groups has been given to careers officers and, in 1977, some 20 specialist staff were appointed in an effort to offer more effective service.[34]

While the careers service has been conscious of its deficiencies in providing for ethnic minorities, it has paid less attention to handicapped young people. The 1978 Warnock Report on handicapped children and young people reported that 'our strong impression is that existing arrangements for the provision of careers guidance for young people with special needs generally fall far short of what is required'.[34]

In Northern Ireland, there is no separate careers service for young people. Instead it forms part of the general service provided by the Department of Manpower Services (DMS) while the education service provides careers education. Recent reports suggest that the standard of service is lower than in Great Britain in both staffing levels and training. Some efforts are now being made to upgrade the service.[36]

During the 1960s, the Employment Exchanges, as they were then known, became the target of a good deal of criticism because of the relatively weak role they appeared to be playing in the re-development of redundant workers in particular, and for the unemployed and job seekers generally. Critics claimed that the employment service was under-financed and under-staffed, and had inadequate staff training, that it usually occupied dingy, depressing backstreet premises; that it was associated in the public mind with the payment of 'dole' rather than the finding of jobs; and that it was regarded by both employers and workers as a place of last resort. It was decided, therefore, to undertake a progressive modernisation of the service.

The centrepiece of the programme is the provision of Jobcentres (Jobmarkets in Northern Ireland) in modern premises, on High Street sites, where a combination of self-service job vacancy displays, backed by better trained employment advisers, was expected to increase effective use of the service by both workers and employers. By March 1979, 555 new Jobcentres were operating in Great Britain and 5 in Northern Ireland (where the programme began later). The programme has now been slowed down by the revision of public expenditure plans which will reduce the number of planned new centres by seventeen.[37]

Studies undertaken in 1977 show that the effectiveness of the public employment service had been improved, although the majority of jobs were still found through sources such as personal contact, local newspapers, and other informal methods.[38]

Training and experience

Training for employment in Great Britain has been upgraded by successive governments since the early 1960s. The 1964 Industrial Training Act was directed to the improvement of training within industry itself. At the same time, the level of government-provided training was expanded from 2,500 training places in 1962 to 11,000 in 1971. At the latter date, only 3.5 per cent of trainees were women and 0.4 per cent were from ethnic minority groups. In 1972, the *Training Opportunities Scheme* (TOPS) was established and, by 1977, the annual total of workers completing courses was 94.2 thousand, of whom 43.4 per cent were women and 7 per cent from the ethnic minorities.[39]

A review undertaken by the Manpower Services Commission in 1978[40] noted that about half the TOPS trainees in 1977 were unemployed at the time of the acceptance into training. The Commission estimated that TOPS and related training provisions were providing for only a tiny minority (about 3 per cent) of the unemployed at any one time and that very little was known about the training needs of the long-term unemployed. The review team therefore proposed that pilot courses in work preparation combining vocational assessment and re-orientation to work should be undertaken in areas of high unemployment and, if successful, extended nationally in 1979/80. The expansion of this programme will be limited by public expenditure cuts.[41]

The TOPS scheme does not operate in Northern Ireland, but parallel developments have taken place since the 1964 Industrial Training (NI) Act. In 1978, there were 3,300 training places in government Training Centres and a further 1,000 places under the Attachment Training Scheme.[42]

The needs of unemployed young people have been partly met by TOPS, which provided 17.3 thousand places for them in 1977. In 1976, an additional programme, the *Work Experience Programme* (WEP) was introduced in both Great Britain and Northern Ireland. This offered opportunities to learn about different types of jobs through on-the-job experience for periods of up to six months. In October 1977, some 25.6 thousand young people in Great Britain aged 16–18 were engaged in the programme.[43]

In 1977, the MSC, faced with a large increase in unemployment among young people, reviewed its range of programmes – job creation, subsidy programmes, training – for the 16–18 age group. It concluded that, in spite of the temporary, piecemeal and *ad hoc* nature of the previous programmes, they had shown that there were means of tackling the problem of youth unemployment in a constructive way. However, in light of projections of continuing problems for this age group, it was time to engage a more coherent forward planning, and a *Youth Opportunities Programme* (YOP) commenced in 1978.[44]

The goal of the Youth Opportunities Programme is to improve young people's prospects of finding satisfactory permanent employment at the earliest possible moment. It offers an integrated range of work preparation courses and work experience schemes which attempt to be responsive to individual and local needs. Its initial objective was to ensure that no Easter or summer leaver who was still unemployed the following Easter should be without the offer of a place in the YOP. By April 1979, in Great Britain 75,000 young people, between the ages of 16–18, had had a place on the programme.[45] Of those who should have had an opportunity, approximately 1,600 remained uncovered. The Northern Ireland programme has operated on similar lines and offered 6,000 places in all.[46]

The Youth Opportunities Programme is one of the few manpower programmes to be expanded by the present government. The 1979/80 provision was for 210,000 entrants and the 1981/82 programme is to have 250,000 places.

Labour mobility

The Manpower Services Commission have operated three programmes to enable workers to move out of their area to find jobs. Similar schemes operate in Northern Ireland.[47] The *Employment Transfer Scheme* offers grants to assist with rehousing costs, the *Job Search Scheme* pays fares and subsistence to enable unemployed persons to attend interviews beyond daily travelling distance from home and the *Nucleus Labour Force Scheme* offered subsidies for a limited period to workers transferred by their company to new ventures in areas of high unemployment. This last scheme was abolished in July 1978 for lack of custom. In 1978/79 in Great Britain, 22.9 thousand workers moved under the Employment Transfer Scheme. The effectiveness of labour mobility schemes is limited by the widespread nature of current unemployment, by the serious housing shortage in areas where more jobs are available and by the reluctance of workers and their families to move away from areas where they have strong roots. The present government considers more labour mobility ought to be encouraged and has upgraded these schemes.

Discrimination

Discrimination which leads to refusal to hire a worker (or to dismissal) on grounds irrelevant to the ability to do the job can be a serious barrier to employment. *The Race Relations Acts of 1968 and 1976* provided that it was unlawful for an employer to descriminate on the grounds of colour, race, nationality or ethnic or national origin, in engagement, terms and conditions of employment, training, promotion or dismissal. The 1976 Act widened the definition of discrimination to cover the imposition (whether intentionally or unintentionally) of any unjustifiable requirement or condition which, although applied equally to all people, is disproportionately disadvantageous to members of a particular racial group - so-called indirect discrimination. The Race Relations Act does not apply to Northern Ireland, where the racial minority population is very small.

Studies of racial disadvantage in 1966–67 and in 1974[48] have shown that, since the 1968 Race Relations Act, there has been an important reduction in the prevalence of accepted, open and obvious discrimination, and probably some reduction in actual discrimination, but they suggest that methods of discrimination may have become more covert. As already noted, the proportion of minority group workers receiving training has been increased, though concern has been expressed by both the MSC and the Commission for Racial Equality at the relative failure to attract young black unemployed to training and job creation programmes.[49] The problem of racial discrimination in employment has certainly not been overcome and, while it is probably fair to say that, in the absence of race relations legislation, the situation of racial minorities in conditions of general high unemployment would have been far worse, there are no grounds for complacency.

The *1975 Sex Discrimination Act* (and the Sex Discrimination (Northern Ireland) Order 1976) makes unlawful any discrimination made on the grounds of sex or marital status in recruitment, terms and conditions of employment, and opportunities for promotion, transfer or training. As in the Race Relations Act, discrimination is defined as both direct and indirect.

The effect of the Sex Discrimination Act on female unemployment is not easy to ascertain, especially as the unemployment figures do not take into account the unregistered unemployed, the majority of whom are women. In 1977, the Equal Opportunities Commission (created by the Act) indicated that a survey of 500 firms showed that, while advertisements were nondiscriminatory, inquirers were often discouraged from pursuing their application on the grounds of sex and individuals had been reluctant to complain because of the difficulty of proving discrimination. Job segregation, attitudes of employers, unions and fellow workers as well as structural barriers, such as minimum age entry, all still continued to restrict women's employment opportunities.[50]

The *Fair Employment (Northern Ireland) Act 1976* established a Fair Employment Agency whose duties are to promote equality of opportunity in Northern Ireland and to work for the elimination of discrimination on grounds of religion or politics. Lack of statistics which identify the religion of unemployed persons make it impossible to form any judgement on the effect of the Act on unemployment. Given the long-standing nature of this problem in Northern Ireland, and the fact that the general unemployment situation has worsened since the passage of the Act, it would be optimistic to expect rapid progress in this area.

Groups with special needs

There has been an official policy in Great Britain and Northern Ireland to ensure reasonable access for disabled people to employment since 1944 and 1945 respectively. As indicated earlier, under the Disabled Persons (Employment) Act 1944 (and the Northern Ireland equivalent), disabled persons may be registered on a voluntary basis for open or sheltered employment. Less than half of the estimated 1.2 million disabled workers have registered. However, most services are available to registered and unregistered (but registrable) disabled persons alike.

The legislation further provided for the establishment of Employment Rehabilitation Centres (ERCs) and for the appointment to employment offices of Disablement Resettlement Officers (DROs). Every employer of 20 or more employees was required to employ at least three per cent of workers who were registered as disabled – referred to as the quota scheme. Apart from relatively minor adjustments, this legislation is the basis for present day policy, though it has not lacked critics and there have been an endless series of reviews. Detailed figures for programmes in Great Britain are available and these are the basis for the discussion which follows.

A minority of disabled persons, those with very severe disabilities, are placed in sheltered employment. Currently, about 13,000 are so placed, and over 10,000 disabled persons are registered for sheltered employment. The Manpower Services Commission plans a modernisation programme for the workshops, improved methods to find work for and sell the products of workshops, and a modest expansion programme by 200 places a year.[51] There has been criticism of this limited goal and a target of 1,000 additional places a year for the next 10 years has been proposed.[52] The Manpower Services Commission defends its more modest target on the grounds that some persons registered are in fact capable of open employment, while others are not sufficiently fit even for sheltered employment. In addition, sheltered workshops need to be in larger population areas to be viable and must be able to attract work – a task made more difficult by the current economic climate. Moreover, with limited financial resources, sheltered workshops' expansion is not seen by MSC as a top priority.[53]

In 1978, in Great Britain there were 26 Employment Rehabilitation Centres which provide courses for people who, after illness, injury or long unemployment, need mental and physical toning-up to fit them for employment. Disabled trainees are also accepted for TOPS and YOP. In 1977/78, 14,900 disabled persons passed through ERCs (15,670 in 1978/79) and in 1977, 5,166 disabled people completed TOPS courses. Some courses have now been developed under YOP. Figures for employment placement after ERC courses show declining success as general unemployment levels have risen. In 1974, 29 per cent of trainees had not found any work in the six months following training. In 1976, this figure had risen to 43.4 per cent. Separate placement figures for TOPS and YOP disabled trainees are not available.[54]

Disablement Resettlement Officers form a regular part of the employment service. They have a dual task. First, they assist the disabled individual, whether registered or not, to find suitable employment and second, they oversee the quota scheme. During the whole period since 1944, the employment services have preferred to emphasise the placement services and the potential abilities of disabled people, rather than enforce the quota. This order of priority has been re-affirmed by the Manpower Services Commission, which has undertaken an employers' education campaign and introduced a scheme of capital grants for adaptation to premises or equipment and a *Job Introduction Scheme* under which a contribution can be made to the employer's cost of employing a disabled person for a trial period of up to six weeks. Take-up of the capital grants scheme was described by the Manpower Services Commission in 1978 as 'disappointingly low'. The Job Introduction Scheme placed 639 in its first 12 months of operation.[55] While these new policies may have helped to hold the disabled unemployment rate at its new high level, the rate is still excessive and the high level of long-term unemployment among this group is a continuing cause for concern.

The alternative (or additional) policy of enforcing the quota has been the subject of discussion for a number of years, a discussion revived in 1979 by the publication by the MSC of a discussion document on the subject. It notes that the proportion of firms (including government) fulfilling their quota of three per cent has steadily fallen from 61.4 per cent of firms in 1961 to 36.8 per cent in 1978. The average national compliance rate is now 1.7 per cent. The MSC point out that there is a decline in the number of persons registering as disabled and that the maximum national compliance rate which could be achieved if all those on the register were employed would be 2.1 per cent. The Commission has put forward four options for consideration, either separately or in combination. First, a recasting of the quota scheme; second, anti-discrimination legislation; third, obligations placed on employers to review their policy and record on the employment of disabled people; and fourth, the provision of special rights for disabled people.[56]

Certain categories of unemployed have always been recognised as having special difficulties in finding and keeping employment. Workers with poor physical or mental health not amounting to registrable disability, older workers, persons with a prison record, individuals with personality problems and the like. As unemployment has increased and the problems of these individuals in finding jobs have intensified, various attempts were made between 1973 and 1976 to offer them a more specialised service. In 1977, the Manpower Services Commission introduced a *Special Employment Needs Scheme*. Under this, 47 extra staff were allocated for one year to areas with a substantial number of people with special employment needs. The MSC reported in 1979 that in the first ten months of the scheme, 8,500 persons had been assisted and, of these, 37 per cent had been placed in employment and 7 per cent in, or were awaiting, training or rehabilitation.[57] In the review of public expenditure in 1980, this service was withdrawn and no special service for this group is now operated.[58]

Managing unemployment – some comments

This hotch-potch of programmes, developed between 1970 and early 1979, could be regarded as evidence that governments have simply been thrashing around trying to find ways of holding down the numbers of unemployed to a less unacceptable level. Alternatively, they could be viewed as a sign that governments have not been content to adopt a fatalistic attitude towards unemployment, but have shown a willingness to experiment and innovate in an effort to make an impact on a problem which they view with deep concern. It is probable that both elements have existed over the years but, on the whole, the more favourable of the two interpretations seems to be justified.

It has been suggested that funds have been directed to too many relatively small programmes spread over a wide area and might better have been concentrated on fewer, larger programmes focussed on a more limited geographical area and that there have been programmes where expenditure has not been justified by the outcome. The contrary argument is that unemployment is both a widespread and a complex phenomenon, and calls for attack from a variety of standpoints. Moreover, some failure is the price of innovation at a time when well-tried and successful policies are not available.

It may also be true that policies have been based on an over-optimistic assumption that an economic up-turn was just around the corner and therefore all that was needed was short-term programmes to mitigate the worst effects of high unemployment while maintaining the capacity of the labour force to respond to any improvement in the economic situation. Certainly there seems to have been an element of wishful thinking in political circles over the years. However, even if stark realism had always prevailed, there would still have been valid arguments for the adoption of short-term programmes as an interim measure. Whatever long-term economic policy is adopted, there is a need to maintain a sense that government is concerned about the social effects of its policies and that it is striving to offset the worst of these effects.

The policies adopted have had some success in the limited objective of containing unemployment. Table 4.8 shows the numbers of workers in the United Kingdom (in programmes still operating in October 1979) who had their jobs preserved or who have been engaged in programmes which maintained and often enhanced their employability. Though the cost was high, it is worth noting that even a temporary period during which a worker is not drawing social security benefits and is paying income tax, National Insurance contributions and consuming more goods subject to indirect tax, reduces the net cost to goverment of such programmes and it can be argued that this is a more constructive form of expenditure than the passive payment of social security benefits.

Attempts have been made to deal with employment discrimination against certain groups. This is an intransigent problem, even in times of economic prosperity, and it is not yet clear that the anti-discrimination programmes are effective. However, their existence is an

Table 4.8 Expenditure on employment and training schemes and number of jobs and training places provided in the UK

Title of Scheme	Date of commencement	Costs up to[1] 30.9.79 (£m)	Number of jobs or training places provided up to 31.10.79
Training in Industry	2.7.75	175.0	152,060
Community Industry	5.8.75	37.0	6,209
Temporary Employment Subsidy	18.8.75	434.0	540,266
Job Release Scheme	3.1.77	68.0	91,382
Job Introduction Scheme	4.7.77	0.4	2,560
Youth Opportunities Programme	1.4.78	119.2	159,000
Special Temporary Employment Programme	1.4.78	22.0	33,500
Short-time Working Compensation in Textiles, etc.	15.5.78	1.6	15,072
Small Firms Employment Subsidy	1.7.78	35.0	143,529
Adult Employment Subsidy	7.8.78	0.5	1,501
Temporary Short-time Working Compensation	1.4.79	3.9	33,689
Totals		896.6	1,178,768

Source: Derived from Parliamentary written answer, Hansard, 7.12.79.
[1] Gross unadjusted costs

important affirmation of the values of the total society. Thus discrimination on the grounds of race, sex and religion is at least being challenged. No anti-discrimination legislation exists for disabled people, though the possibility is being discussed. There has been little serious discussion on the desirability of combatting discrimination against older workers.

Although the range of anti-unemployment programmes contains something for almost everyone, the main thrust has been towards the problem of the unemployed young worker. They are, of course, a natural target and no doubt a mixture of motives has operated. If the labour force is to be in a condition to respond to an economic upturn, it is important to ensure that the prime age workers of the future have not missed out on the skill training, work experience and 'good' work attitudes that would normally be the outcome of steady employment while they are still young. There is a danger that the young will be 'trained' for unemployment or low paid work because of the lack of normal opportunities at a key period of their lives. There is also an underlying social control motive. While older workers may respond to unemployment by resignation and apathy, and prime age workers, where they fight back, will usually do so through marches, demonstrations, work-ins etc. (all acceptable, if not actively desired democratic methods), the young, it is feared, will turn to crime, vandalism and random violence. Better then to keep them off the streets.

The prime age worker (between the ages of 25 and 49) has been the target of some job creation programmes and, in all probability, many of the subsidy programmes, but insufficient attention has been given to the prime age long-term unemployed.

The most neglected group appears to be the older worker. They benefitted marginally from a number of the special employment programmes, but the only scheme directed at them (the Job Release Scheme) was intended to help them out of the work force to make way for others. Redundancies have always fallen heavily on the older worker. In seeking re-employment, the older worker is at clear disadvantage. While in the 1960s there was a whole literature on the value of the older worker and how he/she could be utilised for the good of the economy, now there appears to be a passive acceptance that the prospects of the older unemployed workers are pretty hopeless.

Present government economic policies, as indicated earlier, are now directed to dealing with inflation as the over-riding priority. Unemployment has substantially increased and is expected to go on increasing, while most measures to manage unemployment have been cut or not expanded in proportion to the increase in the numbers of unemployed. The government's view is that its economic measures are necessary for long-term prosperity; that it is offering special assistance for areas of high unemployment and that its special programme package (YOP, STEP, Community Industry, Temporary Short Time Working Compensation and Job Release, together with improved Employment Transfer and Job Search payments) will help particularly hard hit groups within the level of expenditure the country can afford.

Table 4.9 illustrates the overall expenditure on employment services from 1950 to 1979 and government projections to 1984. The Manpower Services Commission had been expanding and was developing coherent manpower and anti-unemployment policies. Its

Table 4.9 Analysis of total public expenditure on manpower services, UK, 1950–1984

	Current Prices												
	1950	1955	1960	1965	1970	1975	1977	1978	1979	1980–81[1]	1981–82[1]	1982–83[1]	1983–84[1]
Annual expenditure (£m)	20	20	24	45	128	476	963	1125	1014	976	990	950	940
As per cent of total public expenditure	0.49	0.36	0.32	0.31	0.61	0.92	1.55	1.57	1.35	1.30	1.35	1.32	1.31
As per cent of total gross national product	0.17	0.11	0.10	0.14	0.29	0.50	0.76	0.78	0.63	0.55	0.56	0.52	0.52

Sources: Central Statistical Office, *National Income and Expenditure 1961*, 1963–73, 1979; *Economic Trends*, 1980, 1979; *The Governments Expenditure Plans, 1980–81 to 1983–84*. Cmnd 7841, (HMSO, London, 1980)

[1] Estimated expenditure all at 1979 prices.

regular programme reviews and its willingness to experiment and innovate was impressive. While it periodically issued reminders that the demands created by large-scale unemployment must limit the resources available to special groups among the unemployed, until recently it has shown a continuing concern for their problems. Given the present and projected cuts in expenditure on employment services, it is not surprising that the MSC has expressed serious concern about its ability to maintain and develop adequate services to meet the demands of mass unemployment.[59]

Managing the unemployed – social security

The unemployed are 'managed', as the term is used here, through the differential use of social security beyond its relatively neutral role of basic financial support for families temporarily without wage income. Benefits can be kept low and procedures for obtaining benefit made difficult to deter people from remaining unemployed. They can be withheld for a period to 'punish' certain behaviour (such as leaving a job without good reason) or a ceiling can be put on benefits for certain normally low paid workers to avoid creating disincentives to return to work. Benefits can also be paid at a higher level for a time to allow greater choice in employment. When a run down in certain industries in favour of others is desired, lump sum payments can be offered to encourage labour mobility or act as a form of early retirement. Special benefits can be offered to some categories of long term unemployed, for example, those near retirement age, to remove from the unemployment register persons who have little or no hope of obtaining a job. Most of these devices have been used in the last 30 years in UK social security policy for the unemployed.

The National Insurance Act, 1948 established a system under which an employee, together with his employer and the state, contributes to national insurance while he is in employment. In return, he is entitled to unemployment benefit for a maximum of 52 weeks when he is unemployed. This is paid at the short-term rate of national insurance.

During the first six months of unemployment, a second benefit may be available. Since 1966, an earnings-related supplement (ERS) has been payable after three weeks of unemployment for a maximum period of six months, in part with the object of allowing time to choose the 'right' job. Only those eligible for unemployment benefit may receive ERS and the sum is calculated on the amount of earnings on which national insurance contributions have been paid – the so-called reckonable weekly earnings. The supplement may not exceed the amount necessary to bring the claimant's benefit up to 85 per cent of the reckonable weekly earnings and is subject to a maximum figure.

Under the 1948 National Assistance Act and subsequent legislation, for those whose unemployment benefit (and ERS where applicable) is exhausted or is too low to meet their needs, supplementary benefits are available on a means-tested basis. This has no contribution conditions. Payment is made at the supplementary benefit short-term rate (however long the unemployed person is dependent on it), plus a rent addition normally equivalent to the rent and rates payable by the claimant, less income from other sources subject to certain 'disregards'.

Finally, persons made redundant from their jobs who have been continuously employed by the same employer for at least two years of working sixteen hours a week or more or 5 years when working eight hours a week or more have, since the 1965 Redundancy Payments Act, been entitled to lump-sum compensation for the job lost. The sum paid is determined by age and years of service. Redundancy payments are intended as compensation for a lost job and the consequent disruption of a worker's life. An important motive for their introduction was to promote mobility of labour and to ease the pain of (and the hostility to) industrial reconstruction. They are payable whether or not the worker actually experiences unemployment and the sums paid are not necessarily related to the length of unemployment or the income needs of the worker.

These income security provisions are a great deal less handsome than they at first appear. While in a major closure a large proportion of the firm's labour force will receive redundancy payments, overall only a small proportion of the total unemployed are eligible for payments under the Redundancy Payments Act, though they may be entitled to other lump sums from the employer.

Not all workers receive the earnings-related supplement in the first six months of unemployment. The groups most likely to be excluded from benefit are those without an entitlement to unemployment benefit (often because of intermittent unemployment, which has prevented the building up of sufficient weekly contributions) and low paid workers where the supplement is extinguished by the rule that total unemployment payments must not exceed 85 per cent of reckonable weekly earnings. Broadly speaking, the lower the wage received in employment and the more disrupted the employment history, the less likely the unemployed person is to receive ERS or to receive the maximum amount. At its peak in 1975, 235,000 or 21.7 per cent of the unemployed in Great Britain were receiving ERS. The proportion has now fallen below 16 per cent and, at the same time, the number of long-term unemployed whose entitlement to ERS has expired has steadily grown.[60]

The mainstay of the unemployed was always intended to be the unemployment benefit paid under the National Insurance Act of 1948, through which the vast majority of unemployed were to be freed from means testing and dependence on the National Assistance Board. From the beginning, more of the unemployed were dependent on national assistance than had been hoped, but in 1948, 71 per cent of the unemployed in Great Britain depended solely on unemployment benefit and only 16 per cent received national assistance.[61] By May 1961, 51 per cent were dependent solely on unemployment benefit and a further 9 per cent were receiving both unemployment benefit and national assistance. By November 1977, the role of unemployment benefit had shrunk still further. Then 32.6 per cent of the unemployed were dependent on unemployment benefit (including some receiving ERS) and a further 9 per cent were receiving unemployment benefit (and sometimes ERS) and supplementary benefit, the successor of national assistance. Just over 40 per cent were solely dependent on supplementary benefit and 18 per cent received no benefit of any kind. Table 4.10 illustrates the changes since 1961. In Northern Ireland, 55 per cent of the unemployed in 1977 were wholly or partly dependent on supplementary benefit.[62]

Among the 18 per cent receiving no payments will be many workers who will, in due course receive benefit of one kind or another and they include those denied benefit for a period for having left a previous job 'without good reason'. A more important influence on the number receiving unemployment benefit is the contribution rules. As both the duration of unemployment and the incidence of intermittent unemployment has increased, the numbers of unemployed whose benefit entitlement has expired has grown. The youngest unemployed, particularly the large group, of those aged 18 years and under, have in a great many cases not been in employment for sufficiently long periods to build up the necessary contribution record.

Table 4.10 Unemployed persons registered on the first Monday in November analysed by benefit entitlement,[1] *Great Britain, selected years 1961–1977*

	1961		1971		1977	
	Number	*Per cent*	*Number*	*Per cent*	*Number*	*Per cent*
Males						
Total	282	100	722	100	985	100
Flat-rate benefit only	133	47.16	156	21.60	148	15.02
Flat-rate benefit and earnings related supplement[3]	–	–	139	19.25	161	16.34
Flat-rate benefit, earnings related supplement and supplementary allowance[2,3]	–	–	10	1.38	20	2.03
Flat-rate benefit and supplementary allowance[2]	27	9.57	88	12.18	87	8.83
Supplementary allowance only[2]	62	21.98	195	27.00	403	40.91
No flat-rate benefit or supplementary allowance[2]	61	21.63	133	18.42	167	16.95
Females						
Total	101	100	138	100	362	100
Flat-rate benefit only	40	39.60	42	30.43	77	21.27
Flat-rate benefit and earnings related supplement[3]	–	–	15	10.86	54	14.91
Flat-rate benefit, earnings related supplement and supplementary allowance[2,3]	–	–	1	0.72	3	0.82
Flat-rate benefit and supplementary allowance[2]	3	2.97	9	6.52	11	3.03
Supplementary allowance only[2]	12	11.88	28	20.28	136	37.56
No flat-rate benefit or supplementary allowance[2]	46	45.54	44	31.88	81	22.37

Source: Department of Health and Social Security, *Social Security Statistics, 1977*, (HMSO, London, 1979).

[1] 5 per cent sample.

[2] Supplementary benefit, introduced in November 1966 – reference before that date are to national assistance.

[3] Earnings-related supplement was not introduced until October 1966.

Deficiencies in the social security arrangements

During the last decade, there has been a considerable debate about the social security arrangements for the unemployed. The issues can be placed in two broad groups – those related to the system of benefits and those related to the level of benefits.

The basic framework of income security provision for the unemployed was laid down in 1946 and 1948 and added to in the mid-1960s. While it never succeeded entirely in its goal of removing the unemployed from dependence on the National Assistance Board and the Supplementary Benefits Commission, the system could function tolerably well as long as unemployment was low and the duration of unemployment relatively short. These conditions prevailed in the 1950s, judged on the figures for the United Kingdom as a whole, though the unemployment rate for Northern Ireland, Scotland, Wales and the North Region were always higher than the average. As unemployment increased during the 1960s, redundancy payments and earnings-related benefits were introduced and were able to ease some of the strains of industrial reconstruction, while the incidence of long-term unemployment remained fairly low.

Once into the 1970s (as Table 4.3 showed), the numbers of long-term, unemployed in Great Britain alone moved from almost 100,000 in 1970 to almost 350,000 in 1979. This factor, together with the high level of intermittent unemployment and the number of very young unemployed, has produced a situation where a large proportion of the unemployed are ineligible for unemployment benefit and must resort to means-tested benefits provided by the supplementary benefits scheme. Thus the system has been overtaken and out-classed by the inexorable growth in unemployment and this situation can only worsen, given present large-scale unemployment and the predictions of even higher unemployment in the future.

Serious concern has been expressed about the ability of the supplementary benefits scheme to cope effectively with the pressures placed upon it by mass unemployment, especially as public expenditure cuts are likely to limit staff expansion.[63]

A more crucial set of issues revolve around the question of benefit levels in relation to poverty on the one hand and to work incentives on the other. During the 1970s, there was considerable criticism of the earnings-related benefits and redundancy payments scheme which it was claimed were reducing incentives to return to work quickly and thus artificially inflating the unemployment figures.[64]

A review of the supplementary benefits scheme undertaken by a team in the Department of Health and Social Security (DHSS) discounted this. After examining the situation, the review team concluded that while some workers were no worse off in the early weeks of employment than they were in work, this did not appear to lead to reluctance to return to work. Indeed, those with large amounts of ERS, redundancy payments and tax rebates were also those who previously had had high earnings and tended to find new employment quickly.[65]

This claim that the benefit level causes loss of work incentive has also been directed to the ordinary unemployment and supplementary benefit rates for the unemployed, and particularly at the very small gap (and at times overlap) between income in unemployment and income from low paid work. However, studies of this issue suggest that only a small minority of unemployed persons rejected jobs which offered less than benefit income and the DHSS review believed that account had to be taken of the determination of individuals to support themselves rather than rely upon benefits.[66]

In spite of the counter-arguments, these claims that present benefit levels reduce work incentives have been influential in holding general benefits for unemployed persons at the level which is below the poverty line for large numbers of the unemployed. Successive governments have refused to allow the unemployed to qualify for the long-term rate of supplementary benefit, no matter how long they have been unemployed and whatever their realistic chances of re-employment. Such claims have also doubtless contributed to a decision by the present government to phase out earnings-related benefit by 1982 and to uprate unemployment benefit (though not supplementary benefit) at 5 per cent less than the rate of inflation in 1980/81/82. In the circumstances, poverty among the unemployed cannot fail to increase as unemployment and long-term unemployment increases in the next few years.

Future directions for policies on unemployment

The unemployed are being adversely affected by a combination of government policies related to unemployment. First, macro-economic policy has contributed to a very sharp increase in unemployment and is expected to continue to do so. Second, related decisions to cut public expenditure have included cuts in resources devoted to the management of unemployment through the type of programmes described earlier, and restrictions on the resources needed to develop a programme to meet the demands of mass unemployment. Third, decisions on social security arrangements are, at best, holding down and, at worst, reducing the income of the unemployed.

Given the government's view that it is necessary to persevere with the present economic policy, the question now being discussed is how best to cope with the social consequences of this in the immediate future. A number of proposals are being made by public agencies and by the poverty lobby. These include:

(a) Expansion of the Youth Opportunities Programme to make some impact on the severe problem of youth unemployment.
(b) Expansion of the Special Temporary Employment Programme from a current ceiling of 14,000 places in a limited geographic area to a substantially larger number of places available in any part of the country where there is a concentration of the unemployed.
(c) More detailed attention by the Manpower Services Commission to the needs of the long-term unemployed, particularly, but not only, the prime age unemployed. Programmes suggested include more extensive training provision as well as more intensive employment placement services.
(d) A review of the special problem presented by the long-term older unemployed, who have poor prospects of returning to work, even if unemployment begins to fall.
(e) An extension to the long-term unemployed of the right enjoyed by other supplementary benefit recipients to move from the short-term to the higher long-term rate of benefit after twelve months.
(f) A longer term review of the social security system as it relates to the unemployed. This is discussed in more detail at the end of Chapter 5.

Only the first of these is known to form part of government planning, and it is thought that some new initiatives on the older long-term unemployed may be under consideration. The Manpower Services Commission has the issue of programmes for the long-term unemployed under current review, but is expressing little optimism that sufficient funds will be made available for an adequate programme. Prospects for the implementation of the remaining proposals are bleak at present.

Notes

1 Department of Employment, *British Labour Statistics Historical Abstract 1886–1968,* (HMSO, London, 1971), *Department of Employment Gazette,* April 1978.
2 Manpower Services Commission, *Annual Report* 1977–78, (MSC, London, 1978).
3 Ibid, and Office of Population Censuses and Surveys, *General Household Survey 1977*, (HMSO, London, 1979).
4 *Department of Employment Gazette*, August 1979.
5 Department of Finance (Northern Ireland), *Social and Economic Trends Northern Ireland No. 4*, 1978; and *Digest of Statistics Northern Ireland No. 51*, March 1979, (HMSO, Belfast, 1979).
6 *Department of Employment Gazette*, May 1979.
7 Manpower Services Commission, *Manpower Review 1980*, (London, 1980).
8 Department of Employment Gazette, July 1980.
9 Barber, Ann, Ethnic origin and the labour force, *Department of Employment Gazette*, August 1980.
10 *Second Report of the Fair Employment Agency 1977/78*, (HMSO, Belfast, 1979).
11 Manpower Services Commission, *The Quota Scheme for the Employment of Disabled People*, (London, 1970).
12 *Department of Employment Gazette*, April 1962, April 1966, March 1974 and June 1977. Daniel, W. W. and Stilgoe, Elizabeth, *Where are they now? a Follow-up Study of the Unemployed*, (Political and Economic Planning, now Policy Studies Institute, 1977). Daniel, W. W. and Stilgoe, Elizabeth, *The Impact of the Employment Protection Laws*, (Policy Studies Institute, London, 1978). Department of Employment and Productivity, *Ryhope: a Pit Closes, a Study on Redeployment* (HMSO, London, 1970).
13 Manpower Services Commission, *Manpower Review 1980*, (London, 1980).
14 Supplementary Benefits Commission, *Annual Report 1976*, (HMSO, London, 1977).
15 Supplementary Benefits Commission (Northern Ireland), *Annual Report 1977*, (HMSO, Belfast, 1978).
16 Reported in Clark, M., The unemployed on supplementary benefit: living standards and making ends meet on low income, *Journal of Social Policy*, Vol. 7, Pt. 4, Oct. 1978.
17 North Tyneside Community Development Project, *In and Out of Work; a Study of Unemployment, Low Pay and Income Maintenance Service*, (North Tyneside CDP, 1978).
18 The use of this term is discussed on p. 124.
19 Mackay R., The death of regional policy – or resurrection squared?, *Regional Studies*, Vol. 13, No. 3, 1979; and Marquand, J., Measuring the effects and costs of regional incentives, *Government Economic Service Working Paper No. 32*, (Department of Industry, 1980).
20 Ibid.
21 Organisation for Economic Co-operation and Development, *Regional Policies, the Current Outlook*, (Paris, 1977).

22 *Department of Employment Gazette*, June 1979; Manpower Services Commission, *Annual Report 1978–79*, (HMSO, London, 1979).
23 Ibid.
24 Ibid.
25 Northern Ireland Information Service *Ulster Yearbook 1978/79*. (HMSO, Belfast, 1978).
26 Central Office of Information *Regional Development in Britain*. Reference Pamphlet 80. (HMSO, London, 1976).
27 *Department of Employment Gazette*, July 1977.
28 *Department of Employment Gazette*, April 1978.
29 *Department of Employment Gazette*, May 1978 and June 1979.
30 *Department of Employment Gazette*, July 1979.
31 *Department of Employment Gazette*, April 1978.
32 *Department of Employment Gazette*, June 1979.
33. Manpower Services Commission. *Young People and Work*. (London, 1979).
34 Ibid, and Moor, C. H., *From School to Work*, (Sage, London, 1976).
35. Department of Education and Science, *Report of the Committee of Enquiry into the Education of Handicapped Children and Young People – Special Educational Needs* (Warnock Report). Cmnd 7212 (HMSO, London, 1978).
36 *Opportunities at Sixteen*: Report of a study group chaired by Derek Birley, (HMSO, Belfast, 1978).
37 *Department of Employment Gazette*, July 1978; Manpower Services Commission *Annual Report 1978–79*, op. cit.; *Department of Employment Gazette*, June 1979; *Ulster Yearbook 1979/79*, (HMSO, Belfast, 1979).
38 *Department of Employment Gazette*, July 1978; Office of Population Census and Surveys *General Household Survey 1977*, (HMSO, London, 1979); Daniel, W. W. and Stilgoe, E., *Where are they now?, A Follow-up Study of the Unemployed*, op. cit.
39 Department of Employment, *Training for the Future, A Plan for Discussion*, (London, 1972); Manpower Services Commission, *TOPS Review*, (HMSO, London, 1978).
40 Manpower Services Commission, *TOPS Review*, op. cit.
41 Manpower Services Commission, *Manpower Review 1980*, op. cit.
42 *Ulster Yearbook 1978/79*, op. cit.
43 Manpower Services Commission *Annual Report 1978–79*. op. cit.
44 Manpower Services Commission. *Young People and Work*. op. cit.
45 Manpower Services Commission *Annual Report 1978–79*. op. cit.
46 *Ulster Yearbook 1978/79*. op. cit.
47 *Department of Employment Gazette*, June 1976 and June 1979. Manpower Services Commission, *Annual Report 1978–1979*, op. cit.; *Ulster Yearbook 1978/79*, op. cit.
48 Smith, D. J., *The Facts of Racial Disadvantage*, (PEP, London, 1976).
49 Commission for Racial Equality, *Annual Report 1978*, (HMSO, London, 1979).
50 Equal Opportunities Commission, *Annual Report 1977*, (HMSO, London, 1978).
51 Manpower Services Commission. *Developing Employment and Training Services for Disabled People*, (MSC, London, 1978).
52 Jordan D., *A New Employment Programme Wanted for Disabled People*, (The Disability Alliance, London, 1979).
53 Manpower Services Commission, *Developing Employment Services*, op. cit.
54 *Department of Employment Gazette*, January 1978; Manpower Services Commission, *Annual Report 1977–78*, op. cit.; *TOPS Review 1978*, op. cit.

55 Manpower Services Commission, *Developing Employment Services*. op. cit; *Annual Reports 1977–78 and 1978–79*. op. cit.
56 Manpower Services Commission, *The Quota Scheme for Employment of Disabled People*, (MSC, London, 1979).
57 Manpower Services Commission, *Annual Reports 1977–78*, op. cit.
58 Manpower Services Commission, *Manpower Review 1980*, op. cit.
59 Ibid.
60 Department of Health and Social Security, *Social Assistance: A Review of the Supplementary Benefits Scheme in Great Britain*, (London, 1978).
61 Supplementary Benefits Commission, *Annual Report 1976*, (HMSO, London, 1977).
62 Supplementary Benefits Commission, (Northern Ireland), *Annual Report 1977*. (HMSO, Belfast, 1978).
63 Supplementary Benefits Commission, *Annual Report 1979*, (HMSO, London, 1980).
64 Nicholl, S. J., The effect of unemployment and related benefits on the duration of unemployment, *The Economic Journal*, No. 87, March 1979.
65 *Social Assistance*. op. cit.
66 Ibid, and Daniel W. W. *A National Survey of the Unemployed*, (PEP, London, 1974).

5 The Social Security System*

THE basic framework of the UK social security system was established between 1945 and 1948 following the 1942 Beveridge Report. The intention was that the principal form of social security for retirement, sickness, industrial injury, unemployment and widowhood should be national insurance with the national assistance (later supplementary benefit) scheme playing a residual role for those who temporarily or long term were not eligible for national insurance benefits.

The new system was a marked step forward in establishing a wide range of social security rights but it proved to have a number of deficiencies, some of which were foreseeable. The most important of these was the inadequacy of the benefit rates from the outset, and the fact that long-term disability was always poorly provided for. Over the years other factors placed strains on the social security arrangements, in particular the increased numbers of retired people, the growth in the one-parent family group, the changed status of women and the onset of large-scale and long-term unemployment.

Social security has played an important role in alleviating poverty but it has not eliminated poverty among its beneficiaries. From the 1960s onwards, a series of changes introduced, sometimes in a direct attempt to combat poverty and at other times as a response to economic and labour force problems. Four main mechanisms were used. First the use of earnings-related benefits to combat poverty and ease economic dislocation. Second, the use of non-contributory benefits to fill gaps in the system. Third, the encouragement of occupational benefits and fourth, the use of means-tested benefits within a reformed supplementary benefits scheme.

While some of these changes have reduced the incidence of poverty, in particular among elderly people, widows and to a certain extent disabled people, even the best of these programmes have not

* This chapter has been prepared by Joan Brown, drawing extensively on a background paper prepared by Tony Lynes for this study.

been uniform in their outcome or their coverage, and the less satisfactory programmes have offered poor benefit levels. Wage-related benefits are of much greater value to some than to others. Only half of the labour force is covered for occupational retirement pensions. Both the state and occupational pension schemes will take many years to mature, and those who retired before they were established or in the early years of new schemes receive little or no benefit from them. The non-contributory benefit for disabled people and provision for the unemployed has been particularly unsatisfactory. The benefits provided for one-parent families, while improved, are still insufficient.

In spite of all the changes, the supplementary benefits scheme still has a mass role to play both as a primary support and as a supplement to inadequate benefits from other sources. Its allowances, which provide the income floor for the whole social security system, are wholly inadequate at the short-term level and barely adequate at the long-term level. This basic problem has not been resolved by recent reforms of the supplementary benefit scheme. The weaknesses of the whole social security system and of the supplementary benefit scheme in particular are most notable in the region where poverty is most highly concentrated, Northern Ireland.

The adequacy of social security benefits as a means of protecting those eligible for assistance from poverty is determined by various factors of which three stand out as key issues. First, whether the basis on which the benefit is established (and especially the income floor provided by supplementary benefits) adequately reflects the needs of recipients. Satisfactory minimum levels have in fact never been established. Second is the take-up of benefits, which has improved but is still acknowledged to be insufficient. The third determinant is the extent to which the real value of benefits is maintained in relation to the cost of living and to the general standard of living in the community. A coherent and satisfactory uprating policy has never been established and recent legislation has worsened rather than improved current arrangements.

Early development, 1908–1948

The social security system in Great Britain evolved in piecemeal fashion during the first four decades of the 20th century. The Old Age Pensions Act 1908 introduced a small non-contributory pension payable at the age of 70, subject to a means test. This was followed in 1911 by the National Insurance Act, which introduced the principle of compulsory insurance for medical care and sickness, disablement and maternity benefits for most employed workers, as well as unemployment insurance for a few selected industries which were subject to marked fluctuations in employment. In 1920, unemployment insurance was extended to virtually the whole employed population.

In 1925, the Widows, Orphans and Old Age Contributory Pensions Act provided for pensions, financed by contributions and without any means test, from the age of 65. The widow of an insured man also received a pension for life, regardless of her age on becoming a widow and whether or not she had dependent children. In 1940, the age at which a woman qualified for the old age pension was reduced from 65 to 60.

Until 1935, social assistance (previously Poor Law relief) was provided by local Public Assistance Authorities. In that year, responsibility for assistance to the unemployed whose insurance benefit rights had expired was transferred to a newly created body, the Unemployment Assistance Board. In 1940, the Board was also made responsible for the payment of supplementary pensions, subject to a means test, to old age pensioners and widow pensioners over 60, and the word 'unemployment' was dropped from its title. The same body, renamed the National Assistance Board, was to take over the remaining cash assistance functions of the Public Assistance Authorities in 1948.

Social security legislation in Northern Ireland developed along roughly parallel lines, though with some variations in the benefits provided. The post-war legislation, based on the principle of a parity for Northern Ireland, provided the same range of benefits as in Great Britain, payable at the same rates in return for the same contributions, and the description of the legislation which follows can be taken to apply to Northern Ireland in all important respects.

The Beveridge Report

The post-war reconstruction of social insurance was based on the recommendations of a report, *Social Insurance and Allied Services*[1], published in 1942. Sir William Beveridge, the author of the report, recommended the unification of the diverse insurance schemes in a single system covering the whole population of working age, including housewives, the self-employed and highly-paid employees. He recommended a number of extensions of the existing range of benefits, of which the most important was a new system of compensation for industrial accident or disease to replace the workmen's compensation scheme based on individual employers' liability. Benefits were to continue for as long as the need existed, and the main benefit rates were to be based on the principle of 'guaranteeing the minimum income needed for subsistence'.[2] The flat-rate benefits were to be financed by flat-rate contributions, varying only between broad economic categories – employed persons, the self-employed, housewives and so on.[3]

Beveridge envisaged a continuing, but diminished, role for social assistance. His proposed insurance scheme would provide a subsistence income in all normal cases. The need for social assistance would then be limited to those who failed to satisfy the contribution conditions for insurance benefits, those disqualified for benefit, those with 'abnormal needs in respect of diet, care and other matters', and those in need through causes not suitable for insurance (e.g. desertion or separation – though Beveridge proposed that, in some cases at least, separated or divorced women should be entitled to the same benefits as widows).[4]

As well as improvements in the range, coverage and level of benefits, the Beveridge report recommended a major administrative re-organisation of social security (including social assistance) under a single Ministry, in place of the fragmented responsibility that had resulted from the incremental legislation of the earlier years of the century. The division of responsibility for cash assistance between central and local government was also to come to an end; there should be 'one authority administering assistance on the basis of a uniform means test'.[5]

Beveridge's recommendation that insurance benefits should be adequate for subsistence, with the implication that they would not normally have to be supplemented by assistance payments, was of fundamental importance. In later years, the limitations of a system of flat-rate benefits became increasingly apparent but, in 1942, it offered the best hope of a rapid improvement in the often inadequate benefits payable under the existing schemes. Beveridge recognised, however, that adequate benefits during periods of interruption of earnings, providing for the subsistence needs not only of the claimant, but of his wife and children, must be matched by a system of family allowance (for all but the first child), payable whether the head of the family was in work or not. He regarded family allowances not as part of his social security scheme, but as one of the three assumptions on which his proposals rested – the other two were the creation of a national health and rehabilitation service, and the maintenance of full employment.[6]

The Postwar Legislation

The social security system that took shape in Britain between 1945 and 1948, and which has remained in existence with numerous additions and amendments since then, was modelled closely on the recommendations of the Beveridge report. The Family Allowances Act 1945 was passed before the end of the war and payment of family allowances of 5 shillings (£0.25) per week for all except first or only children commenced in August 1946. The new system of insurance benefits was introduced by the National Insurance Act 1946 and the National Insurance (Industrial Injuries) Act 1946, and new social assistance arrangements under the National Assistance Act 1948, all of which came into operation in July 1948, coinciding with the introduction of the National Health Service. The new system differed from the original Beveridge proposals in a number of ways. Three of the more important differences were, first, that the National Assistance Board remained a separate government department and, second, unemployment benefit was limited to 30 weeks, though this period could be extended in certain circumstances (and was extended to 52 weeks in 1965). The third related to the National Insurance (Industrial Injuries) Act 1946, which provided a pattern of benefits for the industrially injured which differed from the general insurance scheme.

Deficiencies in the postwar social security system

The most serious weakness of the 1945–48 legislation was the inadequacy of the benefit rates. The Beveridge concept of benefits adequate for subsistence needs was not realised. More exactly – since there was at no time a clear definition of the levels of income required for subsistence – neither the main insurance benefits nor family allowances matched the levels of requirements assumed in the calculation of national assistance payments, which were themselves lower than the poverty line adopted by Rowntree, whose approach was highly influential (see Chapter 2). Moreover, over the whole postwar period, family allowances (now child benefit) have remained far below the level of requirements assumed for a child under 5 in the national assistance (now supplementary benefit) scheme.

The gap between the national insurance benefits and the national assistance scale rates was small, but national assistance was increased by an allowance for housing costs (normally the full amount of rent and rates). Generally speaking, therefore, the national insurance benefits did not fully cover the minimum needs of the claimant and his wife as assessed for national assistance purposes. Provision for the children of national insurance beneficiaries was also inadequate.

The relative inadequacy of national insurance benefits and family allowances, compared with national assistance, had two consequences. First, it meant that the main function of national assistance proved to be the supplementation of national insurance benefits rather than providing for the needs of those not covered by insurance benefits or with special needs that a flat-rate subsistence benefit could not meet. Second, the disparity between family allowances for working parents and the national assistance rates for the children of parents who were not working meant that, in a minority of cases, national assistance could exceed normal earnings. To prevent this, a rule known as the 'wage stop' was carried over from the prewar unemployment assistance scheme. The effect of the wage stop was to restrict the amount of assistance payable to an unemployed man (and the short-term sick) to the net amount he could expect to earn in full time work in his normal occupation. The wage stop was abolished in 1975, when only one per cent of unemployed claimants in Great Britain were affected by it. In Northern Ireland, however, where wages were lower, the wage stop affected 10 per cent of unemployed claimants.

One group of claimants were inadequately provided for from the beginning. While special provision was made for the war disabled and those disabled at work, no insurance benefits were to be offered to 'civilian' disabled as such. A disabled person was categorised as either sick or unemployed and dealt with accordingly, either under the national insurance system or on social assistance. The potential employment problems of disabled people were to be met through the Disabled Persons (Employment) Act of 1944 (described in Chapter 4) on the assumption that adequate employment opportunities could be found for all the employable disabled. This did not prove possible and many disabled people found themselves in the ranks of the long-term sick and unemployed on social assistance.

Other pressures on the system, not all of which could reasonably

Table 5.1 *Numbers of recipients of regular weekly payments of supplementary benefit (national assistance in 1965 and earlier years) on a day in the month shown, Great Britain*

Thousands

	December 1955	December 1960	December 1965	November 1970	November 1975	November 1978
Supplementary pensions:						
Retirement pensioners and national insurance widows	888	1,075	1,239	1,745	1,586	1,631
Others	264	234	181	156	94	107
Supplementary allowances:						
Unemployed – with national insurance benefit	19[1]	42[1]	34	73	135	93
without national insurance benefit	41[1]	85[1]	78	166	406	505
Sick and disabled – with national insurance benefit	110	136	149	164	77	67
without national insurance benefit	136	131	138	159	165	156
National insurance widows under 60	75	65	55	63	30	22
Other women with dependent children	55	71	108	191	276	322
Others	24	18	15	20	24	30
TOTAL	1,612	1,857	1,997	2,737	2,793	2,932

Source: 1955: National Assistance Board, *Annual Report 1955,* Cmnd. 9781, pp. 6–7, (HMSO, London); 1960; National Assistance Board, *Annual Report 1960,* Cmnd. 1410, pp. 8, 10, (HMSO, London); 1965, Department of Health and Social Security, *Social Security Statistics, 1974,* Table 34.30, (HMSO, London); 1970, 1975: Department of Health and Social Security, *Social Security Statistics, 1976,* Table 34.30, (HMSO, London); 1978: *Hansard,* 28 April 1980, p. 399–400.

[1] 1,000 unemployed recipients over pension age have been deducted from the 'with national insurance benefit' figures, although it is not known whether they were in receipt of national insurance benefit.

have been anticipated, developed because of demographic and social change. Not only has there been a very large increase in the numbers of the aged, but at the same time fewer individuals over retirement age remain in the labour force and a shift towards earlier retirement, both voluntary and involuntary, has occured. There has been a substantial growth in the number of one-parent families, a group regarded as marginal in 1948 and suitable for inclusion in the residual social assistance programme. The onset of large-scale and long-term unemployment in the 1970s placed strains on the unemployment benefit arrangements. A problem fundamental to the operation of the whole social security system stems from the change in the position of women. The postwar system was constructed on an assumption of female dependency, which is now challenged, and the very large increase in the size of the female labour force, including a substantial element of part-time employment, has created further problems.

As with problems raised by the inadequacy of benefit, many of the

Table 5.2 Numbers of recipients of regular weekly payments of supplementary benefit on a day in the month shown; Northern Ireland

	December 1970	December 1975	November 1978
Supplementary pensions:			
Retirement pensioners and national insurance widows	46,477	46,196	49,018
Others	12,465	9,013	7,687
Supplementary allowances:			
Unemployed – with national insurance benefit	18,685	4,727	3,512
without national insurance benefit		20,192	30,284
Sick and disabled – with national insurance benefit	7,588	2,596	6,251
without national insurance benefit	10,095	9,287	5,151
National insurance widows under 60	3,230	2,312	1,949
Other women with dependent children	4,154	6,847	12,594
Others	2,122	3,214	
TOTAL	104,816	104,384	116,446

Sources: 1970: Supplementary Benefits Commission (N. Ireland) *Annual Report*, 1974; 1975: Supplementary Benefits Commission (N. Ireland) *Annual Report*, 1975; 1978: *Digest of Statistics* (Northern Ireland), No. 52, S.12, 1979.

new demands came to be dealt with by a substantial and largely unplanned growth in the role of social assistance. Tables 5.1 and 5.2 illustrate this extended role.

Social security and poverty

Table 2.14 showed that three-quarters of all poor families have no economically active person; Table 2.15 showed that many other poor families had suffered unemployment; Table 2.17 showed that 78 per cent of the net incomes of those who were poor both before and after redistribution was provided by state benefits. For those who were raised above the poverty line by redistribution, 70 per cent of net income was in state benefits. The role of the social security system in alleviating poverty is therefore clear, but it is also clear that improvements in that system will have to be incorporated in any programme for the elimination of poverty.

Table 5.3 shows the number of recipients of social security benefits in 1978, including some forms of benefit not yet discussed. Even taking into account the fact that many people are receiving more than one benefit, the numbers are large and the support is given for a wide variety of circumstances. The social security system proposed by Beveridge was to be largely neutral in its attitude to the immediate cause of need. The system was to conquer the giant evil of want by means of subsistence level allowances, differentiated only by the numbers of persons the benefit had to support.[7] Want was caused by interruption or loss of earning power or because of failure to relate income during earning to the size of the family. The concept of individual deficiency, though not entirely absent, did not play a significant part in the plan. Rather, certain common human risks were identified and these risks were to be pooled through an insurance system with tax supplementation. While national assistance was to be regarded as 'less desirable' than national insurance (in order to give those paying contributions a sense of receiving a better deal than those who did not), it was in the main intended to deal with groups whose needs could not be met through insurance, with one exception, the unemployed who deliberately failed to meet the rules laid down in the insurance system.

However, neither neutrality about immediate cause or lack of differentiation in treatment lasted for long. A hierarchy of social security beneficiaries developed. At the top are those of particular 'worth', including the elderly and widows. At the bottom are single

Table 5.3 Numbers of recipients of social security benefits and war pensions (other than non-recurrent grants) on a day in 1978, Great Britain

	Thousands
Maintenance benefits (not means-tested):	
Unemployment benefit	492
Sickness benefit	472
Injury benefit	45
Invalidity benefit	557
Maternity allowance	92
Retirement pension – contributory	8,602
– non-contributory (over 80s)	64
Widow's allowance	36
Widowed mother's allowance	122
Widow's pension – national insurance	336
– industrial injuries	31
– war	80
Non-contributory invalidity pension	111
Housewives' non-contributory invalidity pension	40
Invalid care allowance	6
Disablement benefits	
Disablement pension – industrial injuries	200
– war	281
Attandance allowance	271
Mobility allowance	101
Means-tested benefits:	
Supplementary benefit	2,933
Family income supplement	81

Source: Statistics and Research Division, Department of Health and Social Security.

homeless persons and others of an 'unsatisfactory' way of life, and deserted wives and unmarried mothers. As in the past, the unemployed and the short-term sick hover uneasily between the two main groups, sometimes treated as if their lack of income was due to economic forces or health problems beyond their control and at other times as deliberate idlers, malingerers and scroungers.

As the social security system has been adjusted to meet changing needs, and changes in social attitudes, much of the differentiation by worth has been maintained. Only deserted wives and unmarried mothers have improved their status somewhat. Now called one-parent families, their treatment has been improved, but they remain slightly suspect.

The 1948 social security system underwent only minor changes in the 1950s. However, from the 1960s onwards, with the renewed debate about poverty and the pressing need to adapt to economic difficulties, a series of adjustments was made, sometimes in a direct attempt to combat poverty in certain population groups, (for example, the elderly and one-parent families), and at other times as a response to economic and labour force problems. In the process, a variety of mechanisms were adopted and the original clean lines of the post-Beveridge system were abandoned.

The use of earnings-related benefits to combat poverty and ease economic dislocation

The failure of the 1948 national insurance scheme to produce benefits at or above national assistance level led within a few years to support for a departure from the Beveridge system of flat-rate benefits and increasing awareness of the inadequacy of flat-rate contributions as the main source of finance for social security benefits. The yield of flat-rate contributions would always be limited by what the lowest-paid worker could afford to pay. Even if flat-rate benefits were raised to a level that would leave only a small minority in need of national assistance, they would still be inadequate as a replacement of lost earnings in most cases. To concern about the inadequacy of benefit rates was added the prospect of growing deficits on the National Insurance Fund, resulting from the decision to allow persons who had not been insured before 1948 to draw pensions under the 1946 Act from July 1958.

Industrial injuries

One group of social security recipients has had a flat-rate plus earnings-related supplement since 1948. Those covered by the industrial injuries scheme receive a flat-rate injury benefit for the first 26 weeks of incapacity for work, followed by a disablement pension based on the extent of any continuing 'loss of faculty' plus a special hardship allowance based on earnings loss. These more favourable benefits (than those available to other sick and disabled) and the rules governing them constitute what is known as the 'industrial preference'.

The industrial preference takes three forms. First, industrial injury and death benefit rates are a little more generous than those of the main national insurance scheme. Second, industrial injury benefits are not subject to contribution conditions. Any employed person is covered from the first day of employment and, if injured at work, may be entitled to a disablement pension for the rest of his life. Third and most important, the industrial injuries scheme provides compensation for disablement - as distinct from incapacity for work - on a much broader basis than the attendance and mobility allowances (see p. 152) for those disabled from non-industrial causes. The basis of compensation is loss of faculty - the extent to which a person is prevented from carrying on the everyday activities of life, compared with a person of the same age and sex whose condition is normal. A person assessed as 100 per cent disabled may be capable of full-time work and suffer little or no long-term loss of earnings, but will still get a full disablement pension. The scheme also provides a 'special hardship allowance' for cases where a lower degree of disablement results in a loss of earning power.

Relatively small numbers of the industrially injured require additional payments from supplementary benefits since, for the majority, their combined benefits brings them above the long-term rate. Although this model has existed from 1948, it has always stood apart from the main system and had little influence on it. Changes in other parts of the system arose from different reasons.

The elderly

The first move away from the flat-rate principle in the main system took place in 1961, when the Conservative Government introduced the 'graduated' pension scheme. Under this scheme, employees above a specified threshold of earnings were to pay a percentage contribution on their earnings, in exchange for which they were to receive an increase in their retirement (and widows') pensions.[8] The existing structure of flat-rate contributions and benefits was to continue. The graduated pension scheme never seemed likely to make a substantial difference to the standards of living of the retired population, and it has not done so. The benefits were deliberately pitched at a modest level, to avoid competing with occupational pension schemes, and were not increased in line with inflation.

An important motive for the introduction of the graduated scheme was to place national insurance on a sounder financial basis by providing an acceptable way of increasing its contribution income.[9] The promise of an earnings-related additional pension, however modest, made it possible to levy earnings-related contributions, thus providing a fertile source of additional revenue for the national insurance scheme as a whole. The move away from exclusive reliance on the flat-rate system, however, reflected a genuine realisation of its limitations. In political terms, it was the Conservative Government's response to the Labour Party's proposals, published in 1957, for a more ambitious national superannuation scheme.

After revised proposals from successive governments had failed to reach fruition, the Labour Government produced another version of its national superannuation scheme, which became law as the Social Security Pensions Act 1975. Contributions to the new scheme commenced in 1978 and the first benefit payments were made in April, 1979.

Like the earlier graduated pension scheme, which it replaced, the new pension scheme preserved the existing structure of flat-rate benefits. The basic pension was treated as providing 100 per cent replacement of earnings up to that level. The new scheme was to provide an additional pension of 25 per cent of earnings above the basic pension level and up to the maximum level of earnings on which contributions were to be levied (the 'upper earnings limit'). The Act provides that the upper earnings limit should be approximately seven times the basic pension, which in practice means about 1¼ times average earnings for men. The additional pension will accrue over a period of twenty years. Thus the full 25 per cent addition will be payable only to those reaching pension age in 1998 or later. Pensions becoming payable after 1998 will be based on the pensioner's best 20 years' earnings (not necessarily consecutive). To ensure that pension rights do not lose their value durng the period of accrual, each year's earnings will be revalued to take account of increases in the general level of earnings since the year in question. Once in payment, the additional pension will be increased annually in line with the increase in prices. The 'best 20 years' formula will eventually be of great value to employees whose earnings fluctuate widely, relative to the average, in the course of their careers, including heavy manual workers, whose earning capacity falls in the later years of their working lives, and those whose earnings are reduced or terminated prematurely by disablement.

Since most pensioners are women, a crucial test of the effectiveness of the new state pension scheme will be the extent to which it provides adequate pensions for women. Once the scheme reaches maturity, the best 20 years formula will enable a woman of 60 to draw a full pension calculated on precisely the same basis as that of a man of 65 except that she will normally have fewer years from which to select the best 20 and the earnings from which they are calculated are likely to be lower (see Chapter 3). In addition, a 'home responsibility' protection will ensure that gaps in a woman's (or man's) contribution record for years spent caring for children or severely disabled relatives will not prevent him/her from receiving a full pension. The majority of women, whether single, married or separated, are expected to become entitled to retirement pensions in their own right, and widows will be able to add a retirement pension based on their own earnings to the pension inherited from their husbands.

However effective the 1975 Act may prove to be in improving the position of the elderly in the long term, it does little for the present generation of elderly, and will have only a modest effect on the incomes of those retiring in the next decade. The financial situation of the present elderly generation reflects the long delays that occurred in the development of adequate earnings-related retirement pensions as part of the national insurance scheme. In 1977, the average graduated pension under the 1961 Act was only 41p per week and, as yet, only a small proportion of elderly people, and none of the very old, get any benefit at all from the new scheme.

As a result, despite the growth of occupational pension schemes, 22.5 per cent of retirement pensioners and widows aged 60 and over were in receipt of supplementary pension through social assistance at the end of 1978. When to the 2 million supplementary pensioners (including wives) are added another 750,000 estimated to be entitled to supplementary pensions, but not claiming them, it would appear that about 30 per cent of pensioners are living at or below supplementary benefit level, while as many more have incomes less than 40 per cent above supplementary benefit level. Poverty in old age is thus an inter-generational problem, not only in the sense that retirement or old age pensions, however financed, represent a share in the national income produced by the population currently of working age, but also because pension schemes confer differing levels of benefit on successive cohorts of pensioners.

It is impossible to predict what effect this will have on the numbers of old people qualifying for supplementary pensions at any stage in the future. All that can be said with confidence is that, by the end of this century, whatever other changes may occur, the combined effect of the State pension scheme and occupational pension schemes should lead to a very substantial reduction in the number of supplementary pensioners. Until then, the problem of poverty in old age will remain.

The unemployed

The social security arrangements for the unemployed were discussed in the last chapter. Some comments on the earnings-related supplement introduced in 1966 are appropriate here. Aimed primarily at skilled and reasonably well paid workers (whose labour mobility it was desired to encourage), it was intended to offer a fairly generous level of wage replacement by combining flat-rate benefits with an earnings related supplement. At the same time, the dangers of undermining work incentives for lower paid workers was to be avoided by imposing a ceiling of 85 per cent of former gross weekly earnings on the combined benefit. From the start, the ERS scheme was often less generous than it appeared, owing to the crude method adopted for assessing weekly earnings, and its effectiveness has been further reduced by the failure to adjust the parameters of the benefit formula in line with movements in average earnings.

The present government has decided to abolish ERS in 1982, on the stated grounds that it is no longer an effective scheme. However, this appears to be an economy measure and to be in part motivated by a desire to widen the gap between income in employment and in unemployment. There is no intention to replace the scheme with a more effective one and thus the unemployed will be dependent on redundancy payments where these apply, on flat-rate unemployment insurance and, in a large proportion of cases, on supplementary benefit at the short-term rate. The government has declined to extend the long-term rate to the unemployed, even after a prolonged waiting period. As was seen in the last chapter, this is a recipe for poverty for unemployed people, particularly the long-term unemployed.

The short and long-term sick and disabled

The national insurance and supplementary benefits systems (as opposed to the industrial injuries scheme) do not recognise disability as such,[10] but only incapacity for work. The short-term sickness benefit is payable to those who are, or are deemed to be, 'incapable of work by reason of some specific disease or bodily or mental disablement'. The same condition applies to invalidity benefit which, since 1971, has replaced sickness benefit after 28 weeks of incapacity. Disablement, however severe, which does not result in incapacity for work does not give title to sickness or invalidity benefit. For this reason, many disabled people whose chances of finding jobs are, in present circumstances, remote are classified as unemployed and the benefit system applying to the unemployed applies equally to them.

Both sickness benefit and invalidity benefit are enhanced by earnings-related supplements. In the case of sickness benefit, the rules applicable to unemployed persons since 1966 apply equally to the short-term sick. The deficiencies of the ERS scheme also apply to the sick and the ERS for this group will also be abolished in 1982 leaving the sick dependent on short-term national insurance and/or short-term supplementary benefit. A proportion of the short-term sick are eligible for sick pay from the employer and this will be discussed later in this chapter.

Invalidity benefit is subject to different rules. It is payable at the higher long-term rate of national insurance and continues as long as certified incapacity to work lasts. Its earnings-related element also derives from a more satisfactory base, the 1975 Social Security Pensions Act.

Invalidity benefit covers only those long-term sick and disabled who have an adequate national insurance contribution record and thus excludes those who have never been in the labour force. It serves two purposes. It is a long-term sickness benefit, providing for the needs of those whose earnings are interrupted for a period of more than 28 weeks, but who expect to return to work in due course. It is also a benefit for those who are prematurely retired from work on medical grounds. The advantage of having a single benefit for these two types of case is that the need to predict the duration and outcome of an illness and to label as permanently incapacitated a person who hopes to be able to work again and should be encouraged to do so, is avoided. The disadvantage is that the benefit is unlikely to be equally well adapted to both purposes. As the earnings-related component under the provisions of the 1975 Act matures, invalidity benefit rates may begin to be regarded as unduly generous in relation to the potential earnings of claimants who are expected to be fit for work in the near future. In cases where invalidity benefit is in effect a premature retirement pension on the other hand, it seems reasonable that it should be calculated in the same way as the retirement pension. Those who become permanently incapacitated too young to have paid twenty years' contributions, however, will not get the full earnings-related component. The age-related invalidity allowance (at present rates, £4.90 if incapacity begins under 40, £3.10 if between 40 and 50 and £1.55 if between 50 and 55 for a woman or 50–60 for a man) provides some compensation for this, and the under-40 rate could be increased as the earnings-related element matures. At present, the invalidity benefit does serve to maintain the majority without supplementation for supplementary benefits, and the position will improve further as earnings-related supplements begin to apply.

Widows

The fourth group benefiting from earnings-related supplements under the 1975 Social Security Pensions Act are widows. Widows were already fairly well served by the national insurance system with a widow's allowance for all those under 60 years for the first six months after the death of the husband, a widow's pension for those over 40, the rate dependent on the age of widowhood, and a widowed mother's allowance for those with dependent children, based on the long-term national insurances rate, plus child dependency additions. These benefits can now be enhanced under the Social Security Pensions Act on the basis of the accrued benefits of the late husband.

Another important advantage enjoyed by widows is that, since 1965, their national insurance benefits are not affected by the amount they earn from employment. In this respect, they fare much better than other lone parents on supplementary benefit. Thus, while it cannot be said that all widows are well off (a small proportion still receive supplementary benefit), their needs are relatively well provided for by the national insurance scheme and will be, increasingly, as the earnings-related pension scheme matures. A growing proportion of widows will also benefit from occupational pension schemes of which their husbands were members.

The use of non-contributory benefits to fill gaps in the system

In recent years, there has been a shift from the almost exclusive emphasis on social insurance in the Beveridge report and the postwar legislation, to a more pragmatic approach which recognises the advantages, in some circumstances, of making benefits available without contribution conditions. One reason for this shift was the fact that, although the contribution conditions for entitlement to the basic flat-rate benefits of the national insurance system were not onerous, they inevitably excluded some potential recipients. Indeed, the less stringent the contributions conditions were (and there was a tendency to relax them as the years passed), the more unfair it seemed when a person who would otherwise have been eligible for a benefit failed to qualify because he or she had not had the opportunity to pay the necessary contributions.

Successive governments have been concerned however, to avoid undermining the contributory principle by paying contributory and non-contributory benefits at the same rates in respect of the same contingencies. Where non-contributory benefits have been introduced, they have generally been payable at 60 per cent of the corresponding contributory benefit rates, though dependency increases for a claimant's children were paid at the full contributory rates.

The first group to benefit from the development of non-contributory benefits were people who had been over pension age when the postwar national insurance provisions commenced in 1948 and had not been insured under earlier legislation. They, or their widows, became entitled to an 'Old Persons' Pension' from November 1970. In the following year, these pensions were extended to anybody over 80 who was not already entitled to a retirement pension of at least an equivalent amount.

A more serious anomaly was the fact that those disabled from birth or childhood and unable to take paid employment could not qualify for invalidity benefit. From 1975, therefore, a non-contributory invalidity pension (NCIP) was paid to persons who would have qualified for a contributory invalidity pension, but for the contribution conditions. Like the Old Persons' Pension, it was payable at 60 per cent of the contributory benefit rate. Married women were included from 1979, but only if they were incapable of performing normal household duties. The household duties condition has been strongly criticised as being unfair discrimination against married women and has proved difficult to administer.

Apart from its application to married women, criticism of NCIP has focussed on the 60 per cent rate at which it is paid. A large proportion of those qualifying for it, other than married women, were previously in receipt of supplementary benefit. In most cases, NCIP was not sufficient to raise their incomes above supplementary benefit level and they therefore gained nothing from the new benefit.

A second group of non-contributory benefits has been introduced to meet needs – in particular, the costs arising from disablement – for which no provision was made in the national insurance system. Since the need for these benefits was either unrelated, or only loosely related, to participation in the labour force, contribution conditions would have been a needless complication which would have denied the benefits to many of those for whom they were intended. The two benefits introduced for disabled people have been the attendance allowance and mobility allowance. Unlike NCIP, these are not intended to meet normal living expenses, but are a contribution towards the additional expenses associated with disablement.

Payment of the attendance allowance commenced in December 1971. It is payable to anyone aged two or over who is so severely disabled, physically or mentally, as to need attention or supervision by day and/or by night.

The mobility allowance commenced in January 1976. It is a weekly benefit for people between the ages of 5 and 65 who are virtually unable to walk because of physical disablement. Men and women receiving the allowance at 65 years are allowed to retain it up to the age of 75 years.

A non-contributory invalid care allowance for men and single women of working age caring for a serverely disabled relative was introduced in July 1976, payable at 60 per cent of the basic contributory pension rate, although in this case there is no contributory benefit covering the same contingency. The exclusion of married women was justified on the grounds that they would not normally be breadwinners.

Finally, in the case of one benefit – the lump-sum maternity grant – the government has undertaken to abolish the contribution conditions. In 1982, the contribution conditions will be replaced by a six months' residence test. The maternity grant is a prime example of the anomalies created by contribution conditions which bear no relation to the purpose for which the benefit is intended. Married women have been able to qualify for the grant either on their own contribution record or that of their husband. Unmarried mothers could rely only on their record and were therefore much less likely to qualify. As a result, it is precisely those mothers who most need the grant who have been disqualified by the contribution conditions.

Encouraging the growth of occupational welfare

Governments of both parties have encouraged the growth and/or improvement of employment-based pension and sick pay schemes as a supplement to, or a substitute for, state schemes.

Pensions

Table 5.4 shows the growth of occupational pension schemes in the period 1936 to 1975, when 11.5 million employees were covered. Pensions in payment had also increased from 0.2 million in 1936 and 0.9 million in 1953 to 4.0 million in 1975.[11]

The 1961 state graduated pension scheme was deliberately pitched at a low level to avoid competing with occupational pensions, whose growth the Conservative Government wished to encourage. The 1975 Social Security Pensions Act (from a Labour Government) aimed to produce a much more substantial state earnings-related pension. Both schemes allowed for 'contracting out' from the state scheme, in full or in part by those covered by occupational pensions. A major difference between the approaches of Conservative and Labour Governments to this question was that the Conservatives were anxious to avoid imposing conditions for contracting out which most occupational schemes would be unable to meet, with the result that many employers might feel obliged to wind up their schemes while Labour Governments placed more emphasis on the need for an adequate state scheme for those not in occupational schemes, even if this meant that the contracting out conditions must be more demanding. The Social Security Pensions Act 1975 therefore set quite high standards for contracting out.

The effect of contracting out is that benefits from the occupational scheme replace the earnings-related retirement pension. As a

Table 5.4 Employees in pension schemes 1936–75; United Kingdom.

Millions

Year	Private sector		Public sector		Total
	Men	Women	Men	Women	Men and women
1936	1.3	0.3	0.8	0.2	2.6
1954	2.5	0.6	2.4	0.7	6.2
1956	3.5	0.8	2.9	0.8	8.0
1963	6.4	0.8	3.0	0.9	11.1
1967	6.8	1.3	3.1	1.0	12.2
1971	5.5	1.3	3.2	1.1	11.1
1975	5.0	1.1	3.7	1.7	11.5

Source: *Department of Employment Gazette*, May 1977.

minimum, the occupational benefits must be of approximately the same amount as the benefits of the state scheme which they replace. In the long run, they will normally be considerably more generous than this, since the occupational pension will accrue at a minimum rate of 1½ per cent for each year of contracted-out employment (the same rate as in the state scheme) up to a maximum of 40 years. For various reasons, this does not mean that the occupational pension will be twice as big as the state pension based on only 20 years' earnings, but contracted-out employees can normally expect to receive a higher pension than if they were solely dependent on the state scheme, and one of the most important consequences of the 1975 Act has been a widespread improvement of the terms of occupational schemes to enable them to meet the conditions for contracting out. Some 10 million (of 11.5 million) employees in occupational schemes are now contracted out.

A result of the imposition of relatively high standards on contracted-out schemes was that the government had to accept that it would be necessary for the state scheme to provide additional support for those schemes. Thus, because it was not thought possible to require private pension schemes to guarantee inflation-proofing of pensions in payment, annual inflation adjustments will be provided by the state scheme to the 'guaranteed minimum pension' (i.e. roughly the equivalent of the state pension forgone). Similarly, in requiring that the guaranteed minimum pension of an employee leaving his employment before pension age should not only be preserved but revalued in line with the rise in average earnings between the date of leaving and pension age, the government recognised that the revaluation would have to be under-written by the state scheme. Under the state scheme, a widow will, subject to certain limits, inherit the whole of her husband's earnings-related pension entitlement. If the husband was in a contracted-out scheme, however, that scheme will have to pay the widow only half the guaranteed minimum pension to which her husband would have been entitled, the state scheme providing the remainder.

Occupational pension schemes are already making a significant contribution to the living standards of a substantial proportion of the retired population and their importance is likely to increase. First, many schemes have been set up within the last 20-30 years and have yet to reach maturity. Second, as noted, there has been a dramatic improvement in the quality of occupational schemes, and third, arrangements for the preservation of pension rights of employees leaving before retirement age have been greatly improved.

Short-term sickness

The proportion of employees covered by sick pay schemes has increased rapidly in the last three decades. The proportions covered vary substantially between different industries and between different occupations. Manual workers, especially women, are less likely to be covered than non-manual, as Table 5.5 shows.

To say that an employee is covered by a sick pay scheme, however, is not to say that he will receive sick pay if he falls sick tomorrow. In many cases, there is a qualifying period of employment, which may be as long as one year and tends to be longer for manual than for non-manual workers. Similarly, the maximum duration of sick pay tends to be longer for non-manual workers and they are much more likely to receive full pay, with or without deductions for national insurance benefits, at the commencement of sickness.[12]

Successive governments of both parties have considered whether, with the growth of employers' sick pay schemes, it would by sensible and practicable to transfer statutory responsibility for payments for the early weeks of sickness from the national insurance scheme to employers, and a Green Paper proposing payment of sick pay by all employers was published in April 1980.[13] The main proposal is that, from April 1982, employers should be required to make a standard minimum payment during the first eight weeks of incapacity. The

Table 5.5 Proportions of all full-time employees covered by sick pay schemes: Great Britain, 1974.

Percentages

	Manual	Non-manual
Men	74.0	94.2
Married women	57.9	92.8
Other women	54.4	94.9

Source: Department of Health and Social Security, *Income During Initial Sickness: A new Strategy*, (HMSO, London, 1980).

suggested minimum is roughly the sickness benefit rate for a man with a dependent wife, but is taxable. These proposals must be seen as part of the government's efforts to cut public expenditure rather than as an attempt to achieve higher standards of provision for short-term sickness.

Long-term sickness and disability

Two types of employment-based schemes are available for long-term sickness and disability. The first is provision within the pension scheme for early retirement on health grounds. Surveys undertaken in 1971[14] indicated that less than half of pension scheme members were entitled to receive an accrued pension or something better and manual workers were more poorly provided for than non-manual workers. Less than one-third of members of these schemes were entitled to an ill-health pension without a waiting period and for over half, the waiting period was 10 years or more. Few major improvements have occurred since 1971.

A second form of provision is through long-term sickness benefit schemes, a type of cover which is growing rapidly and which provides payments until recovery or until retirement age (including payment to the occupational pension scheme to preserve pension rights). Such payments are related to salary rather than to years of service and are often higher than the benefits under arrangement for early retirement because of ill-health. They also require qualifying periods of varying lengths.

Occupational welfare arrangements for short and long-term sickness have a useful contribution to make to the enhancement of the income of this group if they are paid in addition to existing state benefits. If they are to replace state benefits (as is proposed for short-term sick pay), then both a more even spread across the labour force and an upgrading of many schemes will be essential.

The use of means-tested benefits – social assistance

The social assistance arrangements created by the National Assistance Act 1948 have survived with modifications up to the present. Changes in the legal framework of the scheme will take effect from November 1980, but the principles underlying the calculation of assistance payments will remain broadly as they were in 1948. Under the 1948 Act, social assistance remained an administratively separate service from the national insurance system, with a distinctive approach which tended to emphasise administrative discretion rather than legal entitlement to assistance. The National Assistance Board was replaced in 1966 by the Supplementary Benefits Commission, a body with more limited powers which was not a separate department but, in effect, part of the newly created Ministry of Social Security (which was later expanded to become the Department of Health and Social Security).

As Table 5.1 showed, the numbers of recipients of national assistance/supplementary benefits increased in Great Britain from 1.6 million in 1955 to 2.9 million in late 1978. Table 5.2 gave Northern Ireland figures. In the UK as a whole supplementary benefit is estimated to support, or part support, some 5 million persons when dependants of recipients are included. Thus social assistance, far from acting as a residual service, has a mass role to fulfil. It supplements national insurance benefits for the elderly, widows, the sick and the unemployed and replaced national insurance where, because of insufficient contributions or because its time limit has expired, national insurance is not payable. It also supplements certain non-contributory benefits for elderly and disabled people.

In all of these cases, social assistance acts in a subsidiary role. However, one group of recipients is excluded from all the provisions des-

Table 5.6 Proportions of full time employees covered by sick pay schemes, by qualifying period for entitlement, Great Britain, 1974.

Percentages

	Qualifying period required				
	None	Less than 6 months	6 months	1 year	Other
Men:					
Manual	28.4	17.8	23.3	25.9	4.6
Non-manual	67.1	12.7	14.1	5.7	0.5
Women:					
Manual	23.8	13.7	33.1	19.9	9.5
Non-manual	65.1	14.0	14.5	6.2	0.2

Source: Department of Health and Social Security, *Income During Initial Sickness: A New Strategy,* (HMSO, London, 1980).

cribed so far and is heavily dependent upon social assistance. These are non-working lone parents, whose status arises from circumstances other than the death of the married partner, i.e. divorced and separated wives (and husbands) with children, and unmarried mothers. Since this is the only group not yet described in any detail, some comments must first be made on them before social assistance can be considered.

One-parent families

One of the unresolved dilemmas of the UK social security system is what kind of provision, and at what level, ought to be made for one-parent families. In numerical terms, the problem is growing rapidly. In 1971, there were about 570,000 families in Great Britain in which children were being cared for by a single adult. By 1978, the number had risen to about 825,000, including single, separated, divorced and widowed mothers, and a smaller group of lone fathers.[15]

Using figures drawn from Family Expenditure Survey for 1978, the National Council for One-Parent Families compared the situation of one-parent families in the UK with that of two-parent families with two children (the average number of children in the one-parent families in the sample was 1.92) and show that while 99.6 per cent of two-parent families had one or more members working, the proportion of one-parent families with a working member was only 61.8 per cent. The average normal disposable household income of two-parent families was £103.88 per week; that of one-parent families £58.67 per week. The proportion of the two-parent families' normal gross income derived from social security benefits was 4.8 per cent, compared with 32.7 per cent for the one-parent households.[16]

Perhaps the most striking fact about one-parent families as a group is the proportion who rely on supplementary benefit. There were 339,000 of them in Great Britain in November 1978, greatly outnumbering the 196,000 two-parent families on supplementary benefit. In addition, there are an estimated 40,000 one-parent families (in 1977, the latest available figure) entitled to supplementary benefit, but not claiming it[17], which means that almost half of all lone-parent families were living on or below the supplementary benefit level. A further 37,000 receive family income supplement.

Apart from the widows' benefits, discussed earlier, the only non-means-tested social security provision for lone parents is the £3.00 child benefit increase (£3.00 per family, not per child), a small additional benefit which has grown from 50 pence in 1977. Its rapid growth under governments of both parties is, in part, attributable to the fact that it is a relatively cheap way of meeting demands for improved benefits for lone parents. The 'premium', as it is sometimes called, is not paid to widows, whose children's needs are met at a preferential rate under the widowed mother's allowance, and although it can be claimed by lone parents receiving supplementary benefit, their supplementary benefit is reduced by the same amount. Thus only a minority of lone parents benefit from the premium, but they include those who are able to work; it is therefore one means of helping lone parents to avoid the need to claim supplementary benefit.

In recent years there has been considerable discussion about the possibility of a specific social security benefit for one-parent families. The case for this was set out in the Report of the Committee on One-Parent Families (the Finer Report), published in 1974.[18] The Committee's central proposal was for a 'guaranteed maintenance allowance' (GMA) above supplementary benefit level. As the name implies, the GMA was intended to 'top up' whatever income the family might receive by way of maintenance payments from liable relatives. Because of the high cost of any worthwhile benefit payable to all lone parents, it was to be part means tested. The new Labour Government, which had just come to power when the Committee reported, and which in principle was opposed to the extension of means testing, rejected the GMA proposal. Apart from any ideological objection, however, the proposal would almost certainly have been rejected on grounds of cost.

Supplementary benefit and family income supplement (discussed in Chapter 3) remain the main forms of social security provision for lone parents other than widows, and some progress has been made in adapting these schemes to their needs. Supplementary benefit claimants are allowed to earn £4 per week, after deducting work expenses, including child-minding, before the amount of benefit payable is affected, but lone parents have an additional disregard of half their net earnings between £4 and £20, a useful provision for those in part-time work.

The family income supplement scheme has also been adapted to the needs of lone parents by a reduction from 30 to 24 in the weekly number of hours they are required to work in order to satisfy the full-time work test. Moreover, the qualifying income levels for FIS are the same for one-parent and two-parent families and is therefore more generous to lone parents in relation to family size.

Supplementary benefit does have some positive features for lone parents. Entitlement begins as soon as the need arises. Widely varying housing costs are allowed for. Special needs can be met both by extra weekly payments and by lump-sum payments, and maintenance orders can be signed over to the local social security office in return for a regular weekly income.

The social assistance benefits arrangements

In accordance with Beveridge's concept of a national minimum, adequate for subsistence needs, the 1948 National Assistance Regulations laid down a single scale of weekly requirements as a basis for determining the amount of assistance payable. This scale applied equally to the sick, the unemployed, the retired, and those such as unmarried or separated mothers who did not fall within the categories entitled to national insurance benefits. Similarly, the same scale of requirements was used for those needing assistance for only a week or two as for those likely to remain dependent on the scheme for the rest of their lives.

Although the basic scale rates were the same for all, there were wide variations in the use made by the Board's officers of their discretionary powers. In particular, the power to award discretionary additions in cases where there were 'special circumstances' was used increasingly to augment the amounts payable to elderly applicants. The use of the discretion, however, was acknowledged to be inconsistent and uneven and, in an effort to replace it, the government in 1966 introduced a long-term addition of 9 shillings (45 pence) per week, payable to all claimants over pension age and to all those, other than the unemployed, who had been on supplementary benefit for two years or more.[19] The power to make discretionary additions for exceptional circumstances was retained, but the first 9 shillings of any extra needs were assumed to be covered by the long-term addition.

Since 1966, the long-term addition has developed in ways which were not originally envisaged. In 1973, it was replaced by long-term scale rates, giving considerably greater preference to long-term claimants. Whatever the original intention, it is now undeniable that long-term claimants – other than the unemployed, who still do not qualify for the long-term rates – have a higher standard of income than short-term claimants, which is not justified by any objective evaluation of their relative needs. Moreover, since 1975, the idea of a fixed long-term addition payable in place of specific additions for special needs has been virtually abandoned. Most of the exceptional circumstances additions (ECAs) now in payment go to claimants whose basic needs are assessed at the long-term rates. The increase in the proportion of claimants receiving ECAs since 1970 is shown in Table 5.7. As well as awarding ECAs to meet extra needs of recurrent nature, the Supplementary Benefits Commission, like the National Assistance Board before it, could make single lump-sum exceptional needs payments. This power is used mainly to make payments for clothing, bedding, furniture and household equipment.[20]

Table 5.7 Proportion of supplementary benefit recipients with exceptional circumstances additions in November of each year 1970–1978: Great Britain and Northern Ireland.

Percentages

	Great Britain		Northern Ireland	
Year	Pensioners	Under pension age	Pensioners	Under pension age
1970	18	13	15	12
1971	16	11	21	11
1972	19	12	20	12
1973	33	17	26	13
1974	43	17	37	14
1975	53	18	54	13
1976	66	26	66	17
1977	72	30	80	21
1978	75	31	82	24

Source: Statistics and Research Division, Department of Health and Social Security.

Northern Ireland and social assistance

Social security benefits in Northern Ireland are in most respects indentical to those provided in Great Britain, but there are differences in social and economic conditions which produce a higher incidence of poverty in Northern Ireland.[20] The cost of living is higher for example, gas is twice as expensive as in Great Britain and electricity costs are 20 per cent above levels in Great Britain.[22] Rents, on the other hand, tend to be lower. As Chapter 3 showed, average earnings in Northern Ireland are lower than in Britain, though the gap has narrowed in recent years.

Higher unemployment rates in Northern Ireland than in Great Britain have meant that, throughout the postwar period, the unemployed have been a major category of recipients of social assistance, constituting 23.3 per cent of recipients in 1952 (against 3.8 per cent in Great Britain)[23] and 29 per cent in 1978 (20.4 per cent in Great Britain). In December 1976, just over 7 per cent of the population of Northern Ireland were in receipt of supplementary benefit; if their dependants are included, the proportion was 12.8 per cent. For Great Britain, the proportion was 5.5 per cent or 8 per cent including dependants.[24]

A report on poverty in Northern Ireland, published in 1976, concluded that 'the greatest weaknesses of income maintenance services in the United Kingdom are in precisely those areas which are of special significance in Northern Ireland'.[25] This is certainly true of benefits for the unemployed, particularly the long-term unemployed. In Northern Ireland, as in Great Britain, large families are a minority, but they are a larger minority in Northern Ireland, and the available evidence suggests that it is families with dependent children who have the greatest difficulty in managing on supplementary benefit. If there are doubts as to the adequacy of supplementary benefits for the needs of families in Great Britain, therefore, those doubts must be accentuated in Northern Ireland.

In addition, until recently, the value of supplementary benefits for a number of beneficiaries has been reduced by the operation of the Payments for Debt (Emergency Provisions) Act 1971, legislation which is restricted to Northern Ireland.[26] This Act was passed as a result of the rent and rates strike which took place as a protest against the introduction of internment in Northern Ireland. It provides that if a person is in debt, money due to him from a government department can be allocated in whole or in part towards the recovery of the debt.

During 1971–72, over 22,000 tenants in the public sector were withholding payment of rent and rates and, in May 1972, about 12,500 were subject to 'benefit allocations'.[27] By 1976, relatively few tenants were still withholding current rent payments, but arrears had reached a high level and the government decided to extend the operation of the Payments for Debt Act to all those in rent arrears. In

1978, it was again extended to allow debts for gas and electricity to be recovered by deductions from benefits. While deductions were made from other social security benefits (and pay in the case of government employees), hardship was probably greatest where deductions were made from supplementary benefit. In March 1980, it was announced that deductions from supplementary benefits under the Payments for Debt Act were to be suspended.

Recent reforms of supplementary benefit

The Supplementary Benefits Commission (Great Britain), in its annual report for 1975, identified five main 'strategic issues' for supplementary benefits which required examination. These were: over-reliance on discretion, an over-complex scheme, frontier problems with other agencies, the problems likely to arise from giving stronger legal status to Supplementary Benefit Appeal Tribunals (to which dissatisfied claimants could resort) and the likely pressure to reduce staff at a time of public expenditure restraints.[28]

None of these five strategic issues related directly to the adequacy of supplementary benefit payments. The main emphasis of the Commission's thinking was on administrative rationalisation and the need to diminish the role of discretion in the scheme. The achievement of these aims would bring advantages to claimants in the form of simplification, quicker decisions, clearer understanding of their rights and higher rates of take-up. However, the Commission[29] expected that these changes might involve increasing benefit rates 'since it is unlikely to be accepted that people should lose when discretion and complexity are eliminated'. In addition, the report foreshadowed the Commission's intention to focus future debate on the adequacy of the rates.

In 1976, the Secretary of State for Social Services commissioned a small team of officials to carry out a review of the supplementary benefits scheme, but they were instructed to consider how the scheme could be reformed without additional expenditure or increases in staff. Accordingly, the review team's report, *Social Assistance*[30], although it discussed many desirable reforms, concentrated on ways of re-allocating resources within the supplementary benefit scheme itself, to adapt it to its 'mass role'.

The Supplementary Benefits Commission, in its response to the review team's report, was at pains to disassociate itself from the nil-cost approach.[31] The Commission's first priorities for reform within the scheme were to shorten the qualifying period for payment of the long-term rate to people under pension age from two years to one, and – the highest priority of all – to remove the discrimination against the unemployed by allowing them to receive benefit at the long-term rates on the same terms as other claimants.[32] It also pressed for the introduction of a comprehensive housing benefit, which would replace both the existing rent and rate rebate schemes and the rent element in the calculation of supplementary benefits and would give the same assistance with housing costs to those in work whose incomes were at supplementary benefit level as to those in receipt of supplementary benefit.[33] This was a reform for which the Commission had been pressing for several years. In addition, it drew attention to the need for more employment opportunities and a comprehensive fuel benefit.[34]

In the Social Security Act 1980,[35] the government introduced changes which would not require additional resources as a first stage in the reform of the scheme: it left open the question of whether more resources might be needed to complete the process of reform.

Given the nil-cost basis of the changes, it was inevitable that most of them would be relatively small. They will, however, have a significant effect on the benefit entitlement of large numbers of claimants. Among the changes that will operate to the advantage of claimants are the reduction of the qualifying period for the long-term rates of benefit from two years to one (although the unemployed are still excluded) and a reduction in the number of different rates for children by raising the rate for those under 5 to the level of the 5–10 age group, and similarly raising the 11–12 age group rate to the same level as for those aged 13–15.

The increased costs generated by these changes were balanced by a number of measures designed to produce savings. The biggest saving was to come from the alignment of the long-term supplementary benefit rates for adults with the national insurance benefit rates, in effect a small reduction, the deferment of school-leavers' entitlement to benefit, and simpler and more stringent rules on the treatment of resources.

A longer-term reform, which will not take effect until November 1983, allows 'breadwinner' wives to claim benefit. This change was necessitated by the EEC Directive on equal treatment for men and women in social security (Directive 79/7).

The most fundamental changes proposed in the Act, however,

were concerned with the legal structure of the scheme. The Commission itself was abolished in November 1980. The voluminous 'rules' issued by the Commission in unpublished codes of instructions, providing detailed guidance on the use of discretion, have been replaced by regulations (on similar policy lines) laid before Parliament, published and legally binding. There are some changes in relation to lump-sum exceptional needs payments (ENPs). Under the new regulations, the broad intention is that claimants should be expected to meet normal living expenses including, in particular, the replacement of clothing out of their weekly benefit payments. Weekly exceptional circumstances additions (ECAs) are to be replaced by 'additional requirements', which are specified in the regulations and broadly follow the policy of the Supplementary Benefits Commission.

Whether the supplementary benefits scheme will provide as effective a service to claimants in the future remains to be seen. The most important gain from the point of view of claimants is the establishment of legal rights where, in the past, they have depended on discretion. Simplification, as far as it goes, may also be regarded as a gain for claimants, though a nil-cost simplification means redistributing resources in ways which result in gains for some claimants but losses for others.

A less tangible loss, which may in the long run prove no less important, is the abolition of the Supplementary Benefits Commission. A new Social Security Advisory Committee (SSAC) will replace the Commission, the separate Northern Ireland Supplementary Benefits Commission, and the National Insurance Advisory Committee. The Commission has been a powerful advocate of reforms, both in the supplementary benefit scheme and in the social security system as a whole, and the Northern Ireland (SBC) has pressed the needs of its claimants. Both have shown particular concern for those groups of supplementary benefit claimants whom they regard as least adequately provided for – especially families with children and the long-term unemployed. The SSAC's much wider remit may enable it to take a more comprehensive view of the problems of the social security system, but may also make it less responsive to the needs of the poor.

Meanwhile, the main structural problems of the supplementary benefit scheme remain largely untouched. The number of claimants will not diminish and the inequalities between those entitled to the long-term benefit rates and those on the much lower short-term rates will remain, though the latter group will be helped by the reduction in the qualifying period for the long-term rates. The exclusion of the unemployed from the long-term rates will continue. It is by no means clear that the relatively minor simplifications proposed will succeed in adapting the scheme to its 'mass role'.

Establishing and maintaining the adequacy of social benefits

The adequacy of social security benefits as a means of protecting those eligible for assistance from poverty is determined by various factors. Of these, three stand out as key issues.

The first is whether the basis upon which benefit is established adequately reflects the needs of recipients. This is particularly important in relation to social assistance, since the supplementary benefit rates are regarded as the minimum below which all social security recipients should not fall. As noted earlier, when both national insurance and national assistance benefit rates were set, it was without a clear definition of the levels of income required for subsistence, and no full examination of the basis of determining needs, either for adults or for children, has taken place since. Moreover, benefits across the whole social security system are not necessarily determined in relation to need, but to the rules of the various parts of the system and to political and moral judgements, and this is particularly noticeable in relation to decisions about the payment of long-term and short-term rates. It is now generally acknowledged that those in receipt of short-term rates for prolonged periods are living in poverty and, as noted in Chapter 1, the children of long-term claimants do not attract a higher rate of benefit. Thus while not all social security recipients are in poverty, those actually on supplementary benefit and those on other social security benefits at or near this level are likely to be poor.

The second issue is the question of take-up benefits. Table 5.8 shows estimates of the take-up of supplementary benefits in Great Britain in 1977. Take-up of supplementary benefits in Great Britain is estimated to be around 74 per cent. Approximately one million eligible persons are not receiving benefits and thus are living below supplementary benefit level. Lack of take-up arises partly from ignorance of available benefits, but also from reluctance to apply for means-tested benefits which, because of public attitudes and press campaigns about 'scroungers' living off the state, are seen to carry a stigma in a way that insurance-based benefits do not.

Table 5.8 Estimates of take-up of supplementary benefit: Great Britain, 1977

Group	Total likely to be entitled	Proportion receiving benefit	Number eligible but not receiving benefit	Average unclaimed benefit (weekly)
	000	*per cent*	*000*	£
Pensioners	2,280	73	610	3.10
Non-pensioners:				
Sick	240	87	30	8.00
Unemployed	920	81	170	10.10
One-parent families	370	89	40	10.50
Others[1]	220	19	180	12.60
All groups	4,040	74	1,030	6.30

Source: Supplementary Benefits Commission *Annual Report 1978*, Table 12.10, (HMSO, London).

[1] The SBC has questioned whether it is right to include many of those in the 'others' category, since claimants below pension age would not normally be allowed to remain unoccupied without good reason while drawing supplementary benefit. Excluding this category entirely would raise the overall take-up rate from 74 per cent to 78.50 per cent.

The third determinant of benefit adequacy is the extent to which the real value of benefits is maintained in relation to the cost of living and in relation to the general standard of living in the community. The development of policy on the 'uprating' of benefits has been a gradual process, involving fundamental issues which have yet to be finally resolved.

Until the end of the 1950s, there was little argument about the principles involved. It was generally accepted that if prices rose substantially, the main benefits should be increased so as to restore their real value. How frequently such increases should take place, or by how much prices should be allowed to rise before benefits were adjusted, were questions of political judgement. In practice, increases in national assistance rates occurred more frequently than increases in national insurance benefits, reflecting the great importance attached to maintaining the value of the minimum income provided by the former. Similary, benefits providing a weekly income were uprated more frequently than those, such as maternity grant and death grant, payable as a lump sum to meet a particular contingency. Family allowances, although making a regular contribution to family incomes, were accorded relatively low priority.

Although, in the late 1950s, there was some recognition of the need to offer social security recipients a share in national prosperity, no steps were taken to give this legislative form. However, wage levels appear to have been taken into account in the setting of rates. This *ad hoc* approach was maintained in 1966, when the national assistance scheme was reformed and renamed supplementary benefit.

In 1973, a differential between short-term and long-term rates was established in both national insurance and supplementary benefit. When the new rates were announced, it appeared that the intention was to increase the short-term rates by the minimum amount needed to compensate for price increases, while long-term beneficiaries were to get an increase broadly in line with average earnings. The stated grounds for the differential were that while those receiving short-term benefits were not, as a rule, dependent on them for long and often had other resources, those receiving pensions and other long-term benefits were more dependent on this source of income.[36]

There can be little doubt that the Conservative Ministers concerned with the 1973 uprating believed that the cost of real increases in the value of benefits could be contained in an acceptable way by limiting them to long-term beneficiaries, while maintaining the real value of short-term benefits in relation to prices.

Considerations of cost led the 1974 Labour Government to follow a similar policy. The uprating formula enacted in 1975 required the Secretary of State to carry out an annual review of national insurance benefit rates 'for the purpose of determining whether they have retained their value in relation to the general level of earnings or prices obtaining in Great Britain'.[37] Short-term benefits were to be inflation-proofed. Long-term benefits were to rise in line with average earnings, but with a fallback provision to protect their real value in the event of prices rising faster than earnings in a particular year. The formula, however, had two weaknesses.

The first weakness was the fact, obvious in retrospect but little understood in 1975 that, in a period of rising real earnings, to increase long-term benefits in line with earnings and short-term benefits in line with prices must produce a wider differential each year. The second weakness of the 1975 uprating formula has become known as the 'ratchet effect'. It rose from the fact that long-term benefits were to be increased each year by the same rate as either prices or earnings which ever had risen faster, without regard to the cumulative effect over a series of years. So long as earnings consistently rose faster than prices, or prices consistently rose faster than earnings, the formula would simply ensure that pensions kept pace with the long-term increase in either earnings or prices. If earnings rose faster in some years and prices in others, however, the long-term increase in pensions would be greater than both prices and earnings, and pensioners' living standards would rise faster than those of the working population.

In practice, between 1975 and 1979, the effects of these defects of the uprating formula were less serious than they might have been, because over that period the rates of increase of prices and earnings did not diverge dramatically. The basic single retirement pension rate (under national insurance) as a percentage of average earnings of male manual workers, which had risen from 19.1 per cent in 1948 to 21.4 per cent in 1975, increased to 23.6 per cent by 1979. A similar comparison of the basic short-term benefit national insurance rates with average earnings over the period from 1972 to 1979 – the period during which the short-term rates diverged from the long-term, rates – shows that they remained at about 19 per cent throughout. The improvement in the position of pensioners thus did not extend to those in receipt of short-term benefits. Changes in supplementary benefit rates have followed a broadly similar path.

In 1979, the Conservative Government decided to repeal the requirement to increase the long-term national insurance benefits in line with average earnings. This decision was implemented in the Social Security (No. 2) Act 1980. For upratings of both long-term and short-term benefits from November 1980 onwards, therefore, the only statutory requirement will be to compensate for price increases. This not only removed the ratchet effect of the 1975 uprating formula; it also deprived pensioners of their legal entitlement to share in rising standards of living as measured by the index of average earnings.

The Social Security (No. 2) 1980 Act made a further change in uprating arrangements. The government wished to bring unemployment and short-term sickness benefit within the tax system and, pending this change, decided that the short-term benefits and invalidity benefit (which, although designed as a long-term benefit, was exempt from tax by analogy with sickness benefit) would, at the next uprating, be increased by '5 percentage points less than would fully reflect forecast price movements'.[38] Similar reductions in the real value of these benefits are to be made in the two following upratings, in 1981 and 1982, and the child dependency addition to national insurance will suffer a similar cut. Retirement and widows' pensions, which are already taxable, are excluded from the 5 per cent cuts. The supplementary benefit rates are excluded, though it is intended that when unemployment benefit is taxed, supplementary benefit paid to the unemployed and to strikers' families should be treated as taxable income. Apart from saving money, the government's main concern was to increase work incentives by reducing the value of benefits for those out of work.

Under pressure from voluntary bodies representing the disabled and from Members of Parliament of all parties, an assurance was given that when invalidity benefit came into tax, it would, subject to the availability of resources, be brought back into line with the basic retirement pension, but no assurance was given on the short-term benefits. The question of how benefits should be adjusted to take account of changes in prices and earnings has certainly not been finaly settled. At a time when both earnings and prices are rising rapidly, the extent to which these changes are reflected in adjustments to social security benefit rates is plainly of crucial importance, both for the adequacy of the benefits and for their relationship with other incomes. The present lack of any coherent policy on this question could therefore have serious consequences.

Future directions for social security policy

One of the few areas of public expenditure which has increased substantially under the present government is social security. This is not in the main because of large-scale improvements in the social security system, but because of a massive increase in unemployment. Some improvements have been made but, by government policy, wherever possible these have been offset by savings in other parts of the system; some of these changes threaten seriously to impair the adequacy of some benefits, though the precise extent to which the process will be carried over the next few years remains to be seen. If resources became available for renewed expansion of the social security system, difficult political choices would have to be made as to the directions in which expansion should take place, and the relative priority to be attached to various possible improvements. It is possible only to pick out some of the more obvious priorities and to suggest some of the aspects of social security policy which require further consideration.

The elderly

The new pension scheme introduced by the Social Security Pensions Act 1975 should, in the long run, greatly diminish the extent of poverty among the retired population. Its effects, however, will be gradual and during the remaining years of this century there will be a growing contrast between the incomes of the younger and older cohorts of pensioners. The growth in numbers of older pensioners will tend to draw attention to their needs and to the larger proportion of them remaining dependent on supplementary benefit for a minimum income. It is arguable that better services for the very elderly should take priority over higher pensions in the allocation of resources. It can also be argued that dependence on supplementary benefit is less objectionable for pensioners than for some other groups. since their needs and resources, once ascertained, normally remain relatively stable. But the fact remains that supplementary benefit, even at the long-term rates for which all those over pension age qualify, provides a relatively low standard of living. It is probable, therefore, that there will be growing pressure for improved pensions for those who are too old to benefit substantially from the new pension scheme. Another way of reducing the number of supplementary pensions over the next few years would be the introduction of a unified housing benefit, as proposed by the Supplementary Benefits Commission. An inter-departmental study of the feasibility of such a benefit has been undertaken and it is expected that the government's intentions will be announced fairly soon. The cost of a viable scheme is likely to be the main obstacle.

As to the future, the standard of living of pensioners will depend increasingly on a combination of state and occupational pensions. There is ample scope for improvements in the occupational sector, especially in the benefits provided for manual workers, and in the preservation of pension rights of employees who leave before pension age.

The unemployed

Of all the groups dependent on social security benefits for their regular income, it is the unemployed for whom existing provision is least adequate and will become still less satisfactory over the next two years. By 1982, the basic unemployment benefit rates will have been reduced in real value by the decision to uprate it by 5 per cent less than the inflation rate in November 1980 and possibly in the two following years; the benefit will be taxed, probably from April 1982; and the earnings-related supplement payable for up to 26 weeks will have been abolished by mid-1982. But even without these cuts, the unemployed fare relatively badly. Unemployment benefit ceases after a year; there is no long-term benefit for the unemployed similar to invalidity benefit for the long-term sick; and they do not even qualify for the long-term supplementary benefit rates which, from November 1980, are payable to other claimants after one year on supplementary benefit.

An urgent priority is thus to improve the situation of the long-term unemployed and of unemployed people with dependent children. For the long-term unemployed, the most promising way forward lies in the direction of a flat-rate benefit, payable at the same rate as the basic retirement and invalidity pensions, accompanied by, on the one hand, more effective job placement and retraining services and, on the other, child benefits at a more adequate level, payable to those in work as well as to the unemployed, to offset fears of loss of work incentive. The restoration of the cuts in the real value of the basic benefit rates made under the Social Security (No. 2) Act 1980 and of the cuts in the child dependency additions are also a high priority. If this were accompanied by the introduction of a unified housing benefit, the proportion of unemployed people who need to have their insurance benefits topped up by supplementary benefit could be reduced to a very low level.

Whatever changes may be made in the insurance benefits provided for the long-term unemployed, there is a strong case for extending entitlement to the long-term rates of supplementary benefit to them, again combined with an increase in child benefit. Indeed, since this could be done quickly and would be far less costly than a comparable non-means-tested benefit for the long-term unemployed, it would seem right to give it a precedence over the introduction of a new long-term unemployment benefit.

One-parent families

For one-parent families, other than widows and their children, the best prospects of improved social security benefits in the short term lie in the child benefit scheme, including the 'premium' for one-parent families, and the supplementary benefit scheme. Child benefit (and family income supplement) help those with earnings and/or maintenance payments which raise them above supplementary benefit level, and if the premium were increased substantially, it would make it possible for more lone parents to earn enough so that they are not dependent on supplementary benefit. For those unable to earn more than a few pounds a week, and not receiving regular and adequate maintenance payments, there is at present no alternative to supplementary benefit and there is little chance of any possible alternative proving to be politically acceptable, partly on grounds of cost. The present trend of government policy is towards allowing lone parents to earn more than other people, while still qualifying for supplementary benefit and this trend could be taken further. Any improvement in provision for children within the supplementary benefit scheme will benefit one-parent families. One such improvement would be the introduction of higher long-term benefit rates for children whose parents qualify for the long-term adult rates.

The sick and disabled

If the government pursues its present intention to make the provision of sick pay by employers compulsory for the first weeks of sickness, it is to employers' sick pay schemes that one must look for improved provision for short-term sickness. A statutory minimum payment at a satisfactory level is essential. In addition, a requirement for employers to pay a high proportion of previous earnings in the early stages of sickness would be in line with the law in a number of other EEC countries and also in line with what many UK employers already do, particularly for their non-manual employees.

With the abolition of the earnings-related supplement and the cuts in the basic rates of sickness benefit (including the child dependency additions), the benefit payable from the point at which sick pay would cease until invalidity benefit commences in the 28th week will be totally inadequate. Hence, as with unemployment benefit, the restoration of the cuts is a high priority and the statutory minimum rate of sick pay should be based on the restored value of sickness benefit, even if no further improvement is initially possible. Further study of the possibilities of an earnings-related benefit to replace employers' sick pay after the statutory period (eight weeks, if the

Green Paper proposal is adopted) is needed.

For the long-term sick and disabled, the priority is to raise the non-contributory invalidity benefit to the full contributory rate, but without the earnings-related element. The study of the possibility of a general disablement allowance, initiated by the Labour Government in 1978, should be resumed and should consider a benefit for partial incapacity, breaking down the rigid distinction between those who cannot work at all and those whose earning capacity is reduced.

Supplementary benefit

Some aspects of the supplementary benefit scheme as it affects particular categories of claimants have been mentioned in the preceding paragraphs. There are some more general issues which demand attention. Of these, the most fundamental is that of the adequacy of the scale rates and the question of future uprating policies.

Whatever view may be taken on the adequacy of the long-term scale rates, the size of the gap between the ordinary and long-term scales is now so great that those subsisting for many months on the ordinary scale rates must, in general, be significantly poorer. So long as both scales are uprated in line with prices, the gap will not grow in real terms and, in principle, the aim should be to reduce it.

The precise effects of the reforms of the supplementary benefit scheme which came into operation in November 1980 are difficult to predict, but it seems certain that there will be a substantial reduction in the availability of lump-sum 'exceptional needs' payments for clothing and other items which are regarded as 'normal requirements'. It will be necessary to monitor closely the impact that this change has, particularly on families with dependent children, and to review the effects of the replacement of discretion by regulation. The new Social Security Advisory Committee constituted under the Social Security Act 1980 could play an important role in drawing attention to the need for such monitoring.

Notes

1 Beveridge, Sir William, *Social Insurance and Allied Services*, Cmd. 6404, (HMSO, London, 1942).
2 Ibid.
3 Ibid.
4 Ibid.

5 Ibid.
6 Ibid.
7 Ibid.
8 Department of Health and Social Security, *Provision for Old Age*, Cmnd. 538, (HMSO, London, 1958).
9 Ibid.
10 See p. 152 for details of later schemes which do recognise disability.
11 11.5 million pension scheme members, *Department of Employment Gazette*, May 1977.
12 Department of Health and Social Security, *Income during Initial Sickness: A New Strategy*, Cmnd. 7864, (HMSO, London, 1980).
13 Ibid.
14 Department of Health and Social Security, *Occupational Pension Scheme Cover for Disabled People*, Cmnd. 6849, (HMSO, London, 1977).
15 *Commons Hansard*, 6 May 1980, Written Answers Cols. 93–94.
16 National Council for One-Parent Families *Information No. 28*. December 1979.
17 Supplementary Benefits Commission, *Annual Report 1978*. (HMSO, London, 1979).
18 Department of Health and Social Security, *Department of the Committee on One-Parent Families* (Finer Report), Cmnd. 5629, (HMSO, London, 1974).
19 *Commons Hansard*, 17 June 1960, Col. 1989.
20 Supplementary Benefits Commission, *Annual Report 1975*. (HMSO, London, 1976).
21 Supplementary Benefits Commission (Northern Ireland), *Annual Report 1978*. (HMSO, Belfast, 1979).
22 Evason, Eileen, *Ends that Won't Meet: a Study of Poverty in Belfast*, (Child Poverty Action Group, 1980).
23 National Assistance Board (Northern Ireland), *Annual Reports 1952, 1953*. (HMSO, Belfast, 1953, 1954).
24 Supplementary Benefits Commission (Northern Ireland), *Annual Report 1976*. (HMSO, Belfast, 1977).
25 Evason, Eileen, *Poverty: the Facts in Northern Ireland*, (Child Poverty Action Group, 1976).
26 *Commons Hansard*, 17 May 1972, Written Answer Cols. 145–6.
27 *Commons Hansard*, 22 May 1972, Written Answers Cols. 281–282.
28 Supplementary Benefits Commission, *Annual Report 1975*, op. cit.
29 Ibid.
30 Department of Health and Social Security, *Social Assistance: A Review of the Supplementary Benefit Scheme in Great Britain*. (HMSO, London, 1978).
31 Supplementary Benefits Commission, *Response of the Supplementary Benefits Commission to 'Social Assistance: A review of the supplementary benefits scheme in Great Britain'*. (HMSO, London, 1979).
32 Ibid.
33 Ibid.
34 Ibid.
35 Department of Health and Social Security, *Reform of the Supplementary Benefits Scheme*, Cmnd. 7773, (HMSO, London, 1979).

36 *Commons Hansard*, Standing Committee F, 17 May 1973, Col. 85.
37 Social Security Benefits Act 1975, Section 4, (HMSO, London, 1975).
38 *Commons Hansard*, 26 March 1980, Col. 1460.

6 Housing and Poverty*

Although two-thirds of all dwellings in the United Kingdom are in private ownership, all housing is profoundly influenced by government policy. Two principles are implicitly recognised: that housing which is considered adequate by current standards should be available to all, in spite of inequality in incomes; and that a free private market cannot achieve this objective without government intervention.

On the other hand, the implicit objective has never been met by a single overall plan for housing, equivalent to those in social security, health or education. The housing system has altered fundamentally in the course of this century as a result of a variety of influences, and policy continues to deal with many problems piecemeal, rather than through major restructuring.

Governments have essentially four housing policy options, although any particular programme may consist of a combination of two or more of these. They can provide housing directly; they can subsidise the owners of housing; they can subsidise the occupiers of housing; and they can introduce legal constraints on the contract between landlord and tenant. All of these options have been used extensively by governments since the war. It is clear that the quantity and quality of housing available to the poor, as well as to others, have been substantially improved, even though there remain problems for certain groups, notably in Northern Ireland, in the private rental sector, among immigrants, and for the single homeless.

In any analysis of housing policy, the theme must consist of a comparison between the three main tenures. The growth of standard quality public housing at moderate rents has been largely successful in breaking the otherwise inevitable link between poverty and squalor. The expansion of the owner-occupied sector has, however, largely benefited middle and higher income groups, and the system of subsidising owner-occupiers by tax relief has reinforced this

* This chapter has been drafted mainly by Richard Berthoud from material provided by Chris Paris and Stewart Lansley.

advantage, to the extent that council housing may tend to be seen as a welfare sector, reserved for the poor. But, with the exception of improvement grants and some rent allowances, the private landlord and his tenant have been excluded from public subsidy; rents have instead been kept low by regulation. The acute scarcity and poor quality of privately rented housing, which lie behind many housing problems, stem directly from the lack of an adequate policy for this sector.

The ownership of housing

Public municipal housing[1] was introduced in 1919 at a time when, it is estimated, nine-tenths of all homes were rented privately, and the remainder were occupied by their owners. By 1960, 42 per cent of the dwellings in the UK were owner-occupied, 26½ per cent rented from public agencies and 31½ per cent rented privately.[2] By 1978, 54 per cent of homes were owner-occupied, 32 per cent were rented from public agencies and 14 per cent were privately rented.[3] These trends have varied over the country – in particular, London has retained a relatively large private rental sector, while Scotland has a very high proportion of public housing (55 per cent). Public housing also tends to be relatively important in the north of England and Northern Ireland.[4]

Within the private rental sector (in Great Britain), 18 per cent of households rent furnished accommodation; 54 per cent unfurnished accommodation from private landlords; 21 per cent hold their accommodation with their job or business; and 8 per cent rent unfurnished from housing associations.[5] Housing rented from private landlords often represents the worst housing in terms of tenants' rights, overcrowding, physical structure and amenities, and value for money. In one sense, its decline is to be welcomed; in another, the shrinkage in this market for families who have been unable to obtain owner-occupied or public accommodation has exacerbated the housing problem.

Housing problems in the United Kingdom

Access to housing

Clearly the first aim of housing policy is that everyone should have a home. Soon after the war, there was an acute shortage of housing in England and Wales where, in 1951, there were 13.3 million households, but only 12.5 million dwellings. The housing stock has, however, grown rapidly, so that by 1976 England and Wales had 18.1 million dwellings for 17.6 million households.[6] In Scotland, the relative surplus is even greater;[7] there are no equivalent figures for Northern Ireland. This gross surplus does not, of course, mean that there is not a scarcity of housing in many localities.

Data also shows that the number of households which share a dwelling has decreased substantially but the problem has not been eliminated; about 6 per cent of households or potential households in England and Wales do not have a dwelling to themselves (Table 6.1). Progress has also been made in Scotland, where half the housing stock has been constructed since 1945.[8]

Table 6.1 Households sharing, 1951–1976, England and Wales

Thousands

	1951	1976[1]
Multiperson households sharing	1,442	275
Single person households sharing	430	375
Married couples or one-parent families living as part of another household	935	360
Total	2,807	1,010

Source: S. Lansley, *Housing and Public Policy*, (Croom Helm, London, 1979).
[1] Estimates

The improvement in the amount of housing space available is also seen in the level of overcrowding: in 1951, 664,000 English and Welsh households lived at over $1\frac{1}{2}$ persons per room; in 1976, the figure was 150,000.[9] Overcrowding, however, remains a problem in certain sectors: while 4 per cent of households (in Great Britain) are assessed as having fewer bedrooms than they require, the figure is 6 per cent in unfurnished rented accommodation (mainly large families in normal-sized homes) and 14 per cent in furnished accommodation (mainly ordinary-sized families in small flats or rooms).[10] In Northern Ireland, where there are many large families, about 17 per cent of all households are at least one bedroom short of standard requirements.[11]

Physical amenities

The quality of the housing stock has also been improving. In 1951, it was estimated that 7.5 million households were living in unfit or sub-standard dwellings (England and Wales); by 1975, the figure was 1.7 million, or 9 per cent of households.[12] In Scotland, in 1977, about 8 per cent of total stock, or 150,000 houses, were sub-standard.[13] Again, Northern Ireland is worst off, with a 1974 estimate of 35 per cent of dwellings in an unsound condition, including 17 per cent which required replacement.[14] While some older owner-occupied properties are sub-standard, and a small proportion of council properties, the private rental sector is very poor in this respect. Only just under three-quarters of households in unfurnished private accommodation in Great Britain have the sole use of a bath or shower and in furnished accommodation less than half have this amenity.[15] The figures for the sole use of an indoor WC are similar.

Housing costs

The costs of housing average 15 per cent of total household expenditure in the UK.[16] Expenditure on housing is, however, inelastic: households in the top 10 per cent of incomes pay about one-eighth of their expenditure on housing; households in the bottom 10 per cent about one-quarter.[17]

The net cost of buying one's home through a mortgage has been calculated at 47 per cent higher than the average net rent of council housing.[18] However, council tenants continue to pay rent throughout their lives, while owner-occupiers have no direct cost of house purchase once the mortgage has been paid off. The full lifetime cost of owner-occupation may, therefore, be lower than the cost of renting, even though the public sector contains none of the large or luxurious homes available for purchase. Private unfurnished housing costs, on average, 14 per cent less than council housing,[19] but is often of a much lower standard. Private furnished accommodation, which very often consists of a room or two, without private bath or WC, costs on average 69 per cent more than council housing.[20]

While the cost of council housing varies with the size and quality of the accommodation, it also varies between local authorities. But it is in the private sector that the variation is widest. For outright owner-occupiers, the actual cost is nil; but for a young family which has just entered the market, housing costs at the present high prices and high interest rates can easily exceed one quarter of their net income. In the private rental sector, the combination of rent control and security of tenure means that many families pay very low rents, but the same forces often mean that the scarce accommodation on the open market is very costly indeed. The highest decile rent of private unfurnished housing has been calculated at 11 times the lowest decile; the equivalent figure for council housing is less than 4 times.[21] In general, families have little choice over their housing costs, which vary not so much in relation to income or size and quality of accommodation, as in relation to the sector of the market, the time at which the family entered the market, and local scarcity. These 'random' variations mean that some low income families are forced to pay very high rents, and can be reduced to poverty in direct consequence.

The incidence of housing disadvantage

The elderly

Largely because they tend to have remained in homes that they entered many years ago, the elderly have a distinctive pattern of housing. Compared with younger families, a high proportion own their own homes outright, or rent from private landlords. Their costs are low, but their homes are often old and in disrepair; lone old people, in particular, often lack the amenities of a private bath (11 per cent compared with 5 per cent of all other households), a private indoor WC (12 per cent compared with 6 per cent) or central heating (60 per cent compared with 46 per cent).

Young people

Young people experience the opposite problem. Coming new to the housing market, they have difficulty in obtaining access. The capital and interest costs of owner-occupation are very high for first-time buyers, especially affecting young couples with low incomes. In many areas, young couples would have to wait years to obtain the tenancy of a council house; privately rented accomodation is very scarce, and available only at high rents. Rent control and rent regulation tend to benefit existing tenants, rather than those seeking a home. Although many single young people share amenities such as bath and WC with others,[22] this is not considered a very serious problem. But young families who have been unable to secure long-term housing can suffer acute problems, especially following family disputes, which lead them to depend on emergency accommodation for homeless families.

Disabled people

A 1968 government survey[23] of disabled people (including the elderly disabled) found that the accommodation for disabled people was not significantly better or worse than for people in general and that a proportion of them had received local authority assistance (under the 1948 National Assistance Act) to adapt their dwellings to their needs. However, some 200,000 households containing a person severely or appreciably handicapped needed some form of modification to their homes and about 150,000 were, in 1968, living in accommodation not best suited to their needs.

The ethnic minorities

Much of the worst housing in Britain is occupied by families who originated in the West Indies or the Indian sub-continent. While a fair proportion of families of West Indian origin have secured council housing (26 per cent), those of Asian origin have rarely done so (4 per cent), and a remarkably large number of Asians (76 per cent) have bought houses, often old and in run-down areas.[24] Table 6.2 summarises some of the differences between the native white and 'coloured' populations.

Table 6.2 Housing and the ethnic minorities, Great Britain 1978

Percentages

	White UK born	'Coloured'
Building built before 1919	26	49
Fewer bedrooms than requirement	4	19
Lack sole use of bath/shower	6	20
Lack sole use of wc	2	16

Source: Office of Population Censuses and Surveys, *General Household Survey, 1978*, (HMSO, 1980)

Geographical variations

The static nature of the housing stock means that housing problems vary substantially between regions and between towns and cities. As with many other aspects of social disadvantage outlined in this report, the pattern of variations between the regions of Great Britain is insignificant in relation to the comparison between Britain and Northern Ireland. Very few houses were built in the Province during the decades between the partition of Ireland and the end of the Second World War.[25] The rate of public sector construction in recent years has been above the UK average, and the problem may be improving[26] but there is much leeway to catch up. Table 6.3 summarises Northern Ireland's housing problem.

Table 6.3 Housing: Northern Ireland compared with Great Britain

Percentages

	Northern Ireland	Great Britain
Dwellings unfit for habitation	20	7
Households entirely without:		
fixed bath/shower	28	9
internal or external wc	11	1
internal wc	27	11
hot water tap	21	6
Households with fewer bedrooms than requirement	18	4

Source: E. Evason, *Poverty: the Facts in Northern Ireland*, (Child Poverty Action Group, 1976).

In Great Britain, much of the housing problem is concentrated in the older inner areas of the great cities. Wholesale slum clearance programmes have improved the situation in many areas, although doubts are often expressed about the quality of life and the habitability of the very large mass-produced estates which replace them. The most notable problems have been in Glasgow, where large slums of 'tenement' housing have not yet been eliminated, and London, where the enormous pressure on the housing market is illustrated by the preservation of much privately rented accommodation, and by a severe problem of homelessness. In an analysis of the worst housing localities in Great Britain (using 1971 Census data), 28 per cent of the total were in Inner London, and 23 per cent in the Clydeside (Glasgow) conurbation.[27]

Housing disadvantage and poverty

Direct analysis of the relation between income poverty and housing disadvantage is confused by the position of the elderly; they – especially single old people – tend to live in old and often inadequate homes, and also have a high risk of poverty. On this basis, there will be a tendency for both poverty and bad housing to affect the same people, even though there may be no direct link between the two problems.

Among the non-elderly, there is a general tendency for the poor to have an above average risk of bad housing. Table 2.19 showed that 37 per cent of the poor, but only 18 per cent of the non-poor, either lacked some private amenities or were overcrowded. But the link is not a very strong one: the great majority (80 per cent) of those with one of these housing problems are not poor, within the definitions applied in Chapter 2. Studies in particular localities have tended to show little correlation between housing disadvantage and poverty.[28]

This is especially likely to be the case in areas dominated by council housing. The great majority of this is of reasonably satisfactory quality, though the environmental quality of many public housing estates is deteriorating. Not only do local authorities provide reasonable housing, they also charge moderate rents, which are supported by a reasonably efficient rent rebate scheme. Council housing, which now accounts for one-third of all accommodation, has been largely successful in breaking the link between poverty and housing problems, which was inevitable in an unfettered private market.

Housing and income problems will, therefore, be found in two types of case. Old people, prone to both housing and income problems independently of each other, form one group. The other group arises when public housing fails to meet housing requirements. While many, mainly elderly, poor families own their own homes, there is little hope now of a poor or nearly-poor family becoming an owner-occupier. In some areas, there is a chronic shortage of council housing; in most areas, council housing is not promptly available to meet the needs of those with immediate requirements. Poverty and housing problems will coincide when the poor are forced to accept sub-standard accommodation in the privately rented sector; or when those with modest means are forced to pay rents so high as to leave them without enough to live on.

General features of housing policy

Public expenditure on housing

It was noted in Chapter 1 that public expenditure in general rose through the 1960s to a peak in 1975, but has since been cut, and further cuts are planned. Expenditure on housing has been particularly sensitive to changes in expenditure, rising more rapidly during periods of expansion, suffering acutely during the period of retrenchment. Detailed figures are shown in Table 6.4.

Many of the figures on housing problems earlier in this chapter suggest that the massive investment of the late 1960s and 1970s has brought about a substantial improvement in UK housing. There remains work to be done, however, and it is equally important to maintain and replace the current stock. On the evidence provided by the public expenditure figures, it would be safe to assume that there is unlikely to be an improvement in the 1980s equivalent to that witnessed in the past 15 years.

Table 6.4 Public expenditure on housing, 1950–1984, United Kingdom

Year	£ billion (1975 prices)
1950–63[1]	1.4
1964–72[1]	2.4
1973	3.5
1974	5.4
1975	4.5
1976	4.5
1977	4.0
1978	4.4
1979	3.4
1980–81	3.0
1981–82	2.4
1982–83	2.0
1983–84	1.8

Sources: Central Statistical Office, *National Income and Expenditure* (various years) (HMSO, London); *The Government's Expenditures Plans, 1980/81 to 1983/84*, Cmd 7841, (HMSO, London, 1980)

[1] Annual averages

Tenure policy

Throughout the postwar period, until 1979, government policy has had the twin aims of developing the stock of public housing, while at the same time encouraging owner-occupation. The two have increased at similar rates: owner-occupation increased by 63 per cent between 1960 and 1978 and public housing by 54 per cent.[29] Although council houses are actually constructed and owned by local authorities, governments have been able to expand this sector more or less directly, through the allocation of public expenditure. There is no direct control over owner-occupation, but governments have sought to encourage private building, and have reduced the cost of house purchase by relieving mortgage interest payments of tax.

Although Labour Governments have had little sympathy for private landlords, there has not been a deliberate policy to reduce the private rental sector. It has declined throughout the century for two reasons: partly, this decline is simply a converse of the expansion of owner-occupation, and a consequence of slum clearance programmes, in which poor quality private housing has been replaced by council building; partly, it has stemmed from improvements in tenants' rights (see p. 193) and control or regulation of rents, which have made it virtually impossible to rent out non-luxury housing at a worthwhile profit. The latter policy has undoubtedly improved the lot of families in rented accommodation, except where landlords have attempted to circumvent the law, but it has meant that families who have been forced to look for privately rented housing now find it extremely difficult.

On the margin between public and privately rented housing lies the housing association – non-profit making bodies providing housing for rent or under co-ownership schemes. These associations have a history going back to 1830, but it was in the early 1960s that governments attempted to encourage them as a means of replacing the private rental sector. The public Housing Corporation provides loan finance, and registers and controls associations, but they still account for only one per cent of all homes[30] and play, at best, a marginal role in the market, helping, in particular, certain special groups such as young single people, the elderly and disabled.

Owner-occupation is undoubtedly the tenure preferred by most families in the United Kingdom. For those now owning their homes, its expansion has clearly been desirable. Meanwhile, council housing has provided satisfactory accommodation for the majority of the remainder of the population. However, the continued expansion of owner-occupation to become the accepted norm may in time place council tenants in the status of a deprived class. This possibility is enhanced by the fact that, as more people in the middle income ranges have bought houses, low income groups have become concentrated in council housing. Thus the median income of council tenants was only 17 per cent lower than the median income of mortgagors in 1953, but 42 per cent lower in 1977.[31] A similar concentration of low income households can be observed in the private rental sector. If the trend towards owner-occupation continues, and if no means is found for allowing low income households entry into this market, rented housing (public and private) will become the preserve of the poor, and will be seen as a form of poverty.

Policies on housing disadvantage

Increasing the stock of dwellings

Table 6.5 shows the rate of new construction and net gains in the public and private sectors since 1951. As noted at the beginning of this chapter, this has yielded a large increase in the stock of dwellings, so that there is now a net surplus.

Table 6.5 *Annual average changes in the stock of dwellings, United Kingdom, 1951–1979*

Thousands

	1951–60	1961–70	1971–74	1975	1976	1977	1978	1979
Public sector								
Construction	189	170	137	167	169	170	136	106
Other changes	– 2	– 26	– 42	7	– 13	nil	– 20	n.a.
Net gain	187	144	95	174	156	170	116	n.a.
Private sector								
Construction	104	198	183	155	155	143	152	136
Other changes	– 57	– 83	– 58	– 79	– 51	– 55	– 22	n.a.
Net gain	47	115	125	76	104	88	130	n.a.

Sources: Central Statistical Office, *Social Trends, 1980,* (HMSO, London); Department of the Environment *Housing and Construction Statistics* (HMSO, London, quarterly)

Public construction depends directly on government decisions, since subsidies and loans to local authorities come from the centre. Private construction depends more generally on the economic and financial climate. It will be seen that both sectors completed very few houses in 1979, compared with previous years. Moreover, only 80,000 public dwellings were started during 1979,[32] so that the 1980 figure of completions will be lower again than 1979.

Improving the quality of homes

In the immediate postwar period, the acute shortage of housing resulting from war damage and the virtual halt in construction since 1939 meant that the priority was to provide new houses. Apart from repairing war damage, little attention was paid to poor quality in the existing stock. But between 1954 and 1973, one and a half million homes were demolished in Great Britain, usually in slum clearance programmes making way for major redevelopment. Large areas of all British cities have been redeveloped, almost always with council housing. Under these schemes, adequate homes were demolished together with the inadequate, but the net effect was a substantial reduction in unfit housing. This programme now appears to be at its end: in 1978, only 43,000 dwellings were demolished or closed in the UK, compared with an estimated 105,000 in 1971.[33]

In the late 1960s, rehabilitation or 'improvement' began to replace slum clearance as the favoured means of dealing with inadequate property. Cash grants are available to owners to cover a proportion (usually 50 per cent) of the costs of raising the property to an adequate standard. Although the grant is paid by the local authority, the cost is borne by central government, so that councils benefit from grants paid for improvements to their own properties. From 1969, local authorities could declare General Improvement Areas where major new investment was required. In Scotland, the broad equivalent was called the Housing Treatment Area. In 1974, Housing Action Areas were introduced where local authorities could use the grant system to take steps to relieve housing stress; in these areas grants were available at 75 per cent of cost or 90 per cent in cases of hardship. Although improvement grants are available on a voluntary basis to existing owners, whether occupiers or landlords, many failed to take them up and some councils and housing associations have acquired property in Housing Action Areas in order to rehabilitate them.

Table 6.6 shows that there was a peak of improvement activity in the early 1970s, caused partly by rates of grant available at 75 per cent of cost in regions of high unemployment (development and intermediate areas). This option terminated in mid-1974, but there has been a slow steady increase in the number of grants approved since 1975.

Table 6.6 Improvement grants approved, United Kingdom, 1971–1979

Year	Thousands
1961	134
1966	117
1971	235
1972	370
1973	456
1974	302
1975	162
1976	171
1977	206
1978	217
1979	231[1]

Source: Department of the Environment, *Housing and Construction Statistics*, (HMSO, London, quarterly).

[1] The 1979 figure is estimated on the assumption that Scotland and Northern Ireland increased at the same rate as England and Wales.

Policy on the costs of housing

Owner-occupiers

Families who own their home outright have no direct housing costs other than for repairs, and receive no financial help from public sources other than improvement grants. The great majority of owner-occupiers, however, obtain a mortgage loan to cover most of the cost of home purchase, repayable over about 25 years. These loans are principally from building societies (non-profit-making associations), who are encouraged and sometimes assisted by government to keep interest rates as low as possible.

Local authorities also offer mortgages, and often favour those unable to secure loans from building societies – for example, those on low incomes trying to buy older, cheaper houses. Councils normally provide about 7 per cent of all mortgage finance, but this figure was doubled during the peak years of 1973 to 1975.[34]

The main government influence, however, is full income tax relief on all interest payments for house purchase by owner-occupiers. This is, in effect, a subsidy, currently 30 per cent for most families, on the loan cost of purchase. Owner-occupied homes are also exempt from capital gains tax. Families whose incomes are so low as not to gain full benefit of income tax relief have been able, since 1966, to take an 'option mortgage', whereby the rate of interest charged by the building society is reduced; a government subsidy to the society makes up the difference. In 1977, 20 per cent of new mortgages were option mortgages, a relatively large proportion of them having been advanced by local authorities.[35]

While there would be little political support for a complete cessation of financial assistance for house-buyers, the present system of tax relief has been criticised as inequitable. Whereas most forms of public help are geared inversely to income, mortgage tax relief is geared positively in two ways: first, the larger the mortgage payments that can be afforded by a family, the greater the tax relief; second, those high income families who pay tax at high rates are relieved of tax at a similarly high rate. It as been shown that this tax relief rose from £59 per annum for couples with an income below £1,000 in 1974/75 to £369 per annum for couples with an income of £6,000 or more.[36] In 1974, a ceiling was placed on the size of mortgage which qualified for tax relief, but this will prevent only the worst disparities; it is estimated that less than one per cent of new mortgages are at or above the current ceiling of £25,000.[37]

Public tenants

Local authority tenants' housing costs are governed by two independent mechanisms: the level of rent, and rent rebates. Local authority tenants have never paid anything like the full cost of their housing. From 1950 to 1971, subsidies covered about one-third of housing expenditure by local authorities and a major part of these subsidies was borne by central government. In 1972 and 1973, subsidies dropped to 27 per cent and 26 per cent, but averaged 42 per cent between 1974 and 1978.[38]

The 1972 Housing Finance Act sought to phase out general housing subsidies and replace them with a system of 'fair' rents supported by rent rebates for poor tenants. It proved exceedingly difficult to determine 'fair' rents, especially in view of the weakness of the private rental market, and the severe restrictions on its rent levels. Under the Act, rents were intended to rise to a level at which the local authority itself (after allowing for its central government subsidy) would make no loss, and would perhaps a profit, on its housing account, even after paying rent rebates. The 1972 Act, repealed in

1974, was replaced in 1975 by the Housing Rents and Subsidies Act, which reduced the ratio of rents to subsidies as the figures quoted above show. The 1980 Housing Act has again revised the system of housing finance. While it does not contain provisions that would, in themselves, affect rents and subsidies, it leaves the Secretary of State in ultimate control, and the government has indicated its intention to raise rents and reduce subsidies over the coming years.

Rent rebates based on a means test had been operated in certain local authorities prior to 1972, when a central system was adopted. About one million public tenants in England and Wales (out of a total of about five million) now receive a rebate, the average rebate amounting to over half of the average unrebated rent.[39] It is estimated that around three-quarters of those entitled to a rebate take it up. In the United Kingdom as a whole, rebates are in effect a subsidy amounting to 12 per cent of total local authority housing costs, to be added to the central government subsidy of 35 per cent and the local government subsidy of 7 per cent.[40] Thus over half the cost of public housing is borne by the state.

Private tenants

While public housing is directly subsidised and the owner-occupier receives an effective subsidy during the period of his loan, the private rental sector receives no subsidies from the public purse other than improvement grants and rent allowances. The latter are roughly equivalent to the rent rebates in the pulic sector: about 200,000 unfurnished tenants in England and Wales receive these allowances, with a take-up rate estimated between 50–55 per cent. In addition, there are 7,000 rent allowances to furnished tenants,[41] with a take-up rate thought to be as low as 10 per cent.[42] The total help given to private tenants in 1977/78 in Great Britain has been calculated at an average of £39 per annum, compared with £290 for public tenants and £199 for owner-occupiers with a mortgage.[43]

As noted earlier, rents in the unfurnished private rental sector are lower than those for council housing. Although much privately rented housing is older and of relatively low quality, the main reason for this is that governments have controlled and regulated rents.

Under rent control, which dates back to the first world war, landlords are virtually prevented from increasing the rent of unfurnished property for the duration of a tenancy. Since this often meant for the lifetime of the tenant and his wife, and sometimes the lifetime of the tenant's children, controlled rents frequently fall well below market prices. Rent regulation, introduced for unfurnished property in 1965 and furnished property in 1974, allows the tenant to register his rent with the local authority Rent Officer, who would ensure that it was 'fair' in relation to other rents in the area. Regulated rents may be reviewed, for an existing tenant, every three years. Since the comparators used in the evaluation of fair rents inevitably includes subsidised council houses, controlled tenancies and other 'fair' rents adjudicated one or two years previously, 'fair rents' have often been lower than the cost of owning and maintaining the dwelling. Moreover, landlords have not been able to convert controlled tenancies (at fixed rents) into regulated tenancies (at 'fair' rents). The consequences have been low rents for tenants, but also deterioration in the fabric of privately rented dwellings, a severe scarcity on the market and attempts by unscrupulous landlords to circumvent the regulations.

The 1980 Housing Act has sought to re-establish the potential profitability of private rental by converting controlled tenancies to regulated tenancies, and increasing the frequency of review of fair rents from three to two years. A more far-reaching provision is for shorthold tenancies, under which landlords will be free to evict after a fixed term contract of one to five years. A further category of 'assured tenancies' will be free of rent regulation and available to 'approved bodies' such as building societies who, it is assumed, will not exploit their tenants. Hitherto, much of the cost of private rental has been reluctantly assumed by landlords. If governments continue to refuse the subsidies to this sector that they offer to owner-occupiers and council tenants, landlords' costs can be relieved only at the expense of their tenants, many of whom are elderly, or poor, or desperately in need of housing.

Supplementary benefit

All of the public policies on housing costs reviewed in the preceding paragraphs are specifically concerned with housing. While tax relief on mortgages will be of little benefit to the poor, low rents in both the public and private sectors will be of general benefit to the poor, since most of the poor are renters. Rent rebates and allowances are directly intended for the relief of poverty; indeed, there is some debate as to whether they should be considered as a form of housing subsidy or a form of income support. The final form of public aid to the housing costs of the poor is outside the housing system. Families whose head is not in full time work who apply for supplementary benefit have their full rent (or mortgage interest payments) included in the calculation of their 'needs'. For them, therefore, supplementary benefit will bear much of, or the full cost of, their housing. In 1979 in Great Britain, the Supplementary Benefits Commission estimated that the annual amount of their outlay for householders' housing costs was approximately £900 million.[44] This figure is substantial in relation to the items more usually considered in calculations of the state's contribution to housing finance.

Policy on security of tenure

Tenants' rights have been transformed in the course of this century. Not only do more than half of all households now own their own homes, but now only those who ren. rooms from a resident landlord can be evicted at will. Security of tenure, which was introduced for controlled tenants during the first world war, was extended to unfurnished tenants in 1965 and to furnished tenants in 1974. Council tenants, who were far less frequently evicted in any case, have received legal security under the Housing Act of 1980. The principal remaining problems in this field occur when unscrupulous landlords evict tenants outside the law, or take advantage of tenants' ignorance of their full rights. It remains to be seen whether the new short-hold tenures introduced in 1980 will give rise to a problem when contracts come to an end.

Housing for special groups

The elderly

The elderly have become recognised as requiring a separate housing policy both because many of them occupy old, sub-standard property and because of their special needs. The rapid increase in the numbers of the elderly, especially of very old people living on their own, has required substantial investment in specialised housing. The number of residents of old people's homes has been rising, and reached 167,500 – about 2 per cent of the elderly population – in the UK by 1977.[45] But provision for old people in the community is preferred and during the 1960s and 1970s, local authorities have been encouraged to build or adapt self-contained accommodation especially for their needs. There are now 466,000 special units for the elderly in England and Wales, half with a resident warden[46]; ten per cent of these are provided by housing associations. But special accommodation still accounts for only 8 per cent of all elderly households[47], and local authorities have varied very widely in the extent of their provisions.

Disabled people

In Great Britain, new legislation in 1970 (the Chronically Sick and Disabled Persons Act) opened the way for more intensive efforts to assist disabled people to adapt their homes to meet their needs and placed a duty on local housing authorities to have regard to the special needs of disabled people when planning housing provision. This Act was extended to Northern Ireland in 1978. Action to implement this legislation has varied widely from one local authority to another across the country and figures available to date suggest that many disabled people must still be living in accommodation unsuited to their needs.[48]

Ethnic minorities

The dual housing problem faced by ethnic minority groups, i.e. relative lack of access to council housing, and owner-occupation of sub-standard property, was examined in the mid-1970s. Two forms of action were taken.[49] First, encouragement of closer liaison between groups representing ethnic minorities and local housing authorities to facilitate a flow of information and assistance through which members of ethnic minorities could acquire council tenures. Second, the programme of housing rehabilitation described on page 188 was in part designed to assist the ethnic minorities who tended to live in run-down inner city areas.

The Homeless

Homelessness has been a persistent problem in the period under review, and the continued decline both of the private rental sector and of hostel accommodation may have made it worse, although it is impossible to measure the size of the problem accurately. Responsibiltiy for homeless persons lay uneasily between different authorities, under various statutes, until the Housing (Homeless Persons) Act 1977 finally placed a clear responsibility on local authority housing departments to provide emergency accommodation and then to rehouse, certain categories of the homeless. For those who can establish a claim under the Act – people with dependent children, pregnant women, and 'vulnerable' people such as the elderly or mentally or physically handicapped – statutory provision is now more satisfactory, although authorities vary in the quality of the emergency accommodation provided. They have varied too in the liberality of their interpretation of eligibility, especially of the 'vulnerable' categories, and of a clause which excludes those who are 'intentionally' homeless. Nearly 54,000 cases were accepted by English local authorities in 1979,[50] most commonly in inner London, but also frequently in Birmingham, Liverpool and Newcastle. Equivalent figures are not available for Scotland or Wales; the Act does not apply in Northern Ireland.

While the Act may have solved the problem of homelessness for many families, it has had little effect on the other half of the problem – the single homeless – for which the provision was already inferior. The Supplementary Benefits Commission operates a declining number of Reception Centres, where single people are offered very limited facilities, plus pocket money. There are nine Centres in London, with 1,175 beds, but only 15 Centres, with 1,307 beds, throughout the rest of Great Britain.[51] There are another 674 hostels and other types of centre, with 31,137 beds, run mainly by charitable and private commercial organisations. But while these various sources provide a bed for the night for people who would otherwise have none, they make little or no contribution to permanent housing of the homeless. Even though many single homeless people are elderly or in very poor health, very few of them indeed are transferred to local authority responsibility under the vulnerability clauses of the Housing (Homeless Persons) Act. The pressure group, Campaign for the Homeless and Rootless, has claimed that there may be as many as 100,000 people in Great Britain without permanent shelter[52]; there is little immediate prospect of a solution to their plight.

Future directions for housing policy

Although there are still substantial housing problems, especially in Northern Ireland, there can be no doubt that the nation's housing is more plentiful, of better quality, and more fairly allocated than it was 30 years ago. This overall housing improvement, which stemmed from economic prosperity and massive public investment has, since the mid-1960s, been combined with specialised publicly-funded programmes directed at the more disadvantaged groups who do not always benefit from more generalised policies.

Present government policy is directed first to the continued expansion of the owner-occupier sector, including steps to confer upon public tenants the right to buy their houses at discounted prices; second, to the improvement of the position of private landlords, in an effort to stem the decline and if possible encourage the expansion of the private rental sector; and third, a massive reduction in public expenditure on housing, mainly aimed at a reduction in new building, but inevitably involving cuts in the specialised programmes for the housing disadvantaged.

It is unlikely that the poor will gain any advantage from an expansion of owner-occupation, given current house prices and interest rates on mortgages. However, this policy, together with council house sales, will accelerate the polarisation of the housing market and the tendency for public housing to become equated with poor people's housing. At the same time, the legislation related to the private rental sector can only hope to have a marginal effect on its long and continuing decline, while it will almost certainly disadvantage poor tenants through increased rents and decreased security.

The poor and housing disadvantaged will remain heavily dependent on public housing and to a lesser extent on housing associations. The severe curtailment of public expenditure on housing must inevitably worsen the position of those dependent on public housing and is likely to lead to an increase in homelessness. At times of severe financial restraint, groups such as the single homeless (the nature of whose problems was at last being recognised) are the least likely to receive attention.

This gloomy scenario could only be changed by a reversal of the decision to single out public housing to bear a disproportionate burden of the general expenditure cuts, and a re-appraisal of the vital role played by the public sector for lower income groups in general and the poor in particular.

At the same time, serious attention should be given to the allocation of public resources across the three housing sectors, including the problem of the exclusion of the private rental sector from a reasonable share in the public subsidy system. Among the subjects to be reviewed would be the rent rebate/allowance system. As indicated in Chapter 5, there is pressure from various sources to develop a unified housing benefit and an inter-departmental committee has been established to examine this proposition. While the government has shown a willingness to upgrade rent allowances (as part of its policy to reduce work disincentives for the low paid) it seems unlikely at present that a unified housing benefit, which is expected to be costly in public expenditure, will be implemented.

Notes

1 In Great Britain, public housing is mostly owned by local government, and is generally referred to as 'council housing'. Housing rented from New Town Development Corporations is also public sector. In Northern Ireland, the Northern Ireland Housing Executive has undertaken responsibility for public housing since 1973.

2 Central Statistical Office, *Social Trends, 1980*, (HMSO, London, 1980).

3 Office of Population Censuses and Surveys, *General Household Survey, 1978*, (HMSO, London, 1980).

4 Central Statistical Office, *Abstract of Regional Statistics*, published annually, (HMSO, London).

5 *General Household Survey, 1978*, op. cit.

6 Lansley, S., *Housing and Public Policy*, (Croom Helm, London, 1974).

7 English, J. and Martin, F. M., *Social Services in Scotland*, (Scottish Academic Press, Edinburgh, 1979).

8 Lansley, S., *Housing and Public Policy*, op. cit.

9 *Census 1951*, (HMSO, London 1951–1956); and Department of Environment, *Housing Policy, Technical Volume II*, (HMSO, London, 1977).

10 *General Household Survey*, 1978. op. cit.

11 Evason, Eileen, *Poverty: the Facts in Northern Ireland*, (Child Poverty Action Group, London, 1976).

12 Department of the Environment, *English House Condition Survey*, (HMSO, London, 1976).

13 English, J. and Martin P. M., op. cit.

14 Evason, Eileen, op. cit.

15 *General Household Survey*, 1978. op. cit.

16 The calculation excludes the cost of servicing a mortgage for owner-occupiers but it includes an 'imputed' rent based on a rough valuation of the property.

17 Department of Employment, *Family Expenditure Survey, 1978*, (HMSO, London, 1979).

18 Lansley S., *Housing and Public Policy*, op. cit.

19 Ibid.

20 Ibid.

21 Ibid.

22 *General Household Survey, 1978*. op. cit.

23 Buckle, J. R. *Work and Housing of Impaired Persons in Great Britain*. (HMSO, London, 1971).

24 Smith, D., *The Facts of Racial Disadvantage*, (PEP, London, 1976).

25 Evason, Eileen, op. cit.

26 Ibid.

27 Holtermann, Sally, *Census Indicators of Urban Deprivation, Working Note No. 6, Great Britain*, (Department of the Environment, London, 1975).

28 Syson, Lucy and Young, Michael, The Camden Survey in Young, Michael (editor), *Poverty Report 1975*, (Temple Smith, London, 1975); and *Inner Area Study Lambeth Second Report on Multiple Deprivation*, (Department of the Environment, London, 1977).

29 Central Statistical Office, *Social Trends, 1980*, (HMSO, London, 1980).

30 *General Household Survey, 1978*, op. cit.

31 Department of Employment, *Family Expenditure Survey*, 1953–54 and 1977, (HMSO, London, 1955 and 1979).

32 Department of the Environment, *Housing and Construction Statistics*, (HMSO, London) quarterly.

33 Ibid.

34 Ibid.

35 Ibid and *Building Society Bulletin* No. 16, October 1978.

36 Department of Environment, *Housing Policy Technical Volume No. 1*, (HMSO, London, 1977).

37 *Housing and Construction Statistics*, op. cit.

38 Central Statistical Office, *National Income and Expenditure 1979*, (HMSO, London, 1979).

39 *Housing and Construction Statistics*, op. cit.

40 National Income and Expenditure 1979, op. cit.

41 Housing and Construction Statistics, op. cit.

42 *Commons Hansard*, 17 February 1975, Written Answers Col. 303–4.

43 Central Statistical Office, *Social Trends, 1979*, (HMSO, London, 1979).

44 Supplementary Benefits Commission, *Annual Report 1979*, (HMSO, London, 1980).

45 *Local Housing Statistics*, August 1980, (HMSO, London).

46 Ibid.

47 *Commons Hansard*, 3 March 1980, Col. 93–95; 5 March 1980, Col. 241–2.

48 Chartered Institute of Public Finance and Accountancy, *Personal Social Service Statistics*, 1979, (CIPFA, London, 1979).

49 Department of the Environment, *Race Relations and Housing*, Cmnd. 6232, (HMSO, London, 1975).

50 *Social Trends, 1980*, op. cit.

51 *Commons Hansard*, 29 October 1979, Written Answers Cols. 442–4.

52 Campaign for Single Homeless People, *Putting an End to the Workhouse*, (London, 1978).

7 Health and Poverty*

THE establishment in 1948 of the National Health Service was a landmark in the history of the development of the health services. Since 1948 services throughout the country have markedly improved, and death rates have fallen in all sectors of society. In spite of this, marked disparities between the health status of social class 1 and social class V remain. Health resources are not well distributed across the country and there is some evidence that social class V families do not utilise the health service in proportion to their high health needs.

The relationship between health and poverty is a complex one and badly needs unravelling. It does seem clear that disparities in health between social classes arise from the whole network of poverty and disadvantage suffered by semi-skilled and unskilled manual workers and their families. Changing this situation requires action not only within the health services, but on working conditions, pollution, housing and social security. In addition certain groups are both poor and have high health service needs, in particular the elderly, disabled people and the single homeless.

Within the health services steps have been initiated to redistribute health resources, in order 'to secure, through resource allocation, that there would eventually be equal opportunity of access to health care for people at equal risk', but the formula on which this redistribution is based is generally agreed to lack elements important to poor people, to inner city areas and, in England, to rural areas. Steps taken to remove barriers to poor people's access to health services have been limited. On the other hand the growth of private health services (now being encouraged by government) will tend to increase health disparities unless the NHS is simultaneously strengthened in those geographical and service areas important to the poor.

Legislation has been passed aimed at improving occupational health and safety but insufficient attention is being given to general working conditions adverse to health and the growth of unemploy-

* This chapter has been drafted mainly by Joan Brown.

ment and general economic insecurity is believed likely to be detrimental to health. In both work and unemployment manual workers suffer the greatest disadvantage. While prevention of ill health is receiving greater attention from policy makers, this area of activity is still under-financed and poorly developed.

Three population groups are most subject to ill health and require social support: the elderly, the disabled and the single homeless. Better programmes for the elderly and the disabled were developed in the 1970s but are now suffering from public expenditure cut-backs. The single homeless remain a seriously neglected group.

In general then, while it has been recognised that the adverse relationship between health and poverty has not been overcome, the substantial action required to investigate and develop programmes to deal effectively with this problem has not been forthcoming. The recent rejection by the government of the Black report on 'Inequalities in Health' suggests that this situation will not change in the near future.

Historical background

Provision for the health care of the poor in the UK developed as health provision generally became established. In the 19th century, free care was available in voluntary hospitals and through the Poor Law hospitals and doctors, while a variety of schemes enabled the worker, through weekly contributions, to purchase the right to medical care. In the first half of the 20th century, the state gradually extended its role. Poor Law hospitals were upgraded, medical inspection of school children was introduced in 1907, provisions for medical care of the elderly were extended after 1908, and maternity clinics and infant welfare programmes developed after 1918. In 1912, a system of national health insurance was established and, by the 1930s, covered 77 per cent of men aged 16–64 and about 40 per cent of the total population of all ages. In spite of all this, serious dissatisfaction was felt about the health care arrangements for the community and, in particular, for the lower income groups.

The National Health Service commenced operation throughout the UK in 1948 and had as its objective the provision of a comprehensive service, available to all regardless of ability to pay and without restriction of age, social class, sex, race or religion. It offered freedom from the fear of being unable to afford treatment for acute or chronic illness and the confidence that, as medical knowledge advanced, its benefits would be made available to rich and poor alike. Three decades later, the National Health Service remains one of the most popular of the national institutions[1] and while arguments about the organisation and financing of a health service have been fierce, the right of poor people to have access to good health care is rarely disputed.

The persistence of health disparities

The relationship between poverty and ill health is a complex one and the absence of health data related to income adds to the difficulties of unravelling it. The available data shows that social classes IV and V, that is semi-skilled and unskilled manual workers, experience the greatest health disadvantage and, as this report has shown, these occupational groups also have the highest incidence of low pay and the greatest vulnerability to unemployment including long-term unemployment (see Chapters 3 and 4). The life-long health disadvantage of social classes IV and V flows through into old age but, in addition, ageing brings both increased income poverty and increased ill-health, which can cut across social class barriers. Social

Table 7.1 Child death characteristics by social class 1975–76, United Kingdom

		Legitimate births: Social class:						Illegitimate births:
		I	II	III	IV	V	Total	Total
Stillbirths	Rate [1]	7	8	10	11	14	10	13
Perinatal deaths	Rate [1]	13	15	18	20	26	18	25
Neonatal deaths	Rate [2]	7	8	9	11	14	10	15
Post-neonatal deaths	Rate[2]	3	3	4	5	9	4	7
Infant deaths	Rate [2]	10	11	13	16	23	14	22

Source: Registrar General Medical Statistics Division, *Perinatal/Child Mortality by Class*, (HMSO, London 1979).

[1] Per 1000 Total Births

[2] Per 1000 Live Births

The social class definitions are as follows: I–Professional; II–Employers and managers; III–Intermediate non-manual and skilled manual; IV–semi-skilled manual; V–Unskilled manual.

classes IV and V are the most likely to suffer chronic illness and disability, but it is also true that disabled and chronically ill persons generally are particularly vulnerable to income poverty. Groups like the single homeless suffer both poverty and ill-health, each reinforcing the other.

In spite of an improvement in many aspects of the health of the country's population, as measured by mortality and morbidity rates, the link between illness, death and social class, clearly evident in 1948, has not yet been broken. Table 7.1 shows child death characteristics in 1975–76. At every stage, at and after birth, the rate for social class V children is twice that of children from social class I.

These disparities persist during childhood. Up-to-date figures for the whole of the United Kingdom are not readily available, but figures for 1970–72[2] for England and Wales show that for boys aged 5–9 years, the mortality rate per 100,000 per year was 27.5 for social class I, but 69.1 for social class V. In the 10–14 age group, the figures were 28.3 and 56.6 respectively. Slightly better but still unsatisfactory rates applied to girls.

Table 7.2 Male standardised mortality ratios for ages 15–64 social class, England and Wales 1959–1963 and 1970–1972

Social Class	1959–1963	1970–1972
I	76	77
II	81	81
III	100	104
IV	103	113
V	143	137

Source: Sir John Brotherston, Inequality – is it inevitable?, in Carter, C. O. and Peel, John, (Eds.) *Equalities and Inequalities in Health*, (Academic Press, London, 1976).

Table 7.2, which uses standardised mortality ratios, shows the changes between 1959–63 and 1970–72 for the 15–64 age group males in England and Wales. Social class V as a whole improved its position somewhat and slightly narrowed the gap between the classes, but there was actually a deterioration in the rates for the 35–54 group of males in the 1960s and, in general, major class disparities remain.

Table 7.3 Chronic and acute illness rates by socio-economic group and sex, Great Britain, 1974.

Rates per 1,000

	Professional	Employers and managers	Intermediate and junior non-manual	Skilled manual	Semi-skilled manual	Unskilled manual	All
Men							
Chronic illness:							
Long standing illness	141	185	226	202	222	308	206
Limiting long standing illness	82	113	147	132	147	225	134
Acute illness:							
Restricted activity in two week period	74	83	99	96	99	111	93
Average number of days of restricted activity per person per year	10.8	14.2	14.5	18.6	18.3	23.2	16.8
Women							
Chronic illness:							
Long standing illness	154	176	222	198	280	314	224
Limiting long standing illness	93	115	143	124	198	229	150
Acute illness:							
Restricted activity in two week period	94	88	104	96	108	115	99
Average number of days of restricted activity per person per year	14.2	17.0	18.4	17.5	10.5	21.4	18.3

Source: Office of Population Censuses and Surveys, *The General Household Survey 1974*. (HMSO, London 1977). Presented in Walters, Vivienne. *Class Inequality and Health Care*. (Croom Helm, London, 1980).

Useful morbidity data by social class is harder to obtain. The General Household Survey in Great Britain collects information about self-identified acute and chronic illness. Table 7.3 shows the same pattern of class-based health disparity.

The statistical evidence for social disparities in health status can be criticised on a number of grounds, but the fact that all the available evidence points in the same direction cannot fail to impress and the persistence of considerable disparities in health status by social class is now generally acknowledged by the major health authorities to be a matter for considerable concern.

Policies to deal with the problem of class based health disparities and other issues of health status and poverty have been rather slow to develop. In the first two decades following the establishment of the National Health Service and the setting up of the welfare state, it was assumed that, given time, health inequalities would steadily diminish. Since the late 1960s and particularly during the 1970s, concern has grown about the persistence of these disparities and attempts made to identify the cause of the problem and to devise policies to overcome it. In addition, certain groups have been identified as particularly in need of supportive health and social services.

Policies to reduce health disparities – the reallocation of health resources

Resource allocations and the NHS

While the establishment of the National Health Service in 1948 was a landmark in the provision of health services in the UK, it did not involve the creation of a new health service where none had existed before. The NHS took over an existing structure and built upon it and in so doing, inherited the considerable disparities in the distribution of health care facilities and manpower which had grown up over many decades. From the beginning, there was a desire to distribute health resources more equitably across the country. However, the first task was to upgrade existing services to a reasonable level and to maintain the high standard facilities already available. Substantial improvements were made throughout the country so that within the first decade the benefits of the new NHS were felt by all, but much less impact was made on disparities between different regions of the country.

From 1958 to 1974, there was a threefold division within the health services – Regional Hospital Boards, general practitioner services and local authority health services – each with different boundaries and systems of financing. Allocations to the Regional Hospital Boards (RHBs) were made broadly in proportion to their expenditure for the last year for which figures were available. Thus, given that the RHBs started on an unequal footing, they inevitably finished unequal. Since special account was taken of the need to maintain high standards in teaching hospitals, regions with a number of these hospitals tended to emerge better off. In addition, the system was slow to take account of population changes so that areas with a growing population suffered in comparison with those experiencing population decline.

Local authority health services were funded through local rates and the national rate support grant. These services developed according to local priorities within national guidelines. This method also

Table 7.4 Ratio of revenue expenditure per capita by region, 1971–1972, England

Per cent of mean

		Community Health Services		
Region[1]	Hospital services	Local authority	GP services	Total
S.W. Metropolitan	141	117	110	130
N.W. Metropolitan	134	112	112	126
S.E. Metropolitan	111	106	106	109
N.E. Metropolitan	110	106	89	104
Liverpool	107	96	101	104
South Western	96	98	106	99
Leeds	96	92	97	96
Newcastle	91	100	98	94
Manchester	91	100	99	94
Oxford	90	103	97	93
Wessex	86	91	104	91
Birmingham	85	94	93	88
East Anglia	82	87	98	87
Sheffield	77	92	93	83

Source: Presented in Culyer, A. J. *Need and the National Health Service*. (Martin Robertson, London, 1976), (drawn from Noyes et al, *The Lancet*, 30.3.74).

[1] Pre-1974 Health Regions

produced uneven results, though markedly less uneven than the distribution of hospital services.

Limited impact was made on the distribution of general practitioner (GP) services. Restrictions placed on the establishment of new practices in areas designated as over-doctored and financial inducement given to doctors to practice in less popular areas, had some effect. Redistribution also occurred through the importation of overseas trained doctors.[4] However, by 1973, there had been no dramatic shift in the location of general practitioners.[5]

Overall, the combined effect of historical inequalities, the inevitable inertia built into any massive structure, the methods of financing, demographic drag and lack of policy initiatives was that by 1970, over 20 years after the founding of the NHS, the regional disparities existing in 1948 remained largely intact. Table 7.4 illustrates the position in England in 1971–2. Similar disparities were evident within the Scottish, Welsh and Northern Ireland regions. Indeed Hart, in 1971, suggested there was an 'inverse care law' operating which ensured that the availability of good medical care tended to vary inversely with the need for it in the population served.[6]

In 1974, the health services were reorganised. The country was divided into Health Regions (14 for England and a single region each for Scotland, Wales and Northern Ireland – see Map 4), which were in turn subdivided into Areas and Districts. The new Regional Health Authority was to be responsible for all the health services in its geographical area, and this opened the way for a new approach to resource allocation.

In 1975, a Resource Allocation Working Party (RAWP) was established to recommend how financial resources should be shared between the English regions and, subsequently, parallel working parties were established for Scotland, Wales and Northern Ireland.[7]

RAWP (England) stated as its goal 'to secure, through resource allocation, that there would eventually be equal opportunity of access to health care for people at equal risk' and the other committees endorsed this. Allocation criteria based on previous financing or existing supply were to be abandoned. Instead, decisions were to be needs based. For the allocation of revenue, a formula was produced using population adjusted for age, sex, fertility and marital status and by standardising mortality ratios. Adjustments were made for cross boundary flow of patients and the high costs of providing services in London. Separate allowance was made for part of the costs of

Regional Health Authorities in the United Kingdom: Effective from 1974

Map 4

teaching hospitals. Capital allocations were to be made on a population basis. Similar criteria were to be taken into account by Regional Health Authorities when they in turn allocated funds to areas and districts.

Scotland, Wales and Northern Ireland largely accepted this formula, but made adaptations to meet local needs, including the introduction of a sparsity factor to deal with the problems presented by widely scattered rural and island populations. Northern Ireland, where health and social services are integrated under four Health and Social Services Boards, made the necessary adjustments to meet this special factor.

The result of the calculations based upon the formula was the identification of a number of regions in England and areas or health boards in Wales, Scotland and Northern Ireland, which were relatively over or under-resourced. Figure 7.1 illustrates the position in England. All four working parties were conscious of the problems which would be experienced in any progress towards greater parity, even spread over a number of years. Lead time would be needed, both for cuts and for improved services while, at the same time, plans already underway, including partially completed buildings, could not easily be halted and the growth of the elderly population was everywhere creating new demands. Clearly, the process of change

Effects of proposals on revenue allocations for England 1977/78 (assuming 1.5% national growth). Chart illustrating relationship to target allocation in each health region.

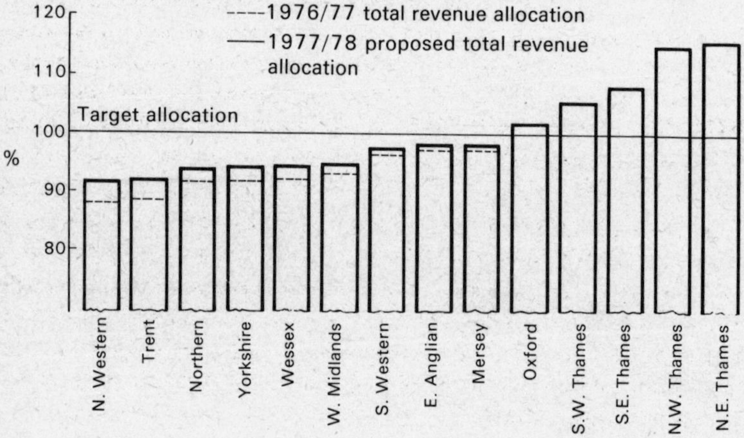

Figure 7.1

would be affected by the overall level of resources made available; the more the resources, the less painful the process. From 1977 onwards, as governments began to implement the RAWP formula, the funding situation deteriorated. In the event, the cries of anguish from relatively over-resourced regions experiencing the effects of RAWP have been drowned by the much greater outcry about overall cuts.

If the RAWP formula could be given a just trial, would it help to reduce the social class based health disparities? Any fairer sharing of resources across the country ought to offer some benefit to deprived groups. Unfortunately, the likely advantages of the new arrangements are reduced because of weaknesses in the formula. It will be noted that morbidity rates do not form part of the formula. All the working parties were concerned about this and searched for a satisfactory way of taking account of morbidity, which they recognised had a more significant social class base than mortality data. No satisfactory formula was found and standardised mortality ratios were accepted as the next best thing. The working parties recommended further attempts to arrive at a satisfactory formula, not only for morbidity but, if possible, other factors related to poverty. In addition, while progress is being made in equalising resources across regions, less progress is evident in achieving equitable allocations within regions, so that more deprived areas and districts do not always receive an appropriate share of available funds.[8]

The difficulties of applying the RAWP formula have been most notable in relation to major cities classified as over-resourced and therefore subject to reduced growth at the very least and, in the present climate, to cuts. Their very vocal complaints have tended to be interpreted as a selfish desire to maintain their favourable position. However, it may well be that part of the difficulty is the failure of RAWP to take into account deprivation factors which related particularly to crowded cities. This led to a suggestion that RAWP should have included a 'conurbation factor', to take into account concentrations of social deprivation in parts of the major cities.[9] In particular, concern has been expressed at the level of health provision available in inner city areas. The Royal Commission on the National Health Service considered that, in some parts of London, the NHS was 'failing dismally to provide an adequate primary care service to its patients' and it drew attention to studies suggesting a relationship between adverse social conditions in other inner cities and health problems.[10]

Table 7.5 National comparisons of resources and standardised mortality ratios, United Kingdom

	Population	Expenditure: 1975/76 £ per capita					SMRs (UK + 100) 1976	
	1976–000's	Hospital services	Community health services	Family practitioner services	Capital expenditure	Total[1]	Male	Female
England	46,418	54.21	5.61	19.11	7.15	92.64	98	98
Wales	2,767	55.37	6.18	21.03	8.35	97.98	106	102
Scotland	5,205	69.11	5.98	19.46	8.18	112.26	112	108
Northern Ireland	1,538	67.82	6.12	22.04	8.52	114.56	111	112

Sources: Regional Statistics No. 13, 1977, (HMSO, London).
Presented in Buxton, M. J. and Klein, C. E. *Allocating Health Resources: A Commentary on the Report of the Resource Allocation Working Party*. Research Paper No. 3 for Royal Commission on the National Health Service. (HMSO, London, 1978).

[1] Includes 'headquarters administration' and 'other services' not shown separately.

The Inner Cities Programme (see Chapter 9) has, since 1977, allocated additional resources for the improvement of conditions and services (including health) in declining inner city areas. In some areas which are part of regions designated as over-resourced by RAWP but which nevertheless received Inner Cities monies, it may be seen as operating against RAWP and this anomaly further illustrates the uncertainty about the level of health resources which ought to go to the major cities on the grounds of social deprivation.

One other issue related to RAWP is the fact that, while each of the working parties discussed how funds should be allocated within its part of the United Kingdom, there was no review of the way funds were distributed between England, Wales, Scotland and Northern Ireland. There are, in fact, quite marked differences, as illustrated by Table 7.5. The Royal Commission pointed out that, while these disparities might well be justified, for example on the grounds of morbidity, mortality or social deprivation data, they had not been explained and that a formula for the distribution of funds within the United Kingdom as a whole ought to be developed.[11]

Private health care

Private health care has existed both within and alongside the NHS from the beginning. Provision was made in 1948 for the continued existence of a limited number of 'pay beds' in NHS hospitals, whilst doctors and dentists practising in the NHS (including hospital consultants) could continue to combine this with private practice and large numbers did so. In addition, some private hospital provision remained.

In the 1970s there was considerable controversy about private provision within the NHS. Claims were made that ability to pay enabled private patients to obtain earlier admission to hospital than others on the waiting list, including those in more urgent need of care. At the same time, there was a growth in the provision of private hospital beds outside the NHS.[12]

Access to private health care is not restricted to the rich. Membership of provident associations (or private health insurance) brings private care within the reach of individual middle income earners, while group and company membership, including union-negotiated agreements, helps to bring such benefits further down the socio-economic scale. In 1978, there were 1.12 million subscribers to provident schemes, of which 869,000 were members of group schemes. Subscriptions often cover more than one person and it is estimated that 2.39 million people were covered in 1978.[13] Details of the occupational and income levels of those covered are not available. However, in spite of the number of group schemes, it would be surprising if many lower income group families were covered.

In 1976, machinery was established, in the shape of the Health Services Board, to arrange an orderly phasing out of NHS pay beds and to exercise some control over the provision of private hospitals. The Royal Commission on the National Health Service considered this machinery was working satisfactorily and took the view that the private health sector was not sufficiently large to constitute a threat to the NHS, though it might be a problem in some localities.[14] The present government has abolished the Health Services Board and indicated it saw no objection to the further growth of the private sector.

The private health services argue that they are not taking money away from the NHS, since their contributors pay the taxes which support the NHS as well as finding additional resources to pay for private care. Moreover, by providing private facilities, they take some pressure off the NHS. Opponents argue that the NHS is subsidising private care by allowing it access to expensive NHS services, such as radiology and pathology, and because private health services provide no training facilities for health staff, but recruit staff trained by the NHS and needed by the public service. There seems little doubt that further growth of the private sector will strengthen the position of higher socio-economic groups as health care consumers and must have the effect of increasing health disparities unless the NHS takes strong measures to upgrade the position of the lowest groups. Such measures are not likely to be possible in times of public expenditure cuts.

Policies to reduce disparities – improving the utilisation of the NHS by low income patients

Data from the General Household Survey suggests that the lower socio-economic groups make less use of the health services in proportion to their needs, as evidenced by morbidity rates, than do the higher socio-economic groups. Table 7.6 giving data for Great Britain in 1972, illustrates the point. Other evidence from the late 1960s and early 1970s shows that under-use of the health services by social classes IV and V extends to ante-natal care, immunisation of children and the use of a range of child health services.[15]

A variety of explanations has been offered to show why the lowest social classes, though having the greatest health needs, nevertheless appeared to be under-utilising the NHS. These explanations can be divided into a number of broad groups.

First are the explanations related to alleged nature of lower class consumers of the health services. It has been suggested, for example, that poorer people are more stoic or resigned about poor health than more affluent groups; that poorer families are more crisis-oriented and therefore will use medical facilities for acute illness, but will do so less for chronic conditions or preventive programmes; and that lower educational levels makes people less well equipped to deal with complex services.

A second group of explanations relates to the costs of health care which occur even though there is no charge for consultation or treatment. While higher socio-economic groups can usually take time off for visits to the doctor without loss of pay, manual workers will usually suffer a loss of income unless facilities are available outside working hours. They are also less likely to have favourable employer-provided sick pay arrangements than non-manual workers. Costs

Table 7.6 Consultation Indices comparing the prevalence of chronic handicapping illness with general practitioner and hospital outpatients consultation rates, Great Britain, 1972

	General practitioner index[1]		Hospital outpatient index[2]	
Social class	M	F	M	F
I	1.20	2.03	1.29	1.56
II	1.01	1.34	0.99	1.08
IIInm	0.91	1.29	1.02	1.05
IIIm	0.84	1.20	0.93	0.84
IV	0.75	0.76	0.66	0.58
V	0.59	0.69	0.63	0.49

Source: Blaxter, M. 'Social Class and Health Inequalities' in Ed. Carter, C. O. and Peel, John, *Equalities and Inequalities in Health*, (Academic Press, London, 1976). (Data from General Household Survey, 1972).

[1] Rate per 1,000 people of general practitioner consultations in a two-week period/prevalence rate per 1,000 people of chronic handicapping illness.

[2] Rate per 1,000 people of hospital outpatient consultation in a three-month period/prevalence rate per 1,000 people of chronic handicapping illness.

may be incurred for transport to and from health facilities, especially where such facilities are poorly distributed between more affluent and poorer areas. All of these factors are thought to deter poorer families from seeking non-urgent health care.

In the third group are conclusions about the nature of the NHS itself which, it is suggested, is better oriented to middle class than to working class patients, perhaps because of the predominantly middle class recruitment to the profession. Studies have shown that the length and content of general practitioner consultations varies between middle and working classes, with the former receiving longer periods of attention with greater clinical content than the latter and, as Table 7.6 showed, more middle class patients are referred by their GPs to outpatient consultants than working class patients (referral by a doctor being a prerequisite).

Suggested solutions to these identified problems have in the past been vague and generalised. The generally agreed goal is straightforward enough. Although it is accepted that the NHS is not responsible for society's inequalities and multiple deprivations which tend to produce low health status, the service should nevertheless function in a way that ensures that the greatest need is matched by the highest standard of service, so that the inequalities might be compensated for as far as possible. Suggested improvements have included more health education, more women doctors, a tier of less highly qualified medical and other staff (health visitors, district nurses, social workers) who would concentrate on deprived families, more health centres with the full range of diagnostic and care facilities in poorer areas, surgery hours which did not clash with hours of work; more effort to recruit non-middle class entry to the medical profession, and selection of target zones for special programmes.

In 1977, the government established a working group to advise on health inequalities. It reported in 1980 (the Black Report)[17] and confirmed and reinforced the findings of earlier studies. It recommended a significant shift throughout the country in NHS and social services resource allocation to strengthen health and welfare services for mothers and pre-school and school-age children, in order to reduce health disparities through the new generation. In addition, it proposed that additional funds for a more broadly based programme should be allocated to ten special areas selected because they had the highest mortality rates.

Among the measures proposed to upgrade the health of mothers and children and to increase the utilisation of services were the introduction of a non-means tested scheme for free milk for infant children; a review of the accessibility and facilities of all ante-natal and child health clinics and the development of plans to increase utilisation by mothers, particularly in the early months of pregnancy; a revitalised school health service linked with general practice; and improvements in the deployment of general practitioners, community nurses and health visitors. The present government has indicated that it cannot at present implement the recommendations of this report.

Policies to reduce disparities – improved conditions of work for manual workers.

An official inquiry into safety and health at work, reporting in 1972 (the Robens report), wrote: 'Every year something like 1,000 people are killed at their work in this country. Every year about half a million suffer injuries in varying degrees of severity. Twenty-three million working days are lost annually on account of industrial injury and disease'.[18] There had been no lack of legislative activity to attempt to improve workers' safety and health. The Robens Committee considered, in fact, that there was too much law, much of it unsatisfactory, and too many administrations involved.[19] Additional legislation existed in Northern Ireland. After the publication of the Robens report, a new Health and Safety at Work Act was passed for Great Britain in 1974. The 1974 Act (largely followed by a Northern Ireland Order in 1978) established the Health and Safety Commission, supported by a Health and Safety Executive, responsible for all aspects of health and safety at work. In addition, the protection of health and safety law was extended to more than 7 million workers who had not been covered previously.

Evidence on occupational accidents shows that manual workers from social class V have the highest mortality rate, followed by skilled manual workers and semi-skilled workers from social class IV.[20] An examination of 1979 data on days of certified incapacity and numbers of deaths attributed to injury at work in relation to lowest decile wage levels does not show a straightforward relationship between pay and risk.[21] However, lower paying industries which employ large numbers of manual men rank fairly high on industrial injury and death. High rankings for industrial injury include construction (ranked 2nd), transport and communications (3rd), distributive trades (5th), public administration (7th) and miscellaneous services (9th). High rankings for deaths include construction (2nd again), transport and communications (3rd), agriculture (4th), textiles (5th) and the distributive trades (7th). These figures relate to both manual and non-manual workers, but as the accident mortality statistics suggest, the probability is that manual workers are over-represented in these statistics.

Since its establishment, the Health and Safety Executive has developed a vigorous programme to reduce occupational accidents and illness. So far this has not shown up in markedly lower figures and this is in part due to the extended coverage of the legislation (by 7 million workers) and in part to more efficient reporting systems. The necessary machinery for improved health and safety is in place, though there is some fear that its effectiveness may be undermined by public expenditure cuts.

A survey undertaken by Townsend in 1968–69 (and reported in 1979)[22] investigated a number of elements of work deprivation, some of which may have an adverse influence on the health of the worker. Townsend found, for example, that 63 per cent of unskilled manual workers in his sample worked mainly outdoors and 89 per cent spent all their working time standing or walking about. Of these, 47 per cent had poor or very poor working conditions, including such factors as lack of a dry and warm place to shelter in heavy rain, lack of a safe and dry place for a coat or change of clothing, no facilities for washing and no lavatory. On all the criteria investigated, the position of the unskilled manual worker was substantially worse than that of non-manual workers and rather poor in comparison with semi-skilled and skilled workers.

This problem has received little attention over the years from governments or from the union movement. The 1980 Black Report on health inequalities drew attention to the need to upgrade the working conditions of manual workers and proposed action by government departments and agencies, the trade unions and industry to draw up minimally acceptable and desirable standards of work, security, conditions and amenities, pay and welfare or fringe benefits.[23]

It has been suggested by Brenner[24] on the basis of studies undertaken in the United States and in England and Wales, that the relative lack of financial and employment security of the lower socio-economic groups is a major source of their higher mortality and morbidity rates. He puts forward the view that economic insecurity, in particular recessions followed by rapid economic growth, leads to dislocation in the lives of certain vulnerable groups (for example, unskilled workers or workers whose skills are no longer needed) which in turn produces earlier mortality. The overall effect is not so much a rise in the national mortality or morbidity rates, but a deceleration of a downward trend which would otherwise have taken place. If this is correct, the present severe economic insecurity which is particularly affecting manual workers (see Chapter 4) will lead to an increase in class-based health disparities.

Policies to reduce disparities – prevention

The question of prevention is important in the discussion of health and poverty for several reasons. First, the incidence of income poverty among sick and disabled people (see Chapters 4 and 5) makes it highly desirable to prevent sickness and disability wherever possible. Second, there is evidence[25] that many preventable conditions are disproportionately suffered by social classes IV and V and third, these social classes[26] make lower use of such preventive services as are available.

Generally speaking, preventive services have been deficient in the UK both inside and outside the health service. Within the NHS prevention has always received the lowest priority in funding. While some successes could be charted (for example, the conquest of poliomyelitis), there were other areas where the evidence suggested that more could be achieved, given concentrated attention and additional funding. Of particular concern has been the question of perinatal mortality and perinatal injury. There is little dispute about the fact that perinatal mortality in the United Kingdom is still unnecessarily high. There is additional concern about the higher incidence of perinatal mortality in social classes IV and V than in Class I–III (see Table 7.1). Perinatal mortality is also unevenly distributed across the United Kingdom, with certain areas having higher than average rates, often linked with concentrations of social inequalities.[27] Recent reports have suggested there were 5,000 preventable perinatal deaths each year and 5,000 babies who survived with 'important handicaps' which could have been prevented,[28] and that a concentrated effort was needed to ensure that mothers from the lower socio-economic groups utilised ante-natal services.[29]

The 1970s have seen an attempt by government to place greater emphasis on the prevention of ill health and disability and, at the same time, a number of community organisations have engaged in both public education and pressure on government to improve preventive measures. Matters under discussion during this period have included the prevention of road and home accidents, the reduction of smoking, improvement in immunisation programmes, pollution problems and the question of perinatal handicap. However, while there is now a general commitment to upgrade preventive activity, this has not so far produced an equal commitment either to devote additional resources to these programmes or to shift the balance of resource allocation in the relevant departments.

Policies for special groups

The Elderly

The proportion of the UK population aged 65 and over will have increased from 11 per cent in 1951 to 15 per cent in 1981. While there will be 51 per cent more elderly (aged 65 and over) in 1981 than in 1951, the increase in the very elderly (aged 75 and over) is even more marked - 149 per cent between 1951 and 1981, and an anticipated further increase by 1991.

It hardly needs saying that health problems tend to increase with age. Other chapters have shown that a substantial proportion of the elderly are poor or near poor. However, an unequivocal connection between poverty and ill-health in old age should not be taken for granted. The illnesses and disabilities of old age are no respecters of income or social class. Clearly the health disadvantages of earlier years flow through into the retirement years, but the social class gap closes in old age as class differentials are overtaken by the common effects of the ageing process.[30]

All of the elderly may at some time require additional health and support services because of their health and mobility problems. The poor elderly clearly cannot afford to purchase these services and must therefore rely on the NHS and, if they live alone, on the Social Services Departments for assistance.

The elderly are by no means the best serviced group in the National Health Service. In the hospital services, they suffer, along with other chronically ill groups, from an under-allocation of resources by the NHS and the persistent staff recruitment difficulties for these less popular specialties.[31] Income and social class do not appear to be the prime determinants of service, though a higher income may enable an elderly person to purchase better institutional health care when long-term hospital or nursing home care is required. The level of community medical care (doctors, district nurses, chiropodists, etc.) is fairly good and most differences in access for the elderly are related to maldistribution of services rather than to social class bias.[32]

Elderly people, particularly the very old living alone, also require support services to maintain their health and social well being. The most important of these are home helps and provision of meals. Studies in 1968 and 1970[33] indicated the need for a substantial expansion in the home help and meals services, whether offered to the poor elderly free or at a reduced cost, or to better off elderly at full cost.

The 1970 Local Authority Social Services Act provided for the reorganisation of the personal social services in local government Social Services Departments (Social Work Departments in Scotland, and Health and Social Services Boards in Northern Ireland). The new departments were encouraged by DHSS to upgrade the home help and meals services for the elderly and others in need. A considerable expansion in both services took place; the level of home help to the elderly grew from 67 per 1,000 people over 65 years in 1971–72 to 95 per 1,000 in 1978–79. However, part of this expansion was achieved by reduction in the number of hours devoted to each elderly person; most help goes to the very elderly. Meals services were also expanded by half and, in late 1978, were being received by about 80 per 1,000 elderly.[34] Under the current programme of public expenditure cuts, expansion has now largely ceased. Cuts in services are being made in some areas and charges for both services are being increased. (The disabled elderly also received assistance under the Chronically Sick and Disabled Persons Act of 1970, which will be discussed later.)

A special health problem of the elderly is accidental hypothermia, i.e. low body temperature caused by external cold. This is a potentially fatal condition which affects, in particular, the very young and the very old. A study undertaken in 1972 estimated that some 700,000 old people in the UK were 'at risk' of hypothermia at the time of the survey.[35]

Although it might be assumed that low income leading to the lack of adequate home heating, winter clothing and blankets would be an important factor in the incidence of hypothermia risk, the relationship is not a straightforward one. Not all low income elderly have inadequate heating. Public housing is often centrally heated, while better off elderly owner-occupiers may live in large homes which are difficult to heat. Not all elderly persons living in cold conditions, with or without adequate incomes, are at risk of hypothermia. However, the survey found that the most vulnerable were the very old dependent upon supplementary benefit income and suggested that a combination of declining physiology and the most deprived social conditions greatly increased the likelihood of an old person becoming a hypothermic. The cost of fuel is a major contributory factor. In the winer of 1975/76, the Inspectorate of the Supplementary Benefits Commission reported that many supplementary pensioners were unduly restricting their heating because they were worried about high fuel costs, leading not only to risk of hypothermia, but also to increased vulnerability to potentially dangerous illness such as bronchitis and influenza.[36]

The problem of hypothermia among the elderly has been approached mainly through various forms of fuel benefit (see Chapter 9). Social Services Departments also have powers to assist with aids and appliances, additional blankets and certain home adaptations, but do not always make full use of these powers.[37]

Disabled people

Disabled persons are particularly vulnerable to income poverty. As suggested earlier the incidence of deprivation among disabled people makes it highly desirable to prevent disability wherever this is possible and there is also a need to ensure that where disability has occurred, effective services which minimise the effects of disability are available, and that support services are offered to disabled people in the community.

Rehabilitation services for disabled people have come under criticism by a number of committees of inquiry, including the Tunbridge Committee in 1972.[38] Its report expressed concern at 'the failure on the part of administration, the medical and para-medical professions and the general public to appreciate the importance of effective rehabilitation'. The rehabilitation content of medical education was regarded as inadequate, thus perpetuating the problem. Poor liaison between different elements of the health services led to disjunctions in the patients' programme and to a gap between the completion of the main medical rehabilitation programme and the commencement of the employment rehabilitation programme provided by the Department of Employment.

While some forward steps have been taken in medical education and the provision of facilities, many of the inadequacies identified by the Tunbridge Committee in 1972, and by reports before and since, remain untouched. Follow-up studies still show that the rehabilitation needs of the majority of patients are not considered while they are in hospital and gaps between hospital and community medical and social services and vocational rehabilitation remain.[39]

The slow pace of change reflects the overall bias in the medical profession and the health services towards acute care and the relative neglect of those with chronic conditions. Expenditure cuts are likely to have a further adverse effect on these services.

Support services for disabled people living at home were particularly poorly developed prior in 1970. Provision for these was made in the National Assistance Act in 1948. Local authorities were to establish a register of sick, disabled and handicapped, and could provide both registered and non-registered individuals with a range of services. A survey undertaken in Great Britain in 1969–70[40] found only 5.2 per cent of disabled and handicapped persons were registered and 82 per cent had no knowledge of the existence of the register. In all, some 30 per cent received regular medical or social service help. Seventy-five per cent of those classified as 'severely handicapped' had received assistance of some kind, but regular assistance was available to only 45 per cent of the 'severely handicapped' and 33 per cent of the 'appreciably handicapped'. No survey was undertaken in Northern Ireland, but other reports suggested an equally unsatisfactory situation, with low registration levels and limited service.

The passage of a private member's bill which finally emerged as the Chronically Sick and Disabled Persons Act in 1970 was hailed as a considerable step forward in the position of disabled people in Great Britain. The Act was not extended to Northern Ireland until 1978. The CDSP Act placed a duty on all local authorities to inform themselves of the number of disabled people in their area and to provide services such as aids and adaptions in the home or to the house, provision of meals, holidays, radio and television, telephone, transport and assistance to take part in recreational or educational activities.

While the high hopes raised by the Act have by no means been fulfilled, it has resulted in an increase in the level of services for disabled people. The weakness of the Act lies in the failure of many local authorities to take proper steps to identify disabled people in their area[41] and the extent to which they have chosen to provide for disabled people within their budgets. Expenditure per head has varied widely between local authorities.[42] The lengthy delay in extending the Act to Northern Ireland was a cause for great concern. In Northern Ireland, a full scale house to house survey in the Province is underway to identify disabled people.

In 1980, cuts in social services budgets are affecting the level of services under the CDSP Act in many areas, though some local authorities have held their expenditure under this head at 1979 levels and a few have actually increased it.

Homeless people

Homelessness, especially among single people, shows a clear connection with poor physical and mental health. Wood says: 'There is a marked prevalence of ill health among (the single homeless); they live in gross material poverty and they are cut off from their families'.[43]

The voluntary organisation CHAR (Campaign for the Homeless and Rootless) reports that homeless single people commonly suffer from chronic bronchitis and tuberculosis. In addition, only a minority of single homeless people are registered with a general practitioner, many have tried to register and been refused, and up to half the facilities provided for them had no provision for medical services.[44] High levels of mental illness are also found among the single homeless.[45] Homelessness among families, while exhibiting much less drastic symptoms, is believed to produce morbidity caused by stress.

In 1980, the health problems of homeless single people remain largely untouched and no major proposals are emerging to assist them or homeless people in general.

Future directions for health policy

After a period of relative complacency on the extent to which the reforms of the 1940s had dealt with the adverse relationship between health and poverty, the 1970s saw a re-awakening of concern about class, area and poverty related health disparities. Examination of this problem has focussed to a considerable extent on the role, funding

Table 7.7 Analysis of total public expenditure, on national health services and personal social services, United Kingdom, 1950–1984

£ million

	1950	1955	1960	1965	1970	1975	1977	1978	1979	1980–81[1]	1981–82[1]	1982–83[1]	1983–84[1]
National Health Services													
Annual expenditure	478	585	865	1,275	2,018	5,182	6,727	7,615	7,322	7,533	7,550	7,700	7,770
As per cent of total public expenditure	10.41	9.36	10.36	9.01	9.22	10.03	10.89	10.67	9.74	10.10	10.30	10.70	10.88
As per cent of gross national product	4.06	3.46	3.87	4.03	4.63	5.49	5.36	5.33	4.59	4.27	4.30	4.29	4.32
Personal Social Services													
Annual expenditure[2]	—	—	—	105	257	998	1,243	1,390	1,380	1,289	1,310	1,340	1,360
As per cent of total public expenditure	—	—	—	0.74	1.23	1.93	2.01	1.94	1.83	1.72	1.78	1.86	1.90
As per cent of gross national product	—	—	—	0.33	0.58	1.05	0.99	0.97	0.86	0.73	0.74	0.74	0.75

Sources: Central Statistical Office *National Income and Expenditu.e* 1961, 1963–73, 1979; (HMSO, London)
Economic Trends 1980, 1979.
The Government's Expenditure Plans 1980–81 to 1983–84; Cmnd. 7841, (HMSO, London, 1979).

[1] Estimated expenditure all at 1979 prices.

[2] Separate PSS figures not available for 1950–1960.

and resource sharing of the NHS, together with action in the related field of social services, but some research has been undertaken to try to identify the extent to which health status can be related to problems such as inadequate or inappropriate housing, homelessness, pollution, working conditions and economic insecurity. In addition, the last decade has seen a growth in interest in preventive policies.

Increased concern about persistent health disparities led the previous government to establish a working party to examine the question in detail. The report was published in 1980 and its recommendations can be broadly categorised in three groups.[46]

(a) The need for improved data and further research to clarify the relationship between health and poverty.
(b) Given the evidence already available, a need to redirect the resources of the NHS to programmes of prevention and to improvement in the availability and accessibility of services of particular importance to low income people generally and to mothers and children in particular.
(c) A series of recommendations based on the belief of the Working Party that the excessive incidence of mortality and morbidity in the lower income groups was directly related to the whole network of poverty and disadvantage in the community. Thus questions of income distribution, family benefits, the income of disabled people, nutrition, housing, and working conditions all required attention by government in a wide ranging programme to upgrade the position of the lowest income groups.

Table 7.7 shows the public expenditure patterns in health and social services and proposals for the next few years. Given the projected increase in the elderly population, the proposed expenditure offers little room for manoeuvre, room that is necessary if a shift in resources between areas, groups and types of service is to take place and it offers no hope for substantial expansion.

Other chapters in this report have shown that the probability of upgrading income, housing and work-related programmes in the near future is not high. Not surprisingly then, the present government has said that it cannot consider implementing the Black report now or in the foreseeable future.

Notes

1 *Report of the Royal Commission on the National Health Service* Cmnd. 7615 (HMSO, London, 1979); and Klein, Rudolf, Public opinion and the National Health Service *British Medical Journal*, 12 May, 1979.

2 Office of Population Censuses and Surveys, *Occupational Mortality 1970–1972*, Decennial Supplement, (HMSO, London, 1978).

3 Department of Health and Social Security, *Inequalities in Health*, Report of a Research Working Group (The Black Report). (London, 1980). 66–67.

4 Hart, Julian Tudor, The inverse care law, *The Lancet*, 27 February 1971.

5 Townsend, Peter, Inequality and the Health Service, *The Lancet*, 15 June 1974.

6 Hart, op. cit.

7 Department of Health and Social Security, *Sharing Resources for Health in England, Report of the Resource Allocation Working Party*, (HMSO, London, 1976); Scottish Home and Health Department, *Scottish Health Authorities Revenue Equalisation*, (HMSO, Edinburgh), Welsh Office, *Report of the Steering Committee on Resource Allocation in Wales*, (Welsh Office, Cardiff, 1977); Department of Health and Social Security (Northern Ireland), *Proposals for the Allocation of Revenue Resources for Health and Personal Social Services (PARR), Report of the Working Group on Revenue Resource Allocations to Health and Social Service Boards in Northern Ireland*, (HMSO, Belfast, 1978).

8 *Inequalities in Health*, op. cit.

9 Avery Jones, Sir Francis, The London hospitals' scene, *British Medical Journal*, Vol. 2, 30 October, 1976.

10 Report of the Royal Commission on the National Health Service, op. cit.

11 Ibid.

12 Ibid, Chapter 18, The NHS and Private Practice.

13 Ibid, and Lee, Michael, *Private and National Health Services*, (Policy Studies Institute, London, 1978).

14 Report of the Royal Commission on the National Health Service, Chapter 18, op. cit.

15 Blaxter, M. Social class and health inequalities, in Carter, C. O. and Peel, John, (Eds.) *Equalities and Inequalities in Health*, (Academic Press, London, 1976); and Cartwright, Ann and O'Brien, Maureen, Social class variations in health care and the nature of general practitioner consultations, in Stacey, Margaret, (Ed.) *The Sociology of the National Health Service*, (University of Keele, 1976).

16 Blaxter, op. cit.; Cartwright, Ann and O'Brien, M. op. cit.; Le Grand, Julian, The distribution of public expenditure: the case of health care, *Economica*, 45; Stacey, M., People who are affected by the inverse law of care, *Health and Social Service Journal*, 3 June 1977; Hart, Julian Tudor, The inverse care law, *The Lancet*, 27 February 1971; Townsend, Peter, Inequality and the Health Service, *The Lancet*, 15 June 1974; Brotherston, Sir John, Inequality: is it inevitable?, in Carter, C.O. and Peel, John, op. cit.

17 *Inequalities in Health*, op. cit.

18 *Safety and Health at Work. Report of the Committee 1970–72* (Robens Report), Cmnd. 5034 (HMSO, London, 1972).

19 Ibid.

20 *Occupational Mortality*. op. cit.

21 *Department of Employment Gazette*, December 1979; and social security statistics for 1979 supplied by the Department of Health and Social Security. See Chapter 3 for discussion of low paid industries.

22 Townsend, Peter, *Poverty in the United Kingdom*, (Penguin Books, Harmondsworth, 1979).

23 *Inequalities in Health*. op. cit.
24 Brenner, M. Harvey, Mortality and the national economy: A review, and the experience of England and Wales 1936–1976, *The Lancet*, 15 September 1979.
25 *Occupational Mortality*, op. cit; Brown, G. W., and Davidson, S., Social class psychiatric disorder of mother and accidents to children, *The Lancet*, Vol. 1. 18 February 1978, and Heller, J., Perinatal mortality 1950, 1973, *Population Trends*, No. 10, Winter 1977.
26 Carter, C. O., and Peel, John, (Eds.) op. cit. and Cartwright and O'Brien. op. cit.
27 Office of Population Censuses and Surveys, Infant and perinatal mortality, *OPCS Monitor*, 26 June 1979; and Lister, Ruth, The urgent need to reduce baby deaths, *New Society*, 16 November 1978.
28 House of Commons Social Services Committee, Session 1979–80. *Perinatal and Neonatal Mortality*, (HMSO, London, 1980.)
29 *Inequalities in Health*, op. cit.
30 Abrams, Mark, *Beyond Three-Score and Ten, A First Report on a Survey of the Elderly*, (Age Concern, London, 1978).
31 *Report of the Royal Commission on the National Health Service*. op. cit.
32 Simpson, R., *Access to Primary Care,* Royal Commissions in the National Health Service Research Paper 6 (HMSO, London, 1979); Institute of Medical Sociology, Aberdeen, *Island Health Care* (Scottish Consumer Council, Edinburgh, 1978).
33 Harris, A., *Social Welfare for the Elderly*, (HMSO, London, 1968); and Hunt, A., *The Home Help Service in England and Wales*, (HMSO, London, 1970).
34 Hunt, A., *The Elderly at Home*, (HMSO, London, 1978); and Department of Health and Social Security, *Health and Personal Social Services Statistics*, 1978, (HMSO, London, 1979).
35 Wicks, Malcolm, *Old and Cold: Hypothermia and Social Policy*, (Heinemann, London, 1978).
36 Supplementary Benefits Commission, Annual Report 1976, (HMSO, London, 1977).
37 Wicks, Malcolm, op cit.
38 Department of Health and Social Security, Central Health Service Council, *Rehabilitation Report of a Sub-committee of the Standing Medical Advisory Committee* (Tunbridge report), (HMSO, London, 1972).
39 Report of the Royal Commission on the National Health Service, op. cit. Central Office of Information, *Care of Disabled People in Britain*, (HMSO, London, 1975).
40 Harris, Amelia I., *Handicapped and Impaired in Great Britain*, Part 1. (HMSO, London, 1971).
41 Brown, O., and Bowl, P., *The CSDP Surveys*. (Social Services Unit, Birmingham University, 1977).
42 Chartered Institute of Public Finance and Accountancy, *Personal Social Services Statistics* 1975/76 and 1979/80. (London, 1975).
43 Wood, Susanne MacGregor, The social conditions of destitution. The situation of men with schizophrenia or personality disorder, *Journal of Social Policy*, Vol. 8, No. 2, April 1979.
44 Walker, Peter, The missing link, *Community Care*, 13 August 1980.

45 Wood, Susanne op. cit.
46 *Inequalities in Health*, op. cit.

8 Education and Poverty*

EDUCATIONAL reform in the 1940s had the dual goal of providing each child with the type of education for which he/she was best adapted, regardless of income and social background, and of contributing to the larger task of reducing and ultimately eliminating social class based disparities and promoting greater social mobility. The key legislation was the 1944 Education Act with its commitment to the right of the individual child to be enabled to develop its full potential.

From the mid 1960s onwards the emphasis shifted somewhat and became more centred on the need to develop an education system which would contribute to national economic and social goals. In this context class-based educational disparities consituted a waste of the human resources in the lower social classes which ought to be utilised.

During the '60s and '70s there was a steady flow of information emerging showing that educational disparities were persisting – between the children of manual workers and those of the professional and managerial classes, between handicapped and non-handicapped children and between the immigrant and the indigenous population. Some educational theorists discounted the usefulness of further educational reform. On the one hand theories based on the natural inferiority of certain classes and certain races suggested that changes in the education system were unnecessary, and often positively undesirable. On the other hand there were those who argued that educational inequality was inevitable as long as society itself was unequal, and that unless societal inequality was attacked, educational reform would be a waste of time.

These two theories have had relatively little influence on policy, but during the 1960s and 1970s a range of theories and matching policies on the causes of educational disparities and means of overcoming them were developed. In reviewing the resulting policies

* This chapter has been drafted mainly by Joan Brown

and programmes, the first impression is that every possible effort has been made to overcome the disparity problem, and if these efforts have fallen short of their goal, it was not for lack of concern or earnest intention. A closer examination shows many shortcomings, including a failure to invest sufficient resources, the ill effects of local authority discretion and the extent of the idological split between the major parties on education which led to see-saw policies, particularly in relation to secondary education. The prolonged and quite powerful influence of the cultural deficit theory has substantially diverted attention from other important theories of disadvantage and still tends to weaken their impact. There has also been a persistent unwillingness to give serious attention to questions of resource allocation within and between local authorities and between educational sectors.

Historical background

The United Kingdom has had state-provided education on a national scale since the Education Act of 1870 and free compulsory elementary education since the Education Act of 1918. The statutory school-leaving age was fixed at 14 years in 1921. From 1902 onwards in England and Wales, a system of state-provided secondary education developed including grammar schools, technical schools, and central schools. These were fee-paying schools, but from 1907 onwards, 25 per cent of places were to be allocated free to children able to pass an entrance examination and, by 1931, 45 per cent of places were allocated free. Similar developments took place in Scotland and Northern Ireland.

Alongside this system of free or part free state-provided education was a parallel system of private education, including voluntary church (denominational) schools, privately run (proprietary) schools and a number of elite public schools. Some of these provided free places for poor children.

Thus by 1939, avenues to secondary education had opened up to children from poorer families and a small minority were able to move into higher education. However, access to secondary education was still influenced by ability to pay and this applied even more forcibly to higher education.

The education system came under close scrutiny in the war years. A 1943 White paper[1] took the view that 'the nature of a child's education should be determined by his capacity and promise and not by the financial circumstances of his parents' and went on to propose a system in which 'all children regardless of background should receive the type of education for which they are best adapted'.

The 1944 Education Act (1945 for Northern Ireland and 1946 for Scotland) established a state system of free primary and secondary education for all. It proposed raising the statutory school-leaving age to 15 years and as soon as practicable to 16 years - provisions carried out in 1947 and 1973 respectively. The Act also provided for further education for children not progressing to higher education - a provision never fully implemented. On the other hand, an extended system of scholarships and grants for university and teacher training was established.

The system which emerged in the immediate postwar period consisted of three sectors. First the free state sector comprising primary schooling until the age of 11 years, when the child moved into one of three types of secondary schools: grammar, technical or secondary modern. Second were direct grant (or grant-aided) schools, substantially financed by government. Many, and in some cases most, places in these schools were free. Third was the private school system, mainly proprietary and public schools. Here entry was almost entirely determined by ability to pay.

The system just described provided for the average child. Provision for physically and mentally handicapped children developed slowly in the 19th century and legislation in the early 20th century only empowered but did not require local authorities to provide schooling for them. A statutory responsibility to provide education for handicapped children was established in a series of Acts between 1914 and 1921.

The 1944 Educational Act confirmed the right of handicapped children to education. Less handicapped children (the majority) were to be educated in the ordinary school system and severely handicapped children in special schools. In fact, the plan that the majority of handicapped children should be educated in ordinary schools, with special attention as needed, was not carried out. Rather until the 1960s, the tendency was to segregate handicapped children in all-age special schools and while many did have their special needs met in ordinary schools, others remained in these schools, without special provision, while awaiting special school vacancies.[2]

Table 8.1 Socio-economic group by age, highest qualification level attained,[1] *males;*[2] *Great Britain, 1977–1978 combined*

Economically active persons aged 20–69 not in full-time education — *Percentages*

Age (years)		Professional	Employers and managers	Intermediate non-manual	Junior non-manual	Skilled manual and own account non-professional	Semi-skilled and unskilled manual and personal service	Total
20–29	Higher education	75	26	54	14	9	3	19
	Other qualifications	24	57	41	72	55	35	49
	No qualifications	-	17	5	14	36	63	32
30–39	Higher education	87	29	51	14	5	2	20
	Other qualifications	13	46	39	54	44	21	39
	No qualifications	-	25	10	33	51	78	41
40–49	Higher education	82	25	43	7	2	1	14
	Other qualifications	14	43	29	46	39	18	35
	No qualifications	4	32	28	47	59	81	51
50–59	Higher education	79	25	30	5	2	1	12
	Other qualifications	16	36	31	34	33	13	28
	No qualifications	5	39	39	61	66	86	60
60–69	Higher education	(57)	14	(19)	3	1	1	9
	Other qualifications	(14)	38	(26)	26	35	17	29
	No qualifications	(5)	49	(31)	70	64	82	63
All	Higher education	81	25	45	9	4	2	16
aged	Other qualifications	17	43	36	50	42	21	37
20–69	No qualifications	2	31	20	40	53	77	47

Source: Office of Population Censuses and Surveys, *General Household Survey, 1978.* (HMSO, London, 1980).

[1] Both full-time and part-time education.

[2] The figures for unqualified females are higher through all age groups, otherwise a similar distribution is evident.

The relationship between education and poverty

A discussion of education and poverty is handicapped by the very limited data available on the relationship between education and income. The bulk of data on the way the education system functions in relation to particular social groups is based on occupation and class, and thus is more a measure of inequality than of poverty. However, as this report has shown, manual workers, and in particular unskilled manual workers, have the least job security and the highest levels of unemployment, are the most likely to be low paid, have the poorest working conditions, the lowest health status and, in many instances, poor housing. This being so, an examination of the way in which the education system serves manual workers and their children is of relevance to the study of poverty in the UK.

In addition to evidence based on occupational grouping, a certain amount of information is available on the educational experience of two other groups who suffer multiple disadvantage including income poverty. These are handicapped people and members of ethnic minority groups. Other available data relates to the persistence of illiteracy in the UK, a problem which has obvious implications for the ability to command an adquate income.

Table 8.1 offers some evidence on the outcome of education in terms of occupation. The lack of educational qualifications even for the youngest age group does not necessarily condemn the individual to the lowest paid jobs, nevertheless a large proportion of the unqualified do gravitate to the bottom end of the labour market. The material presented in this chapter illustrates the persistence of educational disparities. Most of the available data relates to England and Wales. The Scottish and Northern Ireland systems of education are not identical with that of England and Wales and there are some differences in educational traditions. However, other information suggests that Scotland and Northern Ireland show an overall pattern very similar to that found in England and Wales.

Tables 8.2 and 8.3, drawn from a recently published study,[3] show the proportion of boys who attended grammar and technical schools (i.e. schools intended for children of high ability) and university, by the social class of their father. The first two cohorts (born 1913 and 1932) were educated before the 1944 Education Act took effect; the later cohorts benefited from the Act. It will be seen that the proportion of boys attending grammar school and university (though not technical school) increased in all social classes, but the disparities between classes remained throughout the period studied. It is known that further educational disparity exists between skill levels within the large class of manual and agricultural workers.

Table 8.2 Attendance at grammar and technical schools by birth cohort, England and Wales

Percentages

Father's social class[1]	1913–22		1923–32		1933–42		1943–52	
	Grammar	Technical	Grammar	Technical	Grammar	Technical	Grammar	Technical
I, II	27.0	16.2	32.4	17.1	42.1	7.9	35.9	5.5
III, IV, V	14.9	12.8	17.3	20.3	22.1	13.2	23.0	7.1
VI, VII, VIII	6.2	13.5	8.7	16.3	14.8	10.0	14.6	5.9
All	10.9	13.6	13.9	17.6	20.6	10.7	21.2	6.2

Source: Halsey *et al. Origins and Destinations – Family, Class and Education in Modern Britain*. (Clarendon Press, Oxford, 1980).
[1] I, II Professional and managerial; III, IV, V Nonmanual workers; VI, VII, VIII Skilled, semi-skilled and unskilled manual workers and agricultural workers.

Grammar or technical school and university are not of course the only available educational options. Table 8.4, which is not classified on a class basis, shows the opportunities to obtain occupational skills open to young people under 18 years in the UK on entering employment. While a majority of each sex does enter some kind of training programme or a job in which some professional or clerical skills can at least be learned on the job, over one-third of boys and up to 40 per cent of girls enter employment which offers no training opportunities and thus their economic disadvantage is compounded.

Table 8.3 Attendance at university by birth cohort, England and Wales.

Percentages

Father's social class	1913–22	1923–32	1933–42	1943–52
I, II	7.2	15.9	23.7	26.1
III, IV, V	1.9	4.0	4.1	8.0
VI, VII, VIII	0.9	1.2	2.3	3.1
All	1.8	3.4	5.4	8.5
Number	(1846)	(1879)	(1856)	(2246)

Source: Halsey *et al. Origins and Destinations – Family Class and Education In Modern Britain*, (Clarendon Press, Oxford, 1980).

Table 8.4 Destination of school leavers under 18 entering employment, United Kingdom Analysis of boys and girls entering employment by class of employment entered.

Employment entered:[1]	Boys				Girls			
	1964		1974		1964		1974	
	000s	*Per cent*	*000s*	*Per cent*	*000s*	*Per cent*	*000s*	*Per cent*
Apprenticeship	114.5	36	118.2	43	16.9	6	15.5	6
Professional	5.2	1	3.5	1	5.0	2	4.2	2
Clerical	34.0	11	19.2	7	114.9	39	96.3	40
Employment with planned training over 12 months	30.5	10	26.4	10	13.3	5	13.5	6
Employment with planned training 8 weeks–12 months	16.5	5	20.5	7	24.4	8	27.5	12
Other employment	114.2	36	86.9	32	119.0	40	80.9	34
	314.8	100	274.8	100	293.5	100	237.8	100

Source: Wheatley, D. E., '*Apprenticeships in the U.K.*', (Commission of the European Communities, 1976).

[1]The classification embraces training of all types – off-the-job, on-the-job and simple experience training – and includes provision for further education in some instances.

Table 8.5 shows a fuller picture of part-time further education in England and Wales, this time by social class. It is a form of education extensively used by all social classes and increasingly by the children of manual workers, who thus reduce the gap between themselves and the higher socio-economic groups.

As table 8.1 showed, in each successive age group fewer children emerged from the education system without some qualifications,

Table 8.5 Percentage attending part-time education by social class and birth cohort, England and Wales.

Father's social class	1913–22	1923–32	1933–42	1943–52
I, II	50.0	46.2	59.3	45.1
III, IV, V	40.3	41.7	55.1	57.2
VI, VII, VIII	29.9	36.9	46.4	30.8

Source: Halsey *et al. Origins and Destinations – Family, Class and Education In Modern Britain*, (Clarendon Press, Oxford, 1980).

falling for males from 63 per cent of those now 60–69 years old to 32 per cent of the 20–29 years age group, and for females from 75 per cent to 36 per cent, still uncomfortably high figures, but one sign of educational progress. All classes have benefited from educational change. However, the serious disparities between children of professional and managerial fathers and the rest persist through to the groups educated after the 1944 Education Act and up to the 1960s, though the children of manual workers make up ground to a certain extent through the use of part-time further education.

Similar disparities can be found between handicapped and non-handicapped persons. Table 8.6 illustrates this. Too much attention should not be paid to figures for the older age groups, since many of these persons became handicapped in later life and in fact passed through the ordinary school system. However, more of the 16–29 year old group would have been educated in the handicapped school system and, as can be seen, substantially more of them have no qualifications or skills than in the comparable general population – 58 per cent as against 39 per cent. A 1968–71 survey of handicapped school-leavers from special schools[4] showed that only 15 per cent continued at school after 16 years and only one per cent reached higher education. Some 83 per cent of the children were assessed as suitable for further education and/or training, but only 34 per cent had received this three years later. Educationally subnormal (ESN) children were particularly disadvantaged.

As a result of immigration in the 1950s and 1960s, the number of children of West Indian and Asian origin in schools in Great Britain had reached over 131,000 in 1966 and almost 280,000 or 3.3 per cent of the total school population in 1972. Slightly over half of these were in Greater London and in some schools in London in the early 1970s, more than half of the pupils were of immigrant origin.

From the early 1960s onwards, concern was being expressed at the comparative under-achievement of these children. A number of studies[5] showed that immigrant children of the first generation tested for reading and mathematics produced poorer results than indigenous children. However, the longer they had been in the country, the more the gap closed. Most second generation immigrant children, i.e., those born and brought up in this country, achieved at similar levels to non-immigrant children, but children of West Indian origin still lagged behind.

Although the studies suggested that the problem was one of

Table 8.6 Level of qualification obtained by impaired men and women of different age groups compared with level obtained by men and women in the general population, Great Britain

Percentages

Level Qualification	16–29		30–49		50–64		65–74		75 & over	
	Impaired Population	General Population	Impaired Population	General Population	Impaired Population	General Population	Impaired Population	General Population	Impaired Population	General Population
Higher level	3	6	5	8	4	4	4	4	5	4
Middle and lower level	39	55	45	50	40	46	33	38	30	36
No qualifications	58	39	50	42	56	50	63	58	65	60
Number on which percentage based	369	4,461	1,520	7,161	3,456	4,879	3,796	1,965	3,597	1,049

Source: Derived from Buckle, J. R., *Work and Housing of Impaired Persons in Great Britain*. (HMSO, London, 1971).

adjustment (to new country, new school system, new culture, new language) rather than intelligence, 25 per cent of all children in schools for the educationally subnormal in Greater London in 1973 were of immigrant origin, a figure well out of proportion to the number of children of immigrant origin in the school population. The majority of the children concerned were of West Indian origin.[6]

A report published in 1974 estimated that there were at least two million functionally illiterate adults in England and Wales.[7] No figures were given for Scotland and Northern Ireland, but it can reasonably be assumed that the problem extends to those regions. The term 'functionally illiterate' was defined to mean adults (aged 16 and over) who were either unable to read or write at all, or who had a literacy level below that expected of a 9-year-old child.

Studies[8] suggest that problems arise from missed schooling (from illness, truancy, etc.), unsettled home circumstances, poor intelligence, unrecognised learning disabilities, poor teaching, frequent school changes and, in the case of some immigrants, lack of school provision in the country of origin. The postwar education system was also adding new recruits to the illiterate population, because of poor provision for slow learners.[9]

Arrangements to assist adult illiterates were found to be inadequate in both quantity and quality. Only half the education authorities were making any provision at all in 1973 and covered about 5–10,000 adults at any one time.[10]

The background to education policy

Educational reform in the 1940s had the dual goal of providing each child with the type of education for which he/she was best adapted, regardless of income or social background, and of contributing to the larger task of reducing and ultimately eliminating social class based disparities and promoting greater social mobility. Broad consensus on these goals of education lasted until the mid-1960s. The key element was the 1944 Act with its commitment to the right of the individual child to be enabled to develop its full potential.

From the mid-1960s onwards, the emphasis shifted somewhat. The broad goals of education became less child-centred and more concerned with the need to develop an education system which would contribute to national economic and social goals. Education inquiries during the 1960s identified the problem of educational disparities less as an issue of social inequality than as a waste of potential resources and drew attention to the 'reserves of ability left in the lower classes which are not tapped'.[11] While there was considerable agreement between the political parties on this basic thesis, the lessons drawn from it differed. The Labour Party believed the solution lay in promoting greater equality while the Conservative Party tended towards policies which fostered excellence if necessary at the expense of equality. Many areas of agreement remained, but the secondary school system in particular has been subject to see-saw policies as governments came and went.

Against this background of thinking on the broad function of the education system and with a steady flow of information emerging on the persistence of social class based and other educational disparities, the 1960s and 1970s saw the development of a range of theories and matching policies on the causes and means of combatting this problem. Before moving on to discuss these, it will be convenient to deal with two schools of thought which either oppose substantial educational change or discount its usefulness.

The first takes the view that statistical evidence on social class differences in access to selective and higher education should not be regarded as making a case for change in the education system. Instead, it is suggested, the results represent the reality of inherited intelligence, and as long as pathways to selective and higher education are provided for the minority of high ability children of lower socio-economic groups, there is no need to re-organise the whole educational system on egalitarian lines. On the contrary, such steps will lower the general standard of education and impede the production of a well-educated, high-ability elite necessary for the good of the nation as a whole.[12]

At the extreme edge of this school are those who hold that there are racial differences in the inheritance of intelligence, the white race being superior to other races – thus accounting for the apparent under-achievement and disproportionate ESN school placements of immigrant children.[13]

Arguments based on alleged racial inferiority have generally been rejected by governments as a basis for educational policy. Arguments based on class differences in intelligence are possibly more influential, but evidence that high ability children of manual workers were less likely than non-manual workers' children to reach selective schools and higher education has had more influence on policy than theories based on the natural inferiority of certain classes.[14]

The second school of thought also argues that inequality in education is to be expected, but from a rather different base.[15] Here the argument is that it is impossible to achieve equality in education within a fundamentally unequal society and conversely that the promotion of greater equality in the education system will not change society. Education in this view mirrors the inequalities of the general society and at the same time functions to service that unequal society by providing the kind of labour force it needs. If the schools fail to service this need (by, for example, over-producing young people able to go into higher level jobs) then the existing social system will simply re-assert itself once the child leaves school by depressing the advancement of the children of manual workers.

This process can at times act to reduce disparities, though not with that intention. There is evidence that there has been an increase in social mobility, produced by a lower demand for manual workers and an expansion in professional, service and other non-manual occupations. This has required recruitment from 'below' and children of lower socio-economic group parents have moved up to fill these labour force needs.[16] It could thus be suggested that the demand for a better educated labour force has promoted educational change, but a change in labour force demand could in turn slow down social mobility when it ceased to be 'useful'. In any case, this second school of thought appears to have had little influence on policy makers.

Policies to reduce disparities – providing for additional educational needs

Policies and programmes in this group are not based on any particular sociological or educational theory. They recognise that certain groups of children and adults require additional help to function in school or society, or they seek to ensure that the content of teaching does not create barriers between the child and the educational process. They emerge from the practical realities of the classroom and, in the case of adults, the labour force. This description could apply to a very wide range of programmes but here only a few of the larger programmes will be discussed.

Meeting the needs of immigrant children

In the 1960s, particularly in England and Wales, large numbers of newly arrived immigrant children were entering the schools, a process which has continued at a much slower pace in the 1970s.

Many of these children had only a limited command of English or came from homes where English was not the language most commonly used. Throughout the late 1960s and 1970s, three government departments (Education, Environment and Home Office) have had programmes which enabled local authorities to provide or stimulate English language teaching for immigrant children. The implementation of these programmes depended on the willingness of local authorities to act. While a major part of the funding was provided by central government (commonly 75 per cent of expenditure), local government had to organise the programme and fund the balance and even where voluntary agency activity was involved, local education authorities (LEAs) had to give support and approval to the application. In some cases the central government funding had a time limit on it and the LEAs would ultimately have to provide the whole of the funding or close down the project.

Given this situation, it is not surprising that development across the country has been uneven.[17] Some LEAs have special language centres, peripatetic language teachers, specially appointed staff teams with responsibility for immigrant children's education, training programmes for staff and ancillary help for social and liaison work with parents. At the other extreme are authorities relying on the efforts of individual schools without special assistance.

Teaching of English to adult immigrants relies heavily on adult education programmes and on voluntary agencies. This form of organisation is even more haphazard in its outcome with good, poor and non-existent programmes forming an uneven pattern across the country.

An EEC directive also requires the teaching of English to the children of migrant workers from EEC countries. The UK does not have a large migrant worker population, but some major cities do have sizable numbers of European pupils in the schools, as well as children of Moroccan, Filipino and South American workers. The UK has decided not to distinguish between immigrant and migrant children in its language programme, and thus the latter fare as well or as badly as the former.

Although as new immigration has declined the language issue has become less acute, a second, this time cultural barrier between immigrant children and education has persisted into the next generation of school entrants. It took some time for the education system to come to terms with the presence in the schools of cultures whose roots lay outside the United Kingdom. The early assumption was that the immigrant children should be absorbed into British culture as quickly as possible and sometimes directly and more often by inference immigrant cultures were treated as inferior. That this culture clash between the child's home and school would have undesirable effects on the child's school adjustment and educational progress was not recognised for some time, and is still more likely to the appreciated in relation to children of Asian than of West Indian origin.

To an extent the problem has now been identified and some action is being taken to remove an apparent cause of under-achievement among immigrant origin school children. However, the action taken is not extensive in size or coverage and appears likely to be retarded by public expenditure cuts. In 1978, the government established an inquiry into the educational achievements and needs of pupils from ethnic minority groups. This inquiry has not yet reported.

Combatting adult illiteracy

In 1975, an adult literacy campaign was launched jointly by two voluntary organisations, with the Department of Education and the British Broadcasting Corporation (BBC). A government appointed Adult Literacy Resource Agency (ALRA) was established to encourage and fund local activities, and the BBC offered radio and television teaching. With the co-operation of LEAs and the assistance of a large team of volunteer workers (some 40,000 each year), literacy teaching increased to 70,000 students per year in 1977/78. In all about 125,000 adults undertook courses individually or in small groups in the three-year period. By 1978, special programmes were developing for deaf and partially-deaf people, and literacy programmes in penal institutions had both improved in quality and been more closely linked with community programmes. The problem of teaching slow learners has been examined and better teaching techniques for this group were developing.[18]

On the debit side, there was considerable variation in the level of priority given to adult literacy by local authorities. Some authorities had taken full advantage of the funds and staff made available by ALRA and developed excellent programmes. Others were reluctant to become involved because at the end of the three-year period the full cost would fall upon the local education budget. Local authority resource allocations had varied from £3,000 per annum to £80,000 per annum, a disparity far greater than population size or demand could account for. The campaign had been limited in its impact on the 16–19 year old group and the unemployed generally and, given an estimated two million illiterate adults, the 125,000 so far enrolled in tuition programmes represented only the beginning stages of tackling the problem. In 1978, the literacy programme was absorbed in the normal provision of adult and further education. The ALRA's advisory role was taken over by the Adult Literacy Unit for England and Wales[19] and a similar unit in Scotland, but no equivalent body exists for Northern Ireland.

The future of the adult literacy programme must now be in doubt because of the cuts in the education budget, since many local authorities are choosing adult education as one of the areas to be cut or in some cases wholly suspended.

Policies to reduce disparities – compensating for cultural deficits

In the past three decades, a considerable volume of research activity has been based on the theory that a child's level of educational achievement stems not from the influence of the school or the structure of the education system, but from the child's social background. A contrast is drawn between the background characteristics of a manual worker's child and the middle class child. The former often suffers from the disadvantages of poor material conditions (low income, poor housing, overcrowding), limited parental education, lack of stimulation in the home, restricted linguistic and social skills, and lack of parental experience and ability in handling the school system to the child's advantage. The middle class child, on the other hand, grows up in material comfort, in a stimulating home with well-educated, interested and ambitious parents, who are well versed in the functioning of the education system and the child will enter school with quite well-developed linguistic and social skills. Moreover, the school itself is a middle class institution for which the middle class child is readily prepared and in which he has every chance of succeeding, but the same school is alien territory to parents or children from lower socio-economic groups.

This analysis of the cause of class based educational disparities goes on to suggest that if educational opportunities are to be equalised, then compensatory programmes must be offered to the working class child to offset his disadvantaged position and help offered to working class parents to enable them to co-operate successfully with the school system. Critics of this approach suggest that the analysis proceeds from the unwarranted assumption that middle class culture is superior to working class culture. In their view, the school should offer a milieu which enables it to build upon the strengths of working class culture and not one which attempts to teach the child and his parents to behave according to middle class standards. Others have seen the theory as a means of diverting attention from issues related to the structure of the education system and the way resources are allocated. In spite of these criticisms the cultural deficit theory of educational disadvantage carried considerable weight in education circles in the 1960s and 1970s. A number of programmes emerged from this body of theory of which the most important were those related to nursery education.

Nursery education for disadvantaged children

The debate about the provision of nursery education has operated on two levels. If nursery education should be regarded as a desirable part of education for all or most children, the goal would be a large-scale expansion of nursery places in the UK. If nursery education has a specific role to play in reducing educational disparities, by preparing deprived children linguistically, socially and emotionally for entry into primary school on a more equal level with middle class children, the goal would be to discriminate in favour of children from disadvantaged homes/areas in the provision of nursery education. These goals are to an extent contradictory. A compromise solution would be to aim for universal nursery education with specifically designed programmes for disadvantaged children to speed up their progress. This clash of goals has never been resolved, nor has any single goal or compromise been resolutely pursued.

The Plowden Committee, which examined primary school education, found that in 1965 only about 7 per cent of all children under 5 years in England were receiving some form of education.[20] The Committee recommended as a long-term goal that nursery places should be provided for 90 per cent of 4-year-olds and 50 per cent of 3-year-olds. The main expansion programme was not to be started until 1972 and in the meantime new provision should be concentrated in areas of social disadvantage. The proposals thus represented the second of the two goals suggested above with the first goal 'waiting in the wings'.

In 1972, a government White Paper, *Education: A Framework for*

Expansion[21] also wavered between the two goals of nursery education. On the one hand, it announced the formal adoption, in a ten-year expansion programme, of the full Plowden proposals. On the other hand, it said that 'priority will be given in the early stages of the programme to areas of disadvantage'.

In 1972, the children of professional parents were almost twice as likely to be in nursery schools than children of manual workers.[22] By 1976–77, when total attendance had reached 14 per cent of under-5s in Great Britain (Northern Ireland figures were higher), the lowest socio-economic group were approaching parity with the professional and managerial class.[23] However, parity is not positive discrimination. The figures represented 55 per cent of the 4-year-old and 16 per cent of the 3-year-olds, still well short of the target. Thus by 1977 neither goal was fully achieved and the contradiction between goals remained. Within the nursery schools, especially since 1967, there has been a good deal of experimentation in developing special programmes for disadvantaged children, and nursery teaching in general has been influenced by the cultural deficit theory. Research evidence on the outcome has been contradictory.[24]

The thrust towards substantial expansion of nursery education in the UK has faltered since 1977 and now seems likely to halt altogether, as planned cuts in educational expenditure take effect.

Programmes for school-age children

Research projects in 1969–70 found that working class parents were in fact keenly interested in their children's educational and social chances, but were not sure how best to help them and how to relate to their schools.[25] Ways were therefore sought to explain the schools' aims and methods, to encourage parents to recognise their own role in the educational process and so to develop understanding, skill and enthusiasm in the children's homes which would help them to get the maximum benefit from their schools.[26] To this end, programmes of home visiting and various forms of parent-teacher liaison were developed.

It was also felt that the school itself might have to change from its middle class orientation and find ways of achieving harmony between school and community. The notion of the community school was developed. This might mean opening the school to comminity use in the evening and during holidays or it might mean relating the school curriculum more closely to the local community so that children learned to understand their community, to value what was good in it and to challenge what was bad.[27]

It will be noted that as these programmes developed, some of the criticisms of over-emphasis on middle class values in the original theoretical base were taken into account. In spite of this, there has been a shift away from the cultural deficit approach because it appeared to be blaming the victim and allowing major faults in the general education system to escape unscathed. It remains an influential theory among educators, but the main thrust of policy has moved elsewhere. It is of interest to note that a recent study, Rutter *et al., 15,000 Hours*,[28] while accepting the cultural deficit theory, nevertheless argued that there was evidence that the school and its overall 'ethos' played an important role in the child's educational and social development, and this applied whether or not the child came from a deprived area.

Policies to reduce disparities – removing financial barriers

The 1944 Education Act removed the major financial barrier to education by abolishing fees for all state primary and secondary education. In addition, legislation in the 1940s and 1950s made a number of provisions for additional help to poor children to enable them to gain full benefit from education. With memories of the depression years still fresh, educational policy makers sought means to ensure that the education of children would not suffer because they were poorly nourished, could not afford fares to schools at a distance from their homes, or were poorly clad.

School Meals

The legislation required education authorities to provide a cooked mid-day meal to any child requesting it. Charges for these meals could be waived or reduced for poor children. The implementation of the free or subsidised meal provisions was left to the discretion of local authorities. This discretionary element produced considerable disparities between local authorities in the means tests used, the level of income at which a family qualified for assistance, and the extent to which poor families were encouraged to apply for free meals. Children of families in receipt of national assitance, later supplementary benefit, and after 1971 children of recipients of the family income supplement for low earning families, are automatically entitled to free school meals, but other low income families may find that they qualify for assistance from one local authority, but would not be eligible in other areas.

In the 1970s, there was a substantial increase in the provision of free school meals, in part because of publicity campaigns to draw attention to the service. However, as the resources required for school meals have increased, it has become a matter of controversy whether such charges should fall upon the education budget. In the argument, the original reason for its inclusion (i.e. the need to make sure children could benefit from education) appears to have got lost.

The 1979 Education Act repealed the old school meal requirement and instead requires only that the LEAs make such provisions as appear requisite (not necessarily including cooked meals) to provide for children from families on supplementary benefit or family income supplement and others at local authority discretion. As the cost of (paid for) meals has been raised, and the content reduced, overall demand for the school meals service has fallen dramatically, and this threatens the provision for poor children.

Assistance with fares to school

Pupils living beyond a certain distance from school are entitled to free transport and those inside the limit may be assisted subject to means tests. The provision is of particular importance to rural children, especially following the closure of many small village schools, and is available also to children attending more distant denominational schools. The scheme is mandatory and is fully implemented. A recent attempt by the government to revoke it suffered defeat in Parliament.

School Clothing

A 1948 Act empowered local authorities to provide assistance on a discretionary basis to families in need, for the purchase of school clothing and other school equipment. This provision, relying heavily on local authority discretion and without any stipulation of basic standards, has proved the most unsatisfactory of all the assistance programmes. The rules laid down by LEAs have varied to the point of eccentricity[29] and there are no proposals to change this.

Educational maintenance allowances

A further goal of the 1944 Education Act was to remove deterrents to poor parents to keep their children at school beyond compulsory school leaving age. Discretionary powers were given to local authorities to provide educational maintenance allowances (EMAs) to help towards the cost of keeping a child in school.

A fairly standardised system of educational bursaries has developed throughout Scotland, perhaps reflecting the traditional Scottish concern to ensure the access of poor children to educational opportunities. These bursaries are available to children both below and above minimum school leaving age following an assessment of family circumstances. Grants are made through to sixth form education or for approved courses of further education.

In Northern Ireland, the system of selective education in fee paying schools which still prevails is supported by a scholarship system which provides fees for grammar school education. However, any additional EMAs are provided under arrangements similar to those operating in England and Wales.

In England and Wales, the discretionary EMA powers have been exercised in an inconsistent, haphazard and often meagre way across the country. Various proposals put forward from 1957 onwards came to nothing, but plans were developed in 1978 for a mandatory means tested scheme of educational maintenance allowances for 16—19 year olds in school or in further education. The grants would be paid by local authorities with 90 per cent central government grant aid. Public expenditure restraint in 1978 halted this plan and instead a number of pilot EMA schemes was to be established to ascertain the workability and usefulness of the scheme, but a change of government intervened and the plan was dropped. One authority (the Inner London Education Authority) does plan to implement the EMA scheme from its own resources.

The question remains whether improved support schemes and, in particular, EMAs would produce a greater tendency for poor children to remain at school after 16 years. Those arguing in favour of extended support schemes believe that at least some under-achievement in school must be financial in origin. But studies[30] have suggested that the influence of EMAs may not be as great as expected, especially if the level of allowance offered is fairly low, in comparison to grants for higher education and to income from jobs or from manpower training programmes for unemployed young people.

Grants for higher education

The scheme for grants for higher education is a mandatory one. Individuals possessing certain basic qualifications and with an offer of a place to study at an institute of higher education or a college of education are entitled to an award to meet the costs of fees and maintenance. The amount of the award is on a sliding scale taking into account the income of the student's parents or spouse. Thus the poorer the family, the higher the award.

Although administered by local authorities, the scheme is standardised throughout the United Kingdom and has proved both efficient and equitable. It can be said that if children of low income families survive in the education system long enough to qualify for higher education, they are enabled financially to take advantage of this opportunity.

Policies to reduce disparities – re-organising the education system

The system which emerged from the 1944 Education Act has itself been held responsible for the failure to give working class children adequate opportunity to fulfil their potential. Only the state primary system has remained relatively untouched by this debate and subsequent action.

The private school system

The private school system was left largely intact by the 1944 Act. It may have been thought that the provision of free state secondary (including grammar school) education would lead to the natural decline of the private sector. There was some shift across from private to state schools by the less affluent middle class, but in the main the private schools held their position. The private sector has never been large. In Great Britain, it educates about 5 per cent of school age children. In Northern Ireland, more children are in the private sector, but this is a function of denominational education rather than class or income.

Evidence suggests that this minority of children have gained a significant advantage in access to selective and higher education from their attendance at private schools[31] and, since ability to pay is the main determinant of private education, this advantage has accrued to the higher socio-economic classes. Not surprisingly, this has led some to argue that educational disparities will never be eliminated unless the private school system is abolished or, put more politely, integrated into the state school system.

Proponents of private education maintain the right of parents to buy the education of their choice and stress the importance of preserving academic excellence. Those prepared to concede that excellence of education should not be the preserve of higher income groups tend to seek a compromise which maintains the private school system, but opens it up to children from a wider class and income range. The present government has legislated an Assisted Places Scheme for high ability children from the lower socio-economic groups to attend private schools. Such legislation seems unlikely to survive a change of government and though reaction to it has revived pressure to abolish/integrate the private school sector, this proposition is also politically a doubtful starter.

Re-organising the state system

The pattern of state secondary education established after the 1944 Education Act comprised three types of school: secondary grammar, secondary technical and secondary modern. Placement in one of these three types of school was determined by assessment or more commonly by examination (the '11 plus') at the age of 11 years. Some room for review at 13 years did exist, but the number of children transferred between schools was not high. Theoretically the new school system and the 11 plus selection were to be instruments for promoting school placement by merit and not by class, and by streaming different ability groups in different schools, each could develop educational programmes best suited to the child.

By the mid-1950s, these arrangements were already being called into question. First, there was concern at the extent to which secondary modern schools had become working class establishments with an average of 70–85 per cent of pupils whose fathers were manual workers.[32] Once in the secondary modern stream, there was little movement from it and the majority of the children were destined to leave school at 15 years with few or no qualifications. Second, there were questions about the validity of the 11 plus as a determinant of a child's educational career.[33] In 1957, it was estimated that 12 per cent of pupils were being allocated to the 'wrong schools', including the placement of high ability working class children in secondary modern schools.[34]

A third criticism was that although all three school types were intended to have equal status, this was not the case. In fact, the technical school sector did not exist at all in many areas and was declining elsewhere. The public viewed grammar school pupils as successes and secondary modern pupils as failures. Other factors tended to reinforce this. While a large number of new secondary modern schools were built, others were housed in pre-war, sometimes pre-20th century elementary school buildings with sub-standard amenities.[35] Overcrowding, high teacher turnover and difficulties in attracting graduate teachers were said to be features of the secondary modern system.[36]

Finally, many were concerned at the social divisiveness of a system of secondary education which separated children at the age of 11 years and gave them different forms of education, the one opening up substantially greater life chances than the other. The alternative school system proposed was the abandonment of selection in favour of comprehensive schools for all secondary children.

Comprehensive schools, that is secondary schools which provided for all levels of ability, had existed in Great Britain (though not in Northern Ireland) for a number of years. By January 1965, there were 262 in existence.

In 1965, the new Labour Government decided to favour a shift to comprehensive schooling, and asked local authorities to send in plans for re-organising on comprehensive lines.[37] Since 1965, the re-organisation of the secondary school system has proceeded at a very uneven pace. Labour governments have strongly supported the change to comprehensives. Conservative governments, while not wholly opposed,have been reluctant to eliminate the grammar school sector.[38] At the local level, LEAs have responded to local opinion and the practical needs of the area more than to party ideologies. The Department of Education and Science (DES) has offered guidance but tended to avoid controversy and too much interference in local decision-making. Resource allocation has formed only a limited part of pressure to change.

In spite of constant policy changes and the varied enthusiasm or recalcitrance of local authorities and in spite of the limited resources allocated for the task, substantial progress has been made towards re-organising secondary education on comprehensive lines. Table 8.8 shows the changes in England and Wales to 1977, when almost 80 per cent of public sector secondary children were in comprehensive schools. If independent and state supported schools are taken into account, 72 per cent of all secondary pupils were in comprehensives in 1977.

Scottish comprehensive re-organisation has proceeded at a much faster pace than in England and Wales, and by 1977 90 per cent of Scottish secondary children were in comprehensive schools.[39] Northern Ireland, on the other hand, has largely maintained the

Table 8.7 Maintained secondary and middle (deemed secondary) schools 1965–1977, England and Wales

	1965	1970	1974	1975	1976	1977
Number of maintained schools						
Comprehensive and middle (deemed secondary)	262	1,250	2,677	3,069	3,387	3,647
Grammar	1,285	1,038	675	566	477	407
Modern	3,727	2,691	1,509	1,216	1,002	837
Technical and other	589	406	218	184	116	97
Total secondary	5,863	5,385	5,079	5,035	4,982	4,988
Percentage of pupils						
Comprehensive and middle (deemed secondary)	8.5	32.0	62.0	69.7	75.6	79.9
Grammar	25.5	19.9	11.0	9.0	7.5	6.3
Modern	55.2	40.3	23.0	18.2	15.0	12.2
Technical and other	10.8	7.9	3.9	3.1	1.9	1.5
Total secondary	100.0	100.0	100.0	100.0	100.0	100.0

Source: Department of Education and Science, *Statistics of Education, 1977, Vol. 1. Schools*. (HMSO, London 1979).

selective system and only a very small comprehensive sector has developed.

An assessment of the contribution of comprehensive re-organisation to the reduction of class based educational disparities presents some problems. Only in recent years have there been a substantial number of schools, all of whose pupils have spent their whole secondary years in a comprehensive school setting. Allowance must also be made for the inevitable disruption of re-organisation. Some information is now beginning to emerge which shows that, as comprehensive schools settle down, educational results in terms of literacy, numeracy and achievement of qualifications are quite satisfactory and compare quite well with the selective schools.[40] However, there is still insufficient information on the extent to which social class based disparities are being overcome.

Handicapped children

In 1973/74, a Committee of Enquiry into the Education of Handicapped Children and Young People (the Warnock Committee) was established by the government.[41] Its report published in 1978 contained over 200 recommendations and only a few can be discussed here. The Committee recommended that the planning of services should proceed on the assumption that about 1 in 6 children at any one time and up to 1 in 5 children at some time in their school career would require some form of special provision to overcome fairly widely defined educational difficulty. Each child appearing to need special help should be assessed by a multi-professional team and whole age groups should be assessed three or four times during school life. Local Education Authorities should then have a positive obligation placed upon them to meet the needs revealed by this assessment.[42]

For the majority of children with special education needs, the Committee recommended maximum feasible integration within ordinary schools, either by siting special units or classes within the schools or by including the children in ordinary classes except for periods of special teaching. This would require special teacher training programmes, and good support arrangements and facilities.[43]

Separate special schools would still be needed for some categories of children and here stress was placed on the need to maintain maximum contact with the ordinary school system. The all-age school was to be avoided and children placed in primary or secondary special schools with a curriculum as near to ordinary schooling as possible.[44] Other recommendations related to improved provision for children in hospital and children needing home tuition.[45] Additional recommendations were directed to improving access for handicapped children and adults to nursery education and to further and higher education.[46]

The government, in a White Paper in 1980,[47] accepted many of the proposals of the Warnock Report where these related to the identification of children in need of assistance and the structure of educational provision – though it was less than enthusiastic about proposals for maximum integration of the handicapped child in the ordinary school system. However, the government declined to provide the additional resources required for the full implementation of the Warnock proposals on grounds of the necessity to cut public expenditure. At most, it offered to ensure that the special educational budget was not cut and suggested that LEAs and others involved should review the present use of resources in order to make improvements in education for handicapped children wherever possible.

Policies to reduce disparities – re-allocation of resources

In the past 10–15 years, increasing attention has been paid to the influence of resource allocation on the educational opportunitites of children. In the early years, this approach was linked with the cultural deficit theory, but more recently it has been developed as a counter-theory by those who reject the cultural deficit and other sociological theories to explain educational disparities.

Educational priority areas

The Plowden Committee of 1965,[48] heavily influenced by the prevailing cultural deficit theory, noted areas in which there were many socially deprived children who, it considered, were prevented by their home circumstances from benefiting from their schooling. Parallel with this they drew attention to areas in which the problem of social deprivation was compounded by the existence of inadequate and under-resourced schools.

When it considered the way in which resources were allocated, the Committee found a number of problems. Central government allocations through the rate support grant were designed to equalise the financial resources of poorer and wealthier authorities and did so with reasonable fairness, but they did not take account of the need for substantial additional expenditure on specific disadvantaged areas.

Within local authority boundaries, the report noted the redistribution of resources between affluent and less affluent areas was less marked. Some local authorities did discriminate in favour of schools whose 'social needs' appeared to be greatest but many operated on a basis of roughly equal allocations for all their schools, good or bad.

The Plowden Committee recommended a policy of positive discrimination in favour of poor schools in neighbourhoods with the most deprived conditions with the object first of bringing these schools up to the national average and then 'quite deliberately to make them better' on the grounds that below average environments needed better than average schools. To this end, certain areas in

England and Wales were to be designated Educational Priority Areas (EPAs) and extra resources given to them for school building and improvement, attractive salaries for teachers, better teacher/pupil ratios, appointment of teachers' aides, more nursery places and the development of compensatory programmes.[49]

Although the idea of designated Educational Priority Areas received a generally favourable response, no extensive or coherent EPA programme actually developed. Three million pounds of the £54 million to be devoted to school building in 1968–69 was directed to priority areas. The 1969–70 expenditure plans included £16 million for EPA school building, and approval was given for extra allowances for teachers in EPA schools and for increased staffing levels. This school building programme, the teachers' allowances and additional staff, and a research programme proved to be the sum total of the EPA programme.

In light of this, the rather rosy glow the EPA programme left behind seems somewhat unwarranted. Its direct effect on improved resource allocations was very limited. Its influence seems rather to have stemmed from the ideas generated in the flow of reports from the EPA action research projects,[50] ideas directed more to compensatory education than to positive discrimination in the allocation of funds.

Local authority resource allocation

Evidence from the 1950s and 1960s showed that geographical inequalities in the secondary and tertiary stages of education accounted for approximately half of the social inequalities in selecting for grammar and technical education after taking ability into account.[51] Studies in the early 1970s found considerable inequality in the distribution of what was termed 'educational social income' and concluded that 'there is a systematic relationship between the class background of an area and the educational resources available. In general, the higher the social-class composition of an area, the better the provision'.[52]

Examination of expenditure per pupil in primary and secondary schools in 1976/77 found that, apart from London, where high spending corresponded to poor socio-economic conditions, there was no significant tendency for poor social conditions to be associated with high secondary educational expenditure, though primary educational expenditure did tend to be higher in areas suffering from adverse conditions.[53]

A study of local authority resource allocations within one London Borough, concluded that there was maldistribution of resources within the borough so that children from socially deprived areas tended to attend schools which were less well provided than those attended by less disadvantaged children.[54]

In spite of this growing body of evidence, no major initiatives have developed to deal with the resource allocation question.

Table 8.8 Comparative resource allocations according to mode of educational career, England and Wales

Establishments attended during educational career	Total resource allocations[1] over career 1	2
Primary school and secondary school until age 16	100	100
Primary school and secondary school until age 18	148	145
Nursery classes, Primary School and secondary school until age 16	115	116
Nursery classes, primary school and secondary school until age 18	164	161
Primary school, secondary school until age 18 and 3-year University or Polytechnic course	335	320
Primary school, secondary school until age 18 and 3-year College of Education or Institute of Higher Education course	282	270
Nursery classes, Primary school, Secondary school, until age 18 and 3-year College of Education or Institute of Higher Education course	298	287
Nursery classes, primary school, secondary school until age 18 and 3-year University or Polytechnic course	350	337

Source: Own calculations, derived principally from Central Statistical Office, National Income and Expenditure (various years) (HMSO, London).

[1]Calculation of total resource allocation is achieved by assessment of cumulative *and* unit costs, using in Column 1 the retail price index in Column 2 the implied index of total home costs.

Adult and further education – recurrent education

A rather different resource allocation debate has arisen from a consideration of the nature of educational opportunity and of the comparative expenditure per person on different educational careers. Table 8.8 compares unit costs per pupil/student, and shows that the child receiving the full range of education from nursery class through to university or polytechnic received approximately $3\frac{1}{2}$ times as much investment of educational resources as the child receiving the minimum compulsory education. As this chapter has shown, the children most likely to have received relative under-investment in their education are manual workers' children.

For more than a century, organisations both official and voluntary have endeavoured to provide further educational opportunities for young people over compulsory school leaving age and for adults. But, while a number of advances have been made, adult and further education remained the poor relation of the education system.[55]

In the 1970s, a fresh attempt was made to improve provision. First there was examination of the needs of the 16–19 year old group, an issue which has been seen as increasingly urgent because of the marked increase in youth unemployment, and the decreasing opportunitites available for unqualified persons of all ages. More vocational further education opportunities have been sought for young people and, especially, for the one-third leaving school unqualified and not entering any of the existing full time, part-time or day release training arrangements (see table 8.4). Progress in this area has, however, been slow because of public expenditure cuts, though there has been some expansion of opportunities for the unemployed through the Youth Opportunities Programme (see chapter 4).

The establishment in 1969–70 of the Open University, designed to provide an alternative route to higher education through the use of radio, television and correspondence has proved popular. However, pressure to extend the Open University concept to lower levels of further education has not so far been successful, except perhaps in relation to the Adult Literacy drive discussed earlier.

A Committee of Inquiry to examine non-vocational adult education in England and Wales (reporting in 1973) made no recommendations for drastic re-organisation, though it did propose a doubling of the modest adult education budget.[56] Initially the government of the day promised to implement this proposal in full,[57] but within a year public expenditure restraint reversed this decision. Adult education was not regarded as a priority.

Although the present government expresses a commitment to vocational further education because of the importance of upgrading the skills of the labour force, no major expenditure can be anticipated, except perhaps in relation to the young unemployed. The question of a more equitable sharing of educational resources among the post-16 year olds is not being seriously addressed and little progress seems likely towards developing the potential of adult education for assisting the educationally and socially disadvantaged.[58]

Future directions for educational policy

The problem of social class based educational disparities and the need to direct special attention to socially deprived children has been well documented in the UK and continues to command the interest and concern of educational researchers and policy makers. In considering this policy area, the first impression is that every possible effort has been made to overcome this disparity problem and, if these efforts have fallen short of their goal, it is not for lack of concern or earnest intention. A closer examination, however, reveals a number of problems.

Throughout the period 1950–1980 there has been a consistent failure to invest sufficient resources in promising programmes often combined with a failure to persevere with these programmes long enough for them to be effective.

A recurrent theme in a wide range of programmes has been the problems presented by the exercise of local authority discretion. While in theory local government, because of its closer relations with its own constituency ought not to be tied to national programmes planned in fine detail, the result, as far as policies to combat educational disparity are concerned, has been to produce programmes ranging from the excellent through the deplorable to the non-existent.

A further complication in developing satisfactory policies has been the growth of an ideological split in the political approach to education together with a tendency to classify programmes for poor children as 'welfare' and therefore to be excluded from the education budget. While the removal of education from politics is neither practical nor indeed desirable, it cannot be denied that a change of policy coinciding with each change of government is likely to retard rather than advance progress towards eliminating education disparities. The tendency to segregate poor children's programmes stigmatises them and leaves them open to the operation of periodic expenditure cutbacks in social programmes.

One group of children - the handicapped - has suffered from exclusion from the general thrust of educational and political debate and been neglected in consequence - suggesting that it is better to be the subject of argument, even if this is sometimes destructive, than to be largely ignored. Although handicapped children have at last received the attention they deserve, they now appear likely to fall vicitim to policies to cut educational expenditure.

The prolonged and quite powerful influence of the cultural deficit theory which, in effect, blamed the victim for his own educational poverty is in marked contrast to the development of poverty theory in other policy areas, which shifted from this approach at a much earlier stage. This theory substantially diverted attention from other important theories of disadvantage and still tends to weaken their impact.

There has been a persistent unwillingness to give serious attention to questions of resource allocation between and within local authorities and between educational sectors. Research on this issue has begun to develop, but there is not much evidence that it has influenced policy makers. It must be marked down as one of the more promising areas for future study and policy development.

The late 1970s have been marked by an active educational debate and the identification of a number of programmes which might improve the quality of education and enhance the opportunities for disadvantaged children. These programmes included a reshaping of the educational arrangements for the handicapped, more nursery provision for socially deprived and handicapped children, more consideration for the needs of ethnic minorities, more development of the community school concept, expansion of further and adult education, literacy programmes and serious attention to the life-long learning needs of the population in a time of technological change. Many of these proposals were based on the assumption that the demographic changes which are producing falling school rolls would release education resources in money, staff, buildings and equipment, which could then be redeployed.

Until 1979, the then government promoted active debate on how the resources released by falling school rolls should be used - for tax cuts, for deployment to other policy areas, for improving the quality of the present education system, for extending programmes for disadvantaged groups or for moving more effectively towards recurrent or life-long education. On the change of government, these options were largely foreclosed. Falling school rolls are now part of the means to achieve public expenditure cuts and any educational improvements must now be achieved within reduced education budgets.

Notes

1 Board of Education, *Educational Reconstruction*, Cmnd. 6458, (HMSO, London, 1943).

2 This account is drawn from *Special Educational Needs, Report of the Committee of Enquiry into the Education of Handicapped Children and Young People* (The Warnock report). Cmnd. 7212 (HMSO, London, 1978).

3 Halsey, A. H., *et al.*, *Origins and Destinations – Family, Class and Education in Modern Britain*, (Clarendon Press, Oxford, 1980).

4 Tuckey, Linda *et al.*, *Handicapped School-leavers: Their Further Education, Training and Employment*, (National Children's Bureau, London, 1973).

5 Essen, Juliet and Ghodsian, Mayer, The children of immigrants: school performance, *New Community*, Vol. VII, No. 3.

6 House of Commons Select Committee on Race Relations, *Education, Vol. 1, Report* (HMSO, London, 1973).

7 British Association of Settlements, *A Right to Read*, (London, 1974).

8 Haviland, R. Michael. *Survey of Provision for Adult Illiteracy in England*. (Centre for Teaching of Reading, Reading, 1973).

9 Ibid.

10 *A Right to Read*. op. cit.

11 Committee on Higher Education. *Higher Education* (Robbins Report), Cmnd. 2154 (HMSO, London, 1963).

12 This school of thought is best represented by the series of *Black Papers*: Cox, C. B., and Dyson, A. E., (Eds.) *The Black Papers on Education* (Davis Paynter, London, 1971); Cox, C. B., and Boyson, R. (Eds.) *Black Paper 1975* (Dent, London, 1975); and Cox C. B., and Boyson, R., (Eds.) *Black Paper 1977* (Temple Smith, London, 1977).

13 For example, Eysenk, H. J., *Race Intelligence and Education* (Temple Smith, 1971).

14 Halsey, A. H., *et al.*, *Origin and Destinations – Family, Class and Education in Modern Britain*, (Clarendon Press, Oxford, 1980); and Central Advisory Council for Education (England), *Children and their Primary Schools* (Plowden Report), (HMSO, London, 1967).

15 See for example Byrne, David *et al.*, *The Poverty of Education*, (Martin Robertson, London, 1975).

16 Goldthorpe, John H. and Llewellyn, Catriona, Class mobility in modern Britain: three theses examined *Sociology*, Vol. 11, No. 2, May 1977.

17 House of Commons Select Committee on Race Relations and Immigration (Session 1972–73) *Education*, (HMSO, London, 1973).

18 Department of Education and Science, *Adult Literacy in 1977/78: A remarkable Educational Advance*, (HMSO, London, 1978).

19 Ibid.

20 *Children and their Primary Schools,* op. cit.

21 Department of Education and Science, *Education. A framework for Expansion.* Cmnd. 5-714, (HMSO, London, 1972).

22 Department of Employment, *General Household Survey 1972*, (HMSO, London, 1974).

23 Department of Employment, *General Household Survey 1977*, (HMSO, London, 1979).

24 See Woodhead, Martin, *Intervening in Disadvantage*, (National Foundation for Educational Research, Slough, 1976), for a review of research in this area.

25 Payne, Joan, *Educational Priority Vol. 2. EPA Surveys and Statistics*, (HMSO, London, 1974).

26 Halsey, A. H., (Ed.) *Educational Priority. Vol. 1. EPA Problems and Policies*, (HMSO, London, 1972).

27 Ibid, and Midwinter, Eric, *Projections. An educational priority area at work*, (Ward Lock Educational, London, 1972).

28 Rutter, M. *et al.*, *Fifteen Thousand Hours*, (Open Books, London, 1979).

29 Tunnard, Jo., *Battle Royal*. Welfare in Action Series. Child Poverty Action Group, London 1977.

30 Fulton, Oliver and Gordon, Alan, The British pool of ability: how deep, and will cash reduce it, *Educational Studies*, Vol. 5, No. 2, June 1979; and Manpower Services Commission, *Young People and Work*, (HMSO, London, 1977).

31 Halsey *et al.*, op. cit.

32 Central Advisory Council for Education England, *15–18* (Crowther Report), (HMSO, London, 1959); Central Advisory Council for Education England, *Half our Future* (Newsom Report), (HMSO, London, 1963). See also Halsey op. cit.

33 Vernon, P. E., *Secondary School Selection.*, A British Psychological Society Inquiry, (Methuen, London, 1957).

34 Yates, A. and Pigeon, D. A., *Admission to Grammar Schools*, (National Foundation for Educational Research, London, 1957).

35 Newsom Report, op. cit.

36 Crowther Report, op. cit.

37 Department of Education and Science. *The Organisation of Secondary Education.* Circular 10/65, (1965).

38 Department of Education and Science, *The organisation of Secondary Education*, Circular 10/70, (1970).

39 *Scottish Education Statistics 1973* and information from the Scottish Office.

40 Department of Education and Science, *Aspects of Secondary Education in England. A Survey by H.M. Inspectors of Schools*, (HMSO, London, 1979); Rutter, M. *et al.*, *Fifteen Thousand Hours*, op. cit.; and Steedman, Jane, *Progress in Secondary Schools*, (National Children's Bureau, London, 1980).

41 *Special Educational Needs*, op. cit.

42 Ibid.

43 Ibid.
44 Ibid.
45 Ibid.
46 Ibid., Chapters 5 and 10.
47 Department of Education and Science, *Special Needs in Education*, Cmnd. 7996, (HMSO, London, 1980).
48 *Children and Their Primary Schools*, op. cit.
49 Ibid. Chapter 5.
50 Halsey, A. H., *Educational Priority Vol. 1. Problems and Policies*. op cit.; and Payne, J., *Educational Priority Vol. 2. Surveys and Statistics*. op. cit.
51 Douglas, J. W. B., In his Foreword to Byrne, D., *et al.*, *The Poverty of Education*, (Martin Robertson, London, 1975).
52 Byrne, D., *et al.*, op cit.
53 Howick, Christina and Hassani, Habib, Education spending: primary, *Centre for Environmental Studies Review*, No. 5, January 1979; and Education spending: secondary, *Centre for Environmental Studies Review*, No. 8, February 1980.
54 Tunley, P., Travers, T. and Pratt, J. *Depriving the Deprived: a Study of Finance, Educational Provision and Deprivation in a London Borough*, (Kogan Page, London, 1979).
55 Dent, H. C., *The Educational System of England and Wales*, (University of London Press, 1963); and Department of Education and Science, *Adult Education: A Plan for Development* (Russell Report), (HMSO, London, 1973).
56 Adult Education, Ibid.
57 *Hansard*, No. 953, Vol. 806, 1973.
58 See articles Lawson, L., Adult education: The scapegoat of market place economics, *Times Higher Educational Supplement*, 25 April 1980; and Low, G., Night hawks, the status of adult education, *Education Guardian*, 19 February 1980; and Advisory Council for Adult and Continuing Educating, *Present Imperfect*, (London, 1980).

9 Three Decades of Anti-Poverty Policy*

DISCUSSION of UK anti-poverty policy in this report has focussed on six areas of social policy – low pay, unemployment, social security, housing, health and education. From 1944 to 1948 a large-scale legislative programme was enacted and new policies developed with the objective of establishing a society (a welfare state) in which the most vulnerable members would be helped, common risks would be shared and access to important services such as housing, health and education would be determined not by income and class but by need and ability. The full range of policies adopted were expected to reinforce one another and together would eliminate the five giant evils: want, idleness, squalor, disease and ignorance.

Since the implementation of this 'grand design', anti-poverty policies have developed in a markedly less coherent fashion, as different departments and agencies of government and the non-government sectors have tried to come to grips with new difficulties and old but persistent problems. The result, as this report has shown, has been a multiplicity of programmes, some relatively small and *ad hoc*, others well-thought out major attempts to overcome a well-identified deficiency in the social arrangements. Some have been programmes specifically directed at reducing poverty, others have had this as a sub-goal of greater or less importance.

Although this policy development has been undertaken by separate authorities and without any broadly based master plan, much common ground is evident in the approach to poverty and it is possible to review these policies and programmes under a number of broad headings. It should be emphasised that this 'packaging' of policies into various categories is only a convenient way of looking at them. Some categories do correspond fairly well with the way in which policy makers have thought of them. In other cases, the

* This chapter has been drafted mainly by Joan Brown. The section on the voluntary sector is derived from a paper by W. D. Birrell and A. P. Williamson.[1]

commonalities of the programmes are only the result of being derived from roughly similar theory bases and not the result of planned policies. Moreover, a number of programmes can fit into more than one category.

The individual approach

A number of policies and programmes have been directed at individuals in poverty and/or have been based on assumptions of individual deficiencies. The effects of this approach can sometimes be described as malevolent, as for example the assumption that unemployed and sick people are prone to idleness and malingering and will be content to live 'off the state' if social security benefits are not maintained below the level of earnings of low paid workers, in other words below the poverty line.

At other times the approach is benevolent in intention. Individual deficiencies which may give rise to poverty are identified and programmes devised to overcome these deficiencies. Training is provided for unskilled, low paid and unemployed workers; compensatory educational programmes are devised for children from disadvantaged backgrounds; literacy teaching is offered to the illiterate and much of the work of social workers within the personal social services is aimed at assisting individuals and families to overcome personal problems which handicap them socially and economically.

The presence of a 'deficiency' is not always necessary. Job creation programmes and job subsidies are sometimes aimed at overcoming deficiencies (for example, Community Industry for socially and personally disadvantaged young people or the Job Introduction Scheme which subsidises disabled workers), but they may also be aimed at a limited number of unemployed or potentially unemployed individuals specified only by age, length of unemployment, and perhaps the area in which they live (for example, the Adult Employment Subsidy).

As long as individuals suffer poverty, it is of course appropriate that a caring society should develop means to help them directly, especially as broadly based programmes may fail to meet the special needs of some individals. However, as an approach to anti-poverty policy it may also have serious drawbacks. It can merely shift the poverty problem from one individual to another. A low paid worker may be assisted to achieve a better paid job. The low paid job he occupied remains in existence and will be filled by someone else, while the continued existence of the low paid sector acts to depress the income of unemployed people.

In addition, programmes directed to individuals can rarely help more than a small minority of those in need, for example training programmes in 1978 were reaching only 3 per cent of the unemployed and the literacy campaign in three years met the needs of only 125,000 of the estimated two million illerates in England and Wales. While those reached by the programme may benefit considerably, the majority of poor people in the same situation are not helped. It becomes essential then to ensure that the existence of such programmes does not create the illusion that the problem is being dealt with adequately.

The population group approach

Certain population groups have been identified as particularly vulnerable to poverty and as having certain common needs or common disadvantages to which anti-poverty policy can be directed.

The elderly

The population group approach can be seen at its best in relation to the elderly. The problem of poverty among the elderly is well identified. Unfavourable attitudes towards some poor groups do not extend to the elderly and the allocation of resources to meet the needs of this age group generally meets with popular approval.

As a result, when social security benefits are being improved and services are expanding, the elderly often receive preferential treatment. They have been actively encouraged to apply for supplementary benefit to increase their income, they are entitled to the higher long-term rate without a waiting period, and have always benefited more than other supplementary benefit recipients from additional grants and allowances under the scheme. One of the most substantial changes in the social security system, the introduction of the improved earnings related pension in the 1975 Social Security Pensions Act is designed to improve the income of the elderly over the next two or three decades and the encouragement given by governments to occupational pension schemes has also been influenced by the desire to reduce poverty among the elderly.

In the field of housing, more priority is being given to providing satisfactory and affordable accommodation for older people through sheltered housing programmes. The elderly are exempt from (or pay at a reduced rate) certain charges in the National Health Service, for items such as prescriptions, glasses, dental care or chiropody. As personal social services have expanded, support schemes for the elderly such as home helps and meals services have been given priority.

In spite of all this, 63 per cent of the poor are elderly and 30 per cent of pensioners live at or below supplementary benefit levels and as many again only marginally above. Over the next three decades, the new pension arrangements will greatly improve the incomes of many of the elderly, but the immediate problem remains and the position of the present generation of elderly is being adversely affected by cuts in public expenditure on services essential to them.

These problems are in part attributable to the slowness with which adequate policies for the elderly have been developed, but they relate also to deficiencies in the population group approach. The approach concentrates on those past retiring age, but does not address issues arising during the working years which will tend to produce poverty in old age. Low pay, sex discrimination, periodic unemployment and disability not only prevent the acquisition of resources which would serve to cushion the drop in income experienced at retirement, but will ultimately affect pension levels. In recent years, the incidence of long-term unemployment among older workers has produced a severe drain on the resources of this group in the years immediately preceding retirement.

Disabled people

Disabled people clearly form a disadvantaged population group and much of this disadvantage is directly related to the common factor of disability. In spite of this, policy makers have been slow to develop distinctive population group based policies for them, except in the case of the industrially and war disabled.

Instead, policies for disabled people of working age are set by reference to the general labour force, and for those of retirement age the reference group is the elderly generally. Although it is recognised that disabled unemployed people have significantly more difficulty in obtaining and keeping work than able bodied workers, they are made subject to the deterrent social security policies applied to all the unemployed and to most of the same contribution rules for the acquisition of earnings-related benefits. The level of non-contributory benefits for those too disabled ever to join the labour force is also set in relation to labour force related benefits, but deliberately at a lower level. In retirement, the additional costs related to disability are taken into account only to a limited extent in social security arrangements.

It could be argued that it is highly desirable that disabled people should not be segregated, but should share common community services to meet needs shared with others in society, provided any additional needs because of disability are taken into account. This, in fact, has been the approach adopted in a number of programmes, including employment and unemployment services, health and education. It has the advantage of giving disabled people access to the full range of available services, but as an approach it also has disadvantages. As a small population group within a much larger general group requiring the service (for example, handicapped children within the school population or disabled people among all those requiring health services) they have frequently been accorded low priority in the allocation of resources in spite of the importance of these services to them. In the same way, a large increase in the number of unemployed may divert services from the disabled unemployed or prevent expansion of services at the very time that disabled people are going to require additional help to regain employment.

The unsatisfactory economic and social position of many disabled people has led to pressure for policies more effectively designed to meet their needs. The passage of the Chronically Sick and Disabled Persons Act in 1970, the introduction of the invalidity benefit in 1971 and the provision of the mobility and attendance allowances are signs of the development of a population group approach. Pressure continues for the introduction of better social security benefits and better services generally for disabled people as a group suffering multiple disadvantage.

One-parent families and other families with children

The population group under discussion here is really children in families. In the absence of children, married couples and deserted, divorced or separated husbands and wives are not made the subject of distinctive policies (though childless widows may be) but share in general community services for common needs. The presence of children in the household, however, brings into play a number of programmes directed at preventing or alleviating child poverty.

Some child-oriented family programmes have developed – the most important of these is the child benefit which is paid to all families with children, whatever their income, but it is of particular benefit to low income families. Other programmes tied to the presence of children in the household include the family income supplement for low paid families and the benefits paid to widowed mothers. However, the desire to prevent poverty among children may be over-ridden by other policy priorities, for example, the decision to depress the income of the short-term sick and the unemployed or to maintain a low tax threshold for revenue purposes.

In addition to policies directed to all families with children, a concentrated attempt has been made in recent years to have one-parent families (that is lone parents other than widows for whom special provision already exists) classified as an appropriate population group upon which to base anti-poverty policies. The one-parent family lobby (voluntary agencies in co-operation with Members of Parliament) has been active in promoting this change and one outcome of their pressure was the appointment of the Finer Committee whose report endorsed the need for population group based policies for one-parent families.

To some extent this has been accepted by government, which has provided a child benefit increase to certain one-parent families and offered the group more favourable terms than other families in the family incomes supplement and supplementary benefit schemes. However, successive governments have been reluctant to make separate social security provision for this group through a one-parent famly benefit, nor have adequate support programmes such as day care and after school care been provided.

Other population groups – ethnic minorities, women, young people, unskilled manual workers

These are four other groups identified as vulnerable to poverty and/or disadvantaged. The ethnic minority population was the first of these to be offered a distinctive policy. The 1968 and 1976 Race Relations Acts sought to protect this group from discrimination which would retard their economic and social advancement and the Commission for Racial Equality (CRE) was established to watch over and promote their interests.

The much larger population of women has been for many years the subject of protective labour legislation which restricted hours of work, type of work and work schedules, but only in the 1970s has there been legislation designed to upgrade the position of women and reduce poverty among them. The 1970 Equal Pay Act and the 1975 Sex Discrimination Act and moves to reduce the effect of the concept of female dependency in social security and taxation arrangements all have elements of population based anti-poverty policies and the Equal Opportunities Commission, like the CRE, is intended to act as a monitor and promoter of the interests of women.

In recent years, a new group - young people - has begun to be identified as a group requiring special attention in anti-poverty policy. The very large growth of youth unemployment and with it the fuller recognition that education and further education services have failed to ensure that all young people are adequately qualified and/or prepared for employment has produced a surge of activity directed to this group. The most obvious examples of this are the Youth Opportunities Programme and the extensive discussion on the need for improved vocational education.

While many problems remain outstanding for the three population groups just discussed, their needs have begun to be recognised and attempts are being made to develop coherent policies. The same cannot be said about unskilled manual workers and their families, a group who suffer from a wide variety of disadvantages and are particularly vulnerable to poverty. Some policies have been developed to combat this disadvantage in the separate fields of education, health, housing, unemployment and low pay, but it cannot yet be said that the full range of inter-related disadvantages suffered by unskilled manual workers has been recognised and coherent anti-poverty policies developed.

Area based policies

Area based anti-poverty policies are not entirely new in the UK. Assistance to economically depressed areas and large-scale slum clearance began in the years between the wars and regional development policies have been pursued to a greater or less degree throughout the postwar period. However, the majority of area based policies stem from the late 1960s.

Regional policies

Table 9.1 shows the extent of the differences between the regions of

Table 9.1 Regional variation in principal social and economic variables, United Kingdom 1978–1979

Index numbers, United Kingdom = 100

	South East	South West	East Anglia	East Mid-lands	West Mid-lands	Yorkshire and Humber-side	North West	North	England	Wales	Scotland	Northern Ireland
Average gross weekly wage, all full time men	110	96	99	99	99	100	101	102	103	100	103	94
Lowest decile weekly earnings, all full time men	111	100	102	105	108	105	108	105	107	104	104	93
Unemployment	65	96	80	88	101	99	129	137	99	143	119	258
Long term unemployment	58	103	74	86	90	98	148	156	101	138	144	255
Expenditure[1] per head on main social security benefits	94	102	88	92	93	102	108	110	98	118	106	110
Expenditure per head on supplementary benefit and family income supplement	91	93	73	83	98	97	123	115	97	115	103	147
Private home ownership as proportion of all tenures	104	117	106	106	102	100	107	85	105	109	65	91
Private and public tenancy as proportion of all tenures	96	80	93	93	98	100	91	117	96	89	141	111
Homelessness[2]	104	100	83	96	79	100	100	142	101	76	118	113
Combined mortality rate[3]	95	105	97	96	91	103	106	104	99	108	105	88
Perinatal mortality rate[3]	88	90	83	96	107	97	105	108	97	104	93	130
Proportion remaining at school beyond compulsory age[4]	125	88	73	78	85	83	70	71	95	106	140	85
Proportion leaving school with no qualifications and not entering any further training	76	67	92	89	110	114	93	83	86	164	n.a.	149
Proportion of population over 65 and under 5 years of age	101	109	101	97	93	100	100	97	100	102	97	114
Gross domestic product per head	113	92	92	96	107	95	97	94	98	88	96	86

Principal Sources: *Regional Statistics, 1980, Social Trends 1980, Social Security Statistics 1979, Local Housing Statistics*, August 1980, *Department of Employment Gazette*, December 1979 and June 1980; *Northern Ireland Housing Statistics* 1979; *Health and Social Services Statistics*, 1979.

[1] Retirement pension; sickness and invalidity benefits; widow's benefit; unemployment, maternity, injury and disablement benefits; death grant; war pensions; attendance and mobility allowances; child and supplementary benefits, and family income supplement.

[2] Households registered with local authority (per 1,000 households) as homeless.

[3] Based on rates per 1,000.

[4] Compulsory age in UK–16.

the United Kingdom. Northern Ireland, Wales, North West and North of England and Scotland stand out as the most disadvantaged regions of the UK on most of the social and economic variables cited.

Regionalism is not a strong element in UK policy. Regional policies have been principally directed to economic development with special assistance programmes to increase job opportunities. In addition, the allocation of health resources was examined on a regional basis through the RAWP process and, following the adoption of a needs-based formula, arrangements commenced to shift resources from over to under-resourced regions within (but not between) England, Wales, Scotland and Northern Ireland.

The existence of a separate Scottish, Welsh and Northern Ireland Office for government services does lend itself to a separate consideration of the needs of those regions. Particular efforts have been made to upgrade the legislation and services in Northern Ireland which had fallen behind the rest of the UK during the period of the Stormont Parliament (until 1972) but, economic development apart, there has been little discrimination in favour of Wales and Scotland or for that matter North and North West England, though it would be true to say that awareness of regional disadvantage does influence the selection of targets for other area based policies.

Rural policies

Rural poverty has not been discussed in any detail in this report. The contraction of rural employment opportunities (as agriculture has declined as a source of employment without being fully replaced by alternatives) has led to high rates of unemployment, low availability of skilled employment, seasonality of employment and lower wage levels in many rural areas. At the same time (and in part in consequence) younger and more mobile families have migrated from rural areas, leaving behind the old and less mobile, who in turn have been reinforced by in-migration of retired people. Typically, this kind of population has low levels of income and capacity for self-support and high requirements for health and social services. Rural services generally have declined as rationalisation of social services, education and health provision has resulted in the concentration of these services in the towns. The progressive decline of public transport has simultaneously rendered these re-organised services less accessible to poor people and to elderly and disabled people without access to private transport, as well as further limiting job opportunities.

In the last decade, rural deprivation has begun to be identified as a problem requiring distinctive policies. Again, economic development and job creation have formed the principal policy initiatives, in part through general regional development policies and in part through special agencies created to meet rural needs. Some attention is being given to improving rural public transport. The health needs of rural areas received some attention under RAWP in Scotland, Wales and Northern Ireland, whose resource allocation formula includes a 'sparsity factor' to take account of the needs of scattered rural and island populations. A start has thus been made, but it cannot yet be said that policies to combat rural poverty are well developed.

Educational priority areas

The EPA programme, which ran for a few years in the late 1960s and early 1970s, was the first of the urban anti-poverty programmes. Additional resources were to be given to schools in selected areas regarded as environmentally sub-standard and having a child population which suffered from multiple disadvantage. The criteria for selection were never very clearly defined and the level of resources invested was not high in relation to the ambitions of the scheme.

The EPA programme was in part aimed at intervening in the process of economic and social decline in selected areas through the upgrading of primary school facilities and in part at intervening in the transmission of a 'culture of poverty' through programmes directed at socially disadvantaged families and children. As the programme developed, the latter proved the stronger of the two elements. However, the EPA programme did not last long, though it did influence the development of subsequent urban programmes.

Urban aid

The urban aid programme was launched in 1968 in a somewhat hasty response to concerns about the state of race relations in the cities. The programme assumed that urban poverty in the UK could be defined in terms of pockets of multiple deprivation affecting individuals in relatively small areas. These problems could best be tackled through projects which improved the functioning of individuals and families and thus enabled them to 'break out' of poverty. This would be reinforced by the improvement of the physical environment.

As with the EPA, the criteria for selecting areas eligible for urban aid were never clearly delineated. Local authorities were to identify areas of 'special social need' and could then apply for grants for specific projects to be run by the local authorities themselves or by voluntary agencies. Originally these projects were to be directed at social problems, and included schemes such as nursery school and play group provision, neighbourhood and advice centres, volunteer bureaux, educational projects for immigrants and other community projects for disadvantaged groups. Later, funding could be sought for industrial, environmental and recreational improvements. This programme is still operating.

Community development projects

The community development programme, established in 1969, involved 12 projects in both urban and rural areas, the former predominating. They were intended to complement the somewhat dispersed urban aid programme by concentrating on a few relatively small areas offering a combination of research and action projects which would identify the causes of disadvantage and explore new ways of meeting the needs of people living in areas of high social deprivation. The main instruments of this were to be the better delivery of services and the tapping of self-help potential. The establishment of the programme was influenced by theories of poverty sub-culture and transmitted deprivation, theories which assumed that the cause of this localised poverty and disadvantage lay within the deprived community or individual.

The CDP teams began by operating on the basis of this diagnosis of the problem, but before long were identifying the causes of local poverty as stemming from factors external to the deprived communities, including the structure of the economy and the policies of local and national government and of multi-national companies. The radicalisation of CDP produced inevitable clashes with central and local government and over time, the drying up of political and financial support.

At the local level, the teams promoted the setting up of law and advice centres, neighbourhood councils, community support groups and a range of small-scale projects for children, youth and old people. They also created an awareness in the community of the nature of their problems and the contribution community action could make to local change.

At the national level, the flow of CDP reports opened up the discussion of poverty as a structural rather than an individual problem, but appear to have had comparatively little direct influence on anti-poverty policy. The lessons drawn by government from CDP appear to have been largely negative, i.e., a desire to avoid in future, programmes which led to confrontation with authority.

The inner cities programme

During the mid-1970s, governments sought, through various experimental programmes and research, to find ways to develop a comprehensive approach to the problems of the inner city areas, an approach which avoided the defects felt to be present in both the urban aid and CDP programmes. Stemming from this activity, a new inner cities programme was introduced in 1978.

The programme focusses on three factors in inner city deprivation – economic decline producing higher rates of unemployment and a mismatch between the skills of the people and the kinds of jobs available; the physical decay of the area; and the preponderance of social disadvantage in the population.

It operates at three levels. First there is a general inner cities programme. This aims to give some priority to inner city areas within general economic, employment and other policies, some priority in the allocation of urban aid grants, as well as additional loans and grants for projects which improve the economic and environmental condition of the area. Second, some 15 programme areas have been selected. These receive additional funds for environmental, recreational, health and education projects as well as benefiting from the general inner cities programme. Third, some 7 partnership areas have been established. In these central and local government, with input from voluntary agencies and the community, are to develop a corporate plan for the area, identifying its problems and proposing action by the departments and agencies involved. The first three year partnership funds based on the corporate plan were allocated in 1979 to develop projects on employment, housing, transport, education, health and social services.

The partnership programme is clearly the most comprehensive and sophisticated attempt to date to combat poverty and disadvantage on an area base. Not surprisingly such an ambitious plan is not without its difficulties, involving as it does the harmonisation of many competing interests and operating in a climate of expenditure cuts which will affect all aspects of the programme. It remains to be seen how effective this approach will be. However, its complexity and cost suggest that it is not likely to be applied to more than a few areas of special disadvantage.

Area based programmes – some comments

Some comments can be made on the small area based approach (i.e., excluding the regional and rural programmes). First, it tends to be hit and miss in its operation. In the case of the educational priority areas programme, only a minority of deprived children lived in EPA areas and indeed only a minority of EPA children were actually deprived. Thus children in EPAs who did not need additional help might benefit while deprived children outside those areas were not touched by the programme. Under urban aid, the extent to which urban populations in need benefited was in part determined by the energy of local authorities in seeking funds as well as their ability to identify useful projects.

Second, even for what the programmes aimed to do, the allocation of resources was quite inadequate in relation to need and, when spread across a large number of areas (as in urban aid), represented only a small addition to local resources. Where large resources were allocated – in the partnership programmes – the numbers of areas which could benefit were restricted. Third, the basic problems of poverty in any area were not and could not be expected to be amenable to a limited area-based approach. As the CDP projects pointed out, many if not most of the local problems arose from developments outside local control. Even the partnership programmes, which are the most wide-ranging, are likely to be limited in their impact on non-local problems.

On the credit side, the area-based programmes have enabled increased citizen involvement in the identification of local problems and in action programmes, official and unofficial, to overcome them. The funds allocated also enabled the voluntary sector to develop many innovative projects. Perhaps most important the failure of the area-based programmes to deal with the problems of the urban areas has produced greater understanding of the nature of urban poverty.

Nationally based policies

Many of the programmes described in previous sections could equally have been classified as nationally based policies. However, policies in this section are characterised by the fact that they are more directed to institutions and systems than to individuals or groups or by the fact that they operate on a mass scale and through the shifting of resources from one part of the population to another.

Institutional re-organisation

The 1944–48 attack on poverty made considerable use of institutional re-organisation as a means of providing more access for poor people to needed services. The reshaping of the education system and the establishment of the National Health Service are two obvious examples of this.

This approach to combating poverty and disadvantage re-emerged in the late 1960s and during the 1970s. The employment services were reshaped, the administration of the heatlh services reformed and new Social Services Departments replaced the old local government welfare and children's departments and took over some health department functions. In education the secondary school system was re-organised on comprehensive lines and changes in the way in which handicapped children should be educated have been proposed. The reshaping of programmes for the homeless is a smaller example of this process.

Institutional re-organisation is normally intended to meet a wide variety of defects in the relevant service and is not usually solely an anti-poverty policy. However, the desire to ensure a better service for disadvantaged people has often been an important motivation and in other cases, the re-organisation has opened the way for desired anti-poverty policies which were hampered by previous administrative arrangements. An occasional shake-up of institutional inertia can be valuable, but it should be noted that it will not necessarily lead to better service for poor people unless positive action is taken to ensure that it does. While discussion about the need for improved access for poor people which occurs prior to and during re-organisation does focus attention on their needs, the capacity of old institutional patterns of service to re-assert themselves in new structure appears to be infinite.

Intervention in the market place

A second group of national policies has involved intervention on behalf of poor people in the normal functioning of the market. The most notable and long-lasting example of this has been the operation of housing policies, which have been based on the assumption that left to itself the housing market would not be able to provide adequately for poor people. The development of public housing programmes, the range of subsidy systems, the setting of 'fair rents' and legislation to provide greater security of tenure for renters have all been aimed wholly or in part at enabling poor people to find and keep satisfactory and affordable housing.

A certain amount of intervention in the labour market on behalf of the low paid has also been undertaken, through the setting up of Wages Councils to protect the most vulnerable workers, through Fair Wages Resolutions, and by means of equal pay. Job protection, health and safety legislation, government subsidies to major industries, and the encouragement of trade unions through supportive legislation are other forms of labour market intervention which can help more vulnerable workers.

While intervention in the housing market has been a consistent policy, intervention in the labour market has often been limited, even tentative at times, for fear of adverse effect on the well-being of industry or of the economy generally. Major steps such as equal pay legislation have been taken quite reluctantly and general minimum wage legislation is still regarded as too risky because of its wider economic consequences.

Redistribution of income and resources

The largest scale national programmes are those designed to redistribute income through the taxation and social security systems.

In general the outcome of taxation policies has been beneficial to poor people, enabling the development of substantial public services such as health, education, social services, housing, employment services and others and, together with national insurance constibutions, the tax system provides the means to pay social security benefits. All of these services are vital to the wellbeing of poor people, a fact which has been highlighted by the adverse effect on anti-poverty programmes of cuts in taxation and public expenditure. However, taxation also undermines the wellbeing of the poor through low tax thresholds and the effects on the cost of living of the growth of indirect taxation.

Social security policies have the most obvious and direct influence on the life of poor people. The system protects large numbers from complete destitution and saves others from periods of serious financial hardship. Originally conceived as a universal programme with a residual means-tested element, the balance has increasingly shifted towards means testing. The growth in the role of the supplementary benefits scheme has been largely unplanned and has stemmed from the inability of the universal insurance programme to keep up with social, economic and demographic change. In addition, a range of means-tested schemes has been added to the original structure to meet the problems of certain groups when the introduction of a universal programme was expected to be a less effective or an over-expensive way to respond. These means-tested schemes have rarely met with wholehearted approval and always suffer from take-up problems which limit their effects. Because of this, pressure has been maintained to develop or improve universal schemes. The social security system is ripe for considerable revision, but the biggest single defect at present is the inadequacy of many of its benefits to take recipients out of poverty.

Redistribution of resources within other social policy areas has also played some part in anti-poverty policy. As noted earlier, an attempt was made to shift health resources from advantaged to disadvantaged regions and the rate support grant, which subsidises local government service, tries to ensure through its formula that most assistance goes where needs are greater. In general, however, inadequate attention has been paid to the way resources are allocated within services and a growing tendency can be detected in some general services (such as education) to begrudge special allocation for 'welfare' purposes.

The partnership between voluntary organisations and the state in the development of anti-poverty policy

At the present time, voluntary organisations in the United Kingdom do little in the way of actual distribution of income to the poor. However, they do play quite a major role in ensuring that people receive their proper entitlement from social security offices, and by informing people of their rights and entitlements. They may also act on behalf of individuals or families in contact with housing departments, health and social services departments or gas and electricity boards.

There is also a significant role for voluntary organisations in the direct provision of services which can raise standards of living for deprived groups through assisting and complementing state provision, undertaking tasks left undone by statutory organisations and reacting quickly to meet needs or filling gaps. This work has mainly involved the provision of residential accommodation plus day care, special educative, recreational, employment or training opportunities and forms of counselling. One of the problems with such voluntary provision is that its spread across the country is very uneven.

Voluntary organisations also help counteract poverty by encouraging the government to adopt new policies to solve problems of need and deprivation, by helping to identify new areas of need, and by criticising defects in the operation of existing poverty programmes. Changes in benefits for the disabled, increases in pensions, taxation changes for widows and travel concessions for the old reflect the efforts by a wide range of voluntary organisations. The activities of a number of voluntary organisations have amounted to an influential 'poverty lobby'.

While the traditional activity of voluntary organisations lay in improving the conditions of individuals and their families, the community development movement has led to a new emphasis on local groups expressing their needs and taking collective action to meet them. This expansion in community groups has led to greater community involvement in provision of services and improved facilities in deprived neighbourhoods. Although the urban programmes had a limited impact on multiple deprivation they encouraged community initiatives and many voluntary projects have generated further resources in terms of donations, premises, and other facilities that would not otherwise have been released. The voluntary sector has demonstrated that it can make an important contribution to tackling a range of problems affecting deprived urban areas.

It is probably unrealistic to suggest that voluntary organisations can make a major impression on poverty and deprivation. A recent study[2] has shown that voluntary organisations are only involved at the margins, in pioneering services or providing something ancillary to statutory provision. It has been argued that community groups have mainly dealt with the individual needs of deprived groups in localities and have not been involved in more radical activities or proposals to change the social structure. Even in Northern Ireland, where there was a large increase in community action groups following civil disturbance and the breakdown or rejection of statutory services, their influence on changing the social structure has been limited. It was only for a brief period in the early 1970s that some regarded community development as the voluntary sector's poverty programme. Community groups can and do perform a useful role in focussing upon immediate issues which are part of day-to-day concern such as redevelopment, slum clearance or welfare needs. Their limitations are that for the most part they are confined in their action to producing self-help services or blocking government proposals.

Successive governments have stressed the importance of the role voluntary agencies play in the welfare state and have extended the range of grant-giving mechanisms accordingly. At present, government is re-emphasising the importance of the voluntary sector, but at the same time cutting public expenditure, a process which flows through to the resources made available to voluntary agencies. Many voluntary organisations are endeavouring to respond to the challenge of social deprivation, but may find themselves handicapped by current funding restrictions.

A new poverty problem – fuel poverty

In the last seven years, governments have had to find ways of meeting a new aspect of poverty – fuel poverty. Poor families have always had difficulty in meeting fuel bills, but the dimensions of the problem have greatly increased in recent years.

The problem became more acute as a result of the large increase in oil prices in the 1970s and was reinforced by government decisions, implemented progressively from 1974 onwards, to bring electricity prices broadly into parity with the price of oil and to phase out a long-established system of domestic fuel price subsidy. Although the real price of gas fell during the 1970s as a result of plentiful supplies from the North Sea, the government has recently determined to raise gas prices too to 'a more realistic level'. The cost of fuel is expected to be twice as high as it is now by the end of the century. A related problem was the relatively poor insulation of UK houses. At the same time, the generally rising standard of living had increased the expectations of rich and poor alike, including a demand for warm homes. The decision to install central heating in new public housing was a reflection of this.

Fuel costs, of course, affect all consumers, but the most seriously affected have been those households with limited budgets which offered little room for manoeuvre. Some have cut the use of essential fuel to the point that they live in cold conditions potentially harmful to health; others have maintained reasonable levels of fuel consumption and cut down on expenditure on food or clothing; others again have run into fuel debt and, unable to find resources to meet high quarterly bills, have had their gas or electricity disconnected until the debt was cleared. Particular concern has been felt for the elderly, disabled people at home all day and families with young children.

Governments were slow to recognise the nature and extent of this problem and have maintained energy policies which give priority to the need for high fuel prices to create incentives for conservation over the need to hold down the cost of essential fuel for poor households. Much pressure had to be brought to bear by official and non-official bodies before action was taken to help poor families and the resulting policies have tended to be tentative, piecemeal and poorly co-ordinated. At present, additions for fuel costs are made to some supplementary benefits and to family income supplement payments, although there are doubts about the suitability of small general income increments limited to certain groups to solve the specific problem of fuel poverty. Schemes have been introduced to facilitate staggered repayment of debts; at first these reduced the number of disconnections, but the disconnection rate is rising again in some areas. Grants have been made via local authorities to assist householders to insulate their homes, but although the rate of grant has been increased by the present government, the total budget available was never adequate and has now been reduced.

These various approaches have not solved the problem, however, and there has been pressure for the introduction of a comprehensive fuel benefit. To date no scheme has been proposed which is not excessively costly and which does not have other serious deficiencies, and the problem remains. The fact that governments' fuel policies were developed without consideration of the effects of these policies on poverty, their reluctance to recognise the problem, and the rivalry between departments and branches of government to pass the responsibility elsewhere do not suggest that policy makers are well geared to react to new poverty problems, even after 25 years of experience of administering the welfare state.

Some general comments

It cannot be doubted that UK governments in the last 30 years have been seriously concerned about poverty, disadvantage and inequality in the country and have sought through a wide variety of mechanisms to reduce them. As new theories of poverty have cast further light upon the problem, policy makers have taken them into account in planning anti-poverty programmes. However, the older theories which see poverty as rooted in individual and group deficiencies continue to have an enormous influence on policy. This applies not only within individual and group based approaches, but can be seen operating in the kinds of programmes which are thought suitable for funding in area-based schemes and in the determination of social security policy. Under the present government, this theory of individual responsibility for poverty has received renewed emphasis.

The failure to overcome poverty in the UK is not simply the inevitable outcome of the intransigence of the problem, though present social and economic structures do operate against any attempt to eliminate poverty. Some blame must be placed on ill-thought out policies, the failure to pursue some policies with sufficient rigour, the inadequate investment of resources in many promising programmes and the reluctance to challenge important interests which stand in the way of effective policies. In justice to UK governments up to 1979, they never lost sight of the goal of a more equitable society and, even in the last 15 years when the economic situation has been a serious cause for concern, efforts to achieve this goal, including quite substantial programmes, have continued. At present, anti-poverty policy is not a priority, but a serious examination of past policies may point the way for the future.

Notes

1 Birrell W. D. and Williamson A. P., *Voluntary organisations in the United Kingdom and their Role in Combatting Poverty* (Unpublished, Coleraine, Northern Ireland, 1980).

2 Hatch, Stephen, *Outside the State* (Croom Helm, London, 1980)

Index